WOMEN AND HEALTH

CULTURAL AND SOCIAL PERSPECTIVES

DREW HUMPHRIES

CRACK

MOTHERS

PREGNANCY, DRUGS,

AND THE MEDIA

Ohio State University Press

Columbus

Library of Congress Cataloging-in-Publication Data

Humphries, Drew.

Crack mothers : pregnancy, drugs, and the media / Drew Humphries.

p.   cm. — (Women and health)

Includes bibliographical references and index.

ISBN 0-8142-0816-9 (cloth : alk. paper)

1. Drug abuse in pregnancy—Moral and ethical aspects—United States.   2. Crack (Drug)—United States.   3. Deviant behavior—United States—Public opinion.   4. Deviant behavior in mass media—United States.   5. Social problems—United States—Public opinion.   6. Social problems in mass media.   7. Public opinion—United States.   I. Title.   II. Series: Women & health (Columbus, Ohio)

HV5824.W6H86   1999

362.29'8'0852—dc21   98-46648
                                                      CIP

Text and jacket design by Diane Gleba Hall.

Type set in Joanna and Meta Plus by Graphic Composition, Inc.

Printed by Braun-Brumfield, Inc.

The paper used in this publication meets the minimum requirements of the American National Standard for Information Sciences—Permanence of Paper for Printed Library Materials. ANSI Z39.48-1992.

9 8 7 6 5 4 3 2 1

In memory of my mother,

Carol Guerin Humphries

Contents

Acknowledgments

From the beginning to this project's end, I was fortunate in having colleagues who took the time to talk about ideas, forward useful materials, read the manuscript, and offer general encouragement. I want to thank Kathleen Boyle, Rose Johnson Bigler, Susan Carengella-MacDonald, Gray Cavender, Lynn Chancer, Meda Chesney-Lynd, Kathleen Daley, Eloise Dunlap, Laura Fishman, Mark Fishman, Carol Garrison, Nancy Jurik, Rene Goldsmith Kasinsky, Dorie Klein, Karen Maschke, Lisa Maher, Alita Merlot, Roslyn Muraskin, Sheigla Murphy, Amanda Noble, Kathleen O'Banion, Barbara Raffel Price, Eileen Stilwell, Inga Sagatun, Mina Silberberg, Nancy Wonders, Robert Wood, and Marjorie Zatz.

In addition to individuals, I want to recognize the importance of conferences or the collective exchange of ideas to the arguments developed in this book. In 1991, a conference on women and criminal justice at John Jay College provided the chance to learn from policy makers, administrators, and judges about the policies used to deal with women who used drugs during pregnancy. As one administrator said, "With so few treatment slots, it makes more sense to admit women who want drug treatment than to force unwilling mothers into programs they do not want and will not complete." I would also like to thank Sandra Carr, director of the Wings Program, a drug treatment program for pregnant addicts at Ricker's Island, for inviting me to see how this approach applied to incarcerated women. At Riker's, I had the opportunity to talk informally with the pregnant women about their involvement in drug treatment. In 1997, I attended a Philadelphia conference on the social history of drugs in America, profiting from the new wave of research on drug scares, an idea pioneered by David Musto, Harry Levine, and Craig Reinarman.

Rutgers University's Faculty Study Leave Program enabled me to complete this project. And with a grant from Rutgers's Research Council, I acquired the videotapes of national network news about women who used crack or cocaine during pregnancy from the archives at Vanderbilt University. For help in acquiring copies of what appeared in printed news sources and other materials, I am indebted to the librarians and staff at Robeson Library: Gary Golden, Susan Beck, John Maxymuk, Jim Nettleman, Elaine Navarra, Debra Goldberg, and Mary Anne Chaney. I thank Neal Thompson, staff reporter for The Enterprise in Brockton, Massachusetts; Pamela Liles, librarian for The Post and Courier in Charleston, South Carolina; and Lorence Givens, librarian for Hackley Public Library in Muskegon, Illinois, for forwarding articles from local newspapers that I would not otherwise have been able to obtain.

My sincere thanks go to our undergraduate majors in sociology, many of whom helped with the research: April Farley, John Dawson, Valerie Cronin, Phyllis Keating, Chris Wisniewski, Jennine Eichfeld, Helen Polak, Kelly Behrens, John Wiener, and Vikki Schulter. Joanne Diogo, a graduate student in Rutgers-Camden's master's program in history, provided research support in the areas of drug treatment, education, and child protective services. Manuscript preparation was speeded along by Loretta Carlisle's expert typing. I want to acknowledge the help of Erin Sarkees, Andrea Tortu, and Tory Tompkins in proofreading.

I am grateful to Charlotte Dihoff, editor-in-chief, and her staff at Ohio State University Press, as well as to Janet Golden and Rima D. Apple, series editors, for their helpful support in bringing this project to fruition. I am indebted to the anonymous reviewers for the press for providing such useful comments. Laura Mansnerus, who kept the project on track and performed editorial miracles on earlier drafts of this book, deserves much credit. In the end, however, the responsibility for the book is mine.

Because time is so hard to come by, some special thanks are in order. I thank my husband, Dan Tompkins, and my daughter, Victoria Humphries Tompkins, for standing in for me on the home front. I am equally grateful to my longtime colleague, Myra Bluebond-Langner, for keeping from my door the typically excessive demands of the workplace. And to my newest colleague, Jon'a Meyer, I can finally say, "Yes, the book is finished!"

Introduction

In October 1988, NBC's television news audience met its first "crack mothers." Tracy Watson, a pregnant black woman, was shown smoking crack, sitting on a narrow bed in a bare New York City apartment (1988, October 24). She spent about $100 a day on crack, smoking up to 20 vials of it, according to the voice-over. Talking to someone just off-camera, Tracy acknowledged knowing that the drug affected her pregnancy. She said she knew that crack could make the baby come prematurely. She said she knew that it could cause the baby to be born addicted. As she smoked, Tracy bared her protruding belly and said, "It kicks when I smoke. It tightens up on one side. It's kicking now."

From Tracy's New York City apartment, the NBC news segment shifted to a Miami hospital, where Erocelia Fandino lay on a maternity-ward bed recuperating from the premature birth of her child. Erocelia, a woman whose Spanish accent softened her English, said that the baby had been born at home, coming so fast that it was delivered still encased in the water sac. Erocelia had smoked crack just hours before delivery. The same segment showed Stephanie, a black "crack mother" who had abandoned her newborn at the hospital to go straight to the crack house. With two "crack babies" already in foster care, Stephanie was one of many crack mothers whom the social worker assigned to her had to track down. Interviewed on a downtown street corner, a disheveled Stephanie mumbled that in her state of mind, she could not care for her children. She explained that she had left her children because she had no money, no support, and no housing.

Mothers like Tracy, Erocelia, and Stephanie, the news report went on, were the tip of the iceberg. Estimates made in the late 1980s put the annual number of cocaine babies born in the United States at 375,000 (CBS, 1989, January 9; NBC, 1989, July 7); local estimates were also high (NBC, 1988, October 24). At Jackson Memorial Hospital in Miami, 1 in 10 mothers used crack within hours of delivery. At Columbus Hospital in Chicago, drug use was so common that drug treatment had become a routine part of obstetrics.

As for the impact on newborns, physicians interviewed in the October 1988 NBC report provided alarming details. Dr. Emmalee Bandstra at the University of Miami explained that cocaine reduced the blood supply and with it oxygen to the developing fetus. An associate described "cocaine syndrome," a condition affecting cocaine-exposed babies that seemingly resulted in neurological damage, hyperactivity, poor concentration, and a limited attention span. In other television reports, birth defects, facial deformity, kidney malformation, and even brain damage and increased infant mortality were attributed to maternal cocaine use (NBC, 1989, August 10; NBC, 1989, September 30; ABC, 1989, November 14; ABC, 1990, January 13; CBS, 1990, April 5).

On the most publicly visible level, it was prosecutors who responded to the plight of cocaine babies (ABC, 1989, July 12). In Florida, prosecutors indicted Toni Hudson for administering an illegal drug to a minor, her newborn baby; and Jennifer Johnson and Cassandra Gethers were both charged with delivering cocaine to their babies—for each, the second born exposed to the drug. An Illinois county prosecutor presented a grand jury with a manslaughter charge against Melanie Green, whose cocaine-exposed daughter had died. Addiction was no excuse, the prosecutors insisted. "If you give drugs to your child because you can't help it, that's child abuse. It's time to say this baby didn't deserve this," commented Florida prosecutor Jeffrey Deen. "Two babies is enough," he said. "We're going to interdict. . . . We're going to intercede in your life for a while" (ABC,

1989, July 12). Paul Logli, the Illinois prosecutor, contended that there was no difference between someone's giving a child cocaine and a pregnant woman's ingesting the drug to the detriment of her baby (CBS, 1989, May 10).

However, not all agreed with this prosecutorial approach—objections were raised. Lynn Paltrow, spokesperson and attorney for the American Civil Liberties Union, argued that the prosecutions set dangerous precedents for women. "It's not just about drug-abusing women; it's about any pregnant woman who might be doing something that could harm her fetus" (CBS, 1989, May 10). By this standard, Paltrow said, any pregnant woman who smokes or drinks or doesn't stay off her feet against her doctor's advice could be subject to arrest.

• • •

From 1988 until 1990 or slightly thereafter, the national news about crack focused on women. A decade later, most people, if asked, would still recall the phrase "crack mothers" and be able to associate it with the women who continued to use crack during their pregnancies. If pressed, most people would probably also acknowledge thinking of crack mothers as poor women of color, inner-city residents who like Tracy Watson, Erocelia Fandino, and Stephanie cared more about crack than about their pregnancies or children. And everyone would remember "crack babies," another popular term used to describe infants who had been prenatally exposed to crack.

The obvious suffering of the newborns and the apparent indifference of their mothers is what seems to have triggered the prosecutions. It was one thing to use drugs—one could be punished for the possession or distribution of illicit drugs. It was an entirely different matter for women to use illegal drugs and place their fetuses at risk—one could not be held criminally liable for violating the moral duties of motherhood. If ever there was a case that justified extending the criminal law to enforce motherhood, maternal crack use seemed to be it.

The illegal substance called crack, or rock, initially perplexed experts. Was it a potent new drug or a formidable derivative of an old

3

one? As it turned out, crack was a little of both (Inciardi, 1997b; Williams, 1990; Morales, 1989). Crack's basic ingredient is powder cocaine, a stimulant that is typically snorted through the inner nasal membrane. Cocaine produces a "rush," a short-term high, followed by a "crash," a period of depression, irritability, and with prolonged use, a craving for more of the drug. By adding water, baking soda, and other additives to powder cocaine and boiling the mixture down until it solidifies, anyone can make crack. The residue is broken down into rocks, placed in vials, and sold.

Crack is still a stimulant, producing the rush and crash associated with cocaine, but it is smoked not snorted. Smoking crack or freebase, another form of cocaine, makes the rush instantaneous and the high explosive. It also intensifies the crash and heightens the depression, irritability, and drug cravings that follow. The combined effects of crack reinforce a periodic pattern of chronic use, or binge behavior.

The decision to smoke crack rather than freebase, the purer form, is based on price. Because several grams of cocaine are required to create enough pure drug to smoke, freebasing increases the price of a single high. Crack, on the other hand, can be stretched. Because a single gram of cocaine plus additives creates many rocks, smoking crack decreases the price of a single high. Crack sells for as little as $5 a rock. It is uniquely suited to a mass market in which the customer buys small quantities and the volume of sales determines profit.

Crack hit the illicit drug market in the mid-eighties, attracting almost as many women as men (National Institute on Drug Abuse [NIDA], 1990). And although the overall popularity of the drug played a role in escalating the war on drugs, its use by women sounded alarms. A similar combination had worried the public in the 1960s, as women who had taken thalidomide, an antinausea medication, gave birth to malformed babies. This incident put to rest once and for all notions that the placenta protected the fetus from toxic substances taken in by the mother. Women who had taken this drug during pregnancy became objects of public sympathy, and the desire to avoid the birth of severely deformed infants legitimated efforts to relax antiabortion laws. Twenty years later, pregnant women who used crack—

4

with or without realizing its destructive effects—became objects of public hostility. In contrast, their pariah status legitimated efforts to control the behavior of pregnant women.

According to the Center for Reproductive Law and Policy, criminal charges were filed against 160 women who had used cocaine or crack during pregnancy in the late 1980s (n.d.). Highly publicized cases against Melanie Green, Jennifer Johnson, Kimberly Hardy, and Lynn Bremer, among others, were intended to discourage other pregnant women from using drugs. Unfortunately, the high-profile cases pushed alternative approaches to combatting drug use to the background.

One such approach, the medical model, had been given the imprimatur of the U.S. Supreme Court, which in 1962 ruled that addiction was a medical condition requiring treatment, not punishment (*Robinson v. California*). The public health approach relied on education and preventive services to reduce drug use. Harm reduction, another approach, concentrated on minimizing the harms associated with drug use rather than on reducing the use of drugs. Needle exchanges, for example, showed visible results in reducing the spread of AIDS. But despite humane alternatives, prosecutors riding a wave of anti-drug hysteria captured the public imagination by bringing cases against drug mothers in the late 1980s and early 1990s (Center for Reproductive Law and Policy, n.d.). Even though most cases were dismissed or overturned on appeal, the prosecutions require attention if only because women have rarely, if ever, been the target of a national campaign to suppress crime.

The crusade against crack mothers was a single episode in the broader war on drugs, the aggressive federal anti-drug crusade launched by President Ronald Reagan and continued by George Bush, conducted by drug czars and waged at home and abroad. In the U.S., Reagan's zero-tolerance policy expanded the scope of the war to emphasize consumers, recreational drug users, and potential new drug users (Inciardi, 1986). Teens and children were high on this list, as were women. According to zero-tolerance philosophy, drug use started with an intentional act (Inciardi, 1986). Even though people might become addicted to a drug, they had the ability to stop. And the

5

reason they did not stop, according to this stringent approach, was that no authority held them accountable. Congress and state legislatures, true to the zero-tolerance philosophy, passed laws requiring mandatory sentences for the possession of illegal drugs.

Of course, dealers and traffickers remained targets in the war on drugs. Legislation intended to remove the profit from drug trafficking required dealers to forfeit any assets—property, cash, or possessions—that had been obtained from or used in a criminal enterprise. A reformulated extradition treaty with Colombia, an important cocaine producer, made it much easier to bring traffickers to justice in the United States. Military technologies—for example, assault helicopters, surveillance balloons, and spy satellites—were mobilized in an effort to stop the flow of cocaine from Colombia (and other producer countries) to the United States. Direct military intervention in Bolivia to shut down cocaine-processing plants gave a real military edge to the metaphorical war on drugs.

In the war on drugs, women who used drugs during pregnancy were not treated like other female drug offenders. Drug offenders typically enter the system by being arrested for the possession or distribution of controlled substances. Street sweeps, undercover investigations, or informants' tips produce arrests. Pregnant drug offenders, on the other hand, entered the criminal justice system through the hospital. Health care providers alerted police or county attorneys to suspected drug use by delivering mothers. Police then arrested mothers on a variety of charges, including manslaughter, child abuse or neglect, and drug distribution.

The arrests raised significant legal questions. Mothers are legally responsible for their children's health and safety, and an abusive or negligent mother can be brought to family court, where the state may terminate her parental rights and remove the child or children from her custody. Depending on the circumstances, an abusive mother may also be prosecuted in criminal court. But that legal duty begins only at birth; the law, for most purposes, does not recognize a fetus as a person independent of the mother, and a pregnant woman cannot be prosecuted in criminal court for injuring her fetus.

Attempts to prosecute women on the basis of drug use during pregnancy called this rule into question, however, and opened up a new front in the abortion-related war over fetal and maternal rights. Pro-life advocates saw in the prosecutions an opportunity to hold women accountable for the well-being of their fetuses. Once a woman recognized her pregnancy and decided to carry the fetus to term, the pro-life standard would legally oblige a pregnant woman to provide for her fetus's health and safety. The implications of this position were not lost on pro-choice advocates like Lynn Paltrow, one of the attorneys who defended crack mothers. If it went unchallenged, the pro-life standard would have recognized the fetus and provided a new basis for pro-life groups to chip away at the reproductive rights of women.

Critical race scholars writing about crack mothers pointed out that black women's experience changes the perspective on reproductive freedoms championed by middle-class white women. As Dorothy Roberts pointed out, black women had neither reproductive freedom nor parental rights under slavery: slave owners exploited their reproductive capacities and sold their resulting children into bondage (1991). At the turn of the century, middle-class standards of parental "fitness" clashed openly with the realities of poverty or the lives of the working poor. Women who earned a living and who by necessity left their children alone were deemed "unfit," and the state stepped in to remove the children (Kasinsky, 1994).

Almost a hundred years later, attempts to prosecute women who used drugs during pregnancy raised slightly different questions. Stereotypes of "crack mothers" demeaned black women's roles as mothers, while restrictions on Medicaid payments for abortion and child-welfare policies that removed children from the home put many mothers in a no-win situation. Those who used drugs during pregnancy had no alternative but to bear the children. And because drug use evidenced bad mothering, the state had grounds to take the children into custody (Roberts, 1991; Greene, 1991).

Finally, the campaign against crack mothers was also about poverty. Conservatives said that poverty persisted because the government paid people to remain poor (Murray, 1984). Remove the payments—

7

services and cash benefits—said the same experts, and the poor will work. So in the early 1980s, the "undeserving poor," those who were fit but chose welfare over work, were slated to be removed from welfare rolls. The "deserving poor" could continue to receive benefits, but AFDC recipients—poor women with dependent children—aroused suspicions. Female-headed households allegedly fit into a pattern of family breakdown and intergenerational welfare dependency, and stereotypes like "welfare queen" and "crack mother" stirred up and reflected opposition to the welfare state (Reeves and Campbell, 1994). The obvious suffering of "crack babies" made it easy to hate "crack mothers"; the antipathy helped the New Right diminish their services and benefits (Humphries, 1993).

• • •

This book approaches the campaign against women who used drugs during pregnancy as a moral panic—as a set of disproportionate, punitive responses to conduct believed to threaten the legal order (Cohen, 1972). The literature on moral panic distinguishes between real and imagined threats. Real threats—grave new types of crime or frightening increases in old ones—can be verified. Companies know immediately when computer hackers destroy data, for example, and homicide rates document the effects of gang warfare in the 1980s and 1990s. Imagined or perceived threats are, on the other hand, more complex. They appear real, but when examined may turn out to reflect something else entirely.

In one such instance, a much publicized crime wave against the elderly in New York City turned out to reflect bureaucratic infighting. Threatened with elimination, a police unit had manufactured a crime wave by selectively feeding crime-against-the-elderly stories to the press (Fishman, 1978). According to the literature, moral panics also link crime to unpopular minorities (Hall et al., 1978). An apparent upsurge in Chicano youth gangs in Phoenix was related to federal funding: by expanding the definition of "gangs," the police department increased their numbers and qualified for federal anti-gang grants

8

(Zatz, 1987). In this example, police connected a frightening new problem—gangs, with their associations with drug trafficking and violence—to a subordinated group, Chicano men. The convergence of images is what amplifies the threat to the level of moral panic.

Panics that involve drugs or alcohol have been called "drug scares." According to Craig Reinarman and Harry Levine, drug scares are "periods when anti-drug crusades have achieved great prominence and legitimacy in the U.S." (1995; see also Musto, 1987; Levine, 1978). A drug scare may develop without an actual increase in drug use; but once a new and frightening substance has been singled out, policy makers, crusaders, and medical experts tend to blame it for a host of endemic problems.

Typically, these drugs become associated with racial or ethnic minorities, working-class immigrants, or troubling groups of young people. At the end of the nineteenth century, the crusade against opium targeted Chinese immigrants, but it rested on Californians' anti-Chinese attitudes as much as on the perceived dangers of the drug (Morgan, 1978; Musto, 1987). Southern white fears of black rebellion precipitated the crusade against cocaine at the beginning of this century (Grinspoon and Bakalar, 1976). According to Stephen Kandall, women used opium, morphine, and cocaine in the nineteenth century, but as long as they remained within the gender confines of mainstream society, women addicts were tolerated (1996). As fears of ethnic minorities grew, however, tolerance for drug use changed, and women were more likely to be "cast as vulnerable sexual victims of these groups" in the anti-opium and anti-cocaine crusades (41). In the South, for example, cocaine was believed to promote black sexual violence against white women. Cocaine and opium addiction were tied to prostitution, which raised fears about white slavery, the selling of white women into prostitution networks used and managed by racial minorities.

It is important to keep in mind that moral panics and drug scares have a natural cycle. Interest builds, peaks, and then tapers off, until the drug and its associations seem to disappear entirely. The news summary about crack mothers cited at the beginning of the introduction is drawn from the middle phase of the crack mothers episode. Public reactions had already reached a fever pitch, as had the official crusade against crack mothers. But this is not the whole story; it is just a slice. To get the full story, we need to know what led up to and what followed the crusade. How had matters grown to the level of panic? What were the circumstances under which maternal crack use emerged as a particularly frightening issue? How had crack become tied to a specific group of women and their children? And what explains the powerful images that triggered a panic?

Equally important to consider are the ways in which these matters were resolved. Under what conditions did the issue of maternal crack use disappear from the national agenda? Was the connection between crack and poor women of color broken? What, if any, new associations replaced the imagery that had fueled the anti-crack crusade against women? Had the problem in fact disappeared? The rise and fall of "crack mothers" as a social problem illustrates the politics of moral panics and drug scares.

In his book *The War on Drugs*, James Inciardi notes with some irony that heroin and cocaine have both been called the "most dangerous substance on earth" (1986, 51, 71). Danger, of course, is not necessarily inherent in the chemical nature of the drug but has to do with what experts, politicians, and the media make of it. While addiction is an ill-defined concept, calling something addictive does make people pay attention. And people paid attention to crack, with its legendary reputation as the *most* addictive drug. Crack users said one puff and you're hooked for life. Drug experts said it made people feel so good that they stopped caring about anything else, including that the drug was killing them. Cocaine's effects on newborns, a matter of medical concern in the early 1980s, were considered severe enough to justify criminal prosecution by the late 1980s.

Like previous drug scares, the crack and cocaine panics were about much more than drug use. Historically, drug use had been tolerated as long as it fit into mainstream society. In the 1970s and early 1980s, cocaine use was tolerated among the rich and famous; but as the price dropped, it trickled down to the middle and working classes, raising concerns about the breakdown of social control. A rash of news reports in the early eighties attributed truck wrecks, train crashes, and other transportation disasters to the use of cocaine by truckers and others. In particular, drug scares have been about poor or marginal, subordinate groups who for one reason or another already trouble the dominant group. It is argued that when lower-class groups take control of the distribution of drugs, relocate markets in outdoor settings, and monopolize the market, dominant groups worry about the loss of control (Reinarman and Levine, 1989; Warner, 1994).

Crack hit the illicit drug markets in 1985, and television news teams interviewed inner-city black and Hispanic crack users on street corners and in open-air drug markets, listening as people described using the drug. The drug use of lower-class women in particular has amplified drug scares, because issues of lower-class sexuality and reproduction have historically bothered elites, with dominant groups tending not to want to provide for poor women and their children (Warner, 1994). So when the media interviewed women who used crack during pregnancy, the emerging stereotype that stressed the mothers' indifference to their suffering newborns reinforced the drive to reduce services and benefits to the undeserving poor and tended to justify punitive responses. The media also raised for a public audience concerns about the breakdown of social control in the areas of sexuality and reproduction. Such issues were so inflammatory that they intensified and extended the life of the war on drugs. The power of a stereotype like "crack mother" to escalate responses to the level of criminal prosecution depended on converging images of drugs, class, race, and gender. In focusing on crack and questioning the moral capacity of inner-city minority women to bear and raise children, the stereotype exaggerated beyond all proportion the social ills that most disturbed the New Right—the fundamentalist Christians, conservatives, and right-wing Republicans who claimed responsibility for Republican success at the polls in the 1980s. Images of addiction and poverty fit into conservatives' discussions about the state's responsibility toward those dependent on the state and acting in a self-destructive manner. Drug use was a matter of choice, they argued, and in order to hold drug users responsible for poor choices, the New Right championed aggressive prosecution and mandatory penalties.

Conservatives preferred the stick to the carrot in matters of poverty, too. Welfare, it was said, rewarded the poor for idleness. At the same time, conservatives exploited racial fears, devising the Willie Horton ad that discredited Governor Michael Dukakis and his run for the presidency in 1988. Willie Horton, a black inmate in the Massachusetts prison system, escaped from a work furlough program to murder an elderly white couple. Republicans blamed the killings on Governor Dukakis, suggesting that he, like other liberals, was too soft on crime. The ad's implicit message played on white Americans' worst fears about the black underclass.

Drug-exposed pregnancies were an apparent new link, but the claims about black mothers spoke specifically to long-standing concerns among legislators and policy makers about the social costs of maintaining dysfunctional black families. And crack-affected pregnancies acquired meaning in the contentious debates about motherhood over the responsibility of mothers toward fetuses and children. Encouraged by the anti-abortion planks in the Republican platforms of the 1980s, the pro-life movement exploited every issue it could in efforts to limit Roe v. Wade (1973). Treating women who used drugs during pregnancy as criminals simplified matters, but concealed beneath the anti-drug label "crack mother" were the anti-poverty, anti-minority, and anti-woman imperatives of the New Right.

If threats can be escalated to the level of a drug scare, then the same threats can be de-escalated. The news media's dwindling interest in the story suggested that the problem itself ceased to generate newsworthy events or, among other things, that a change in the political winds brought new issues to the fore. In their study of the campaign against crack, Richard Reeves and Jimmie Campbell (1994) found that news coverage during the period of denouement conveyed the impression that problems that had caused policy makers to launch the war on drugs were now resolved. They noted that news stories questioning drug-war premises and rehumanizing drug offenders contributed to the emerging sense of closure. Likewise, claims about grave effects of prenatal cocaine exposure had justified the crusade against crack mothers. Now these charges were scaled back. Reports that the mental capacities of crack babies fell within the normal range of intelligence reduced the level of threat. Furthermore, the media humanized crack mothers. Those who appeared on television screens during the concluding phase of the panic were remorseful, eager for treatment, and hopeful about regaining custody of their children.

In addition, the notion of crack mothers receded into the background as social services were seen as providing for drug-using women and their children. Reinarman and Levine use the term "institutionalization" in describing the end of the war on drugs (1989). They argue that to the degree that various institutions are seen as addressing the drug problem—for example, the newly fortified criminal justice system with its anti-drug legislation, law enforcement initiatives, and new prisons—perceived threats may be reduced and disappear from the public's awareness. The failure of the prosecutions meant that maternal drug use would have to be addressed elsewhere, but social services were ill-prepared. Women needed drug treatment, but appropriate interventions were problematic: Custody arrangements for crack-exposed children had to be made, and this involved foster care, a system already in crisis. The children needed education, but special education programs were in turmoil, too. The images of systems in crisis converged. A wave of drug-addicted women and their children loomed on the horizon, threatening to overwhelm troubled social services.

Administrators, service providers, and experts used these images to argue persistently and forcefully that without additional resources the impending crises could not be avoided. After a decade of Republican cutbacks in funding for social services, the newly humanized crack mothers, subtly impaired crack babies, and troubled but teachable school-aged children provided two things. They established a compelling need, and for state agencies a tool to pry loose needed dollars to support services. They also presented manageable problems, and for state agencies, the kind that could readily be absorbed into the existing mix of services. In both regards these images provided social service administrators, treatment experts, and public health professionals with exactly what they needed to advance their separate causes.

That the crack mother episode peaked during the Reagan-Bush cutbacks in federal spending should not lull anyone into thinking either that cost-cutting Democrats would restore federal funds or that restoration would solve problems associated with foster care or special education. While many would see today's expanded social services as the culmination of enlightened social policies, others see failure, attributing this to administrators' incompetence or ill-will or to inadequate resources. A more critical position argues that social services regulate the potentially disruptive poor.

John Hagdorn, however, points out that social services like other bureaucracies tend toward policies of self-perpetuation; that is, they will preserve budgets, staff, and their scopes of operation often at the expense of the delivery of flexible, effective services (1995). In this context, poor clients and compelling need (the plight of crack babies) provided the rationales for exacting the continuous flow of federal dollars that state social service administrators so needed. But federal funding does not always mean improved services. While client-appropriate treatments were judged effective, the release of funds to expand the treatment network did not necessarily translate into a level of services that met demand.

Racial issues persisted both in the need for the culturally sensitive delivery of services and in the controversy over interracial adoptions. Conflicts over mothering remained, but since complaints about abuse or neglect applied to living children, the topic of fetal abuse dropped out of discussions. And as the children reached school age, the arena of struggle shifted to public education, where the issues affecting drug-exposed children concerned rising costs of special education as well as classroom discipline. The struggles over federal funding defined the context in which these issues were resolved.

• • •

This book is organized to answer a central question about "crack mothers": How and with what consequences did an unusually powerless category of women emerge as a threatening symbol of disorder, the unenviable enemy in the domestic war on drugs? I begin considering this question by looking at the media. Based on television news broadcasts from 1983 to 1994, chapter 1 identifies three dramatically different images of maternal drug use. First were the white middle-class women who had recovered from a psychological addiction to cocaine and who recounted, from the safety of home or treatment facility, the horror of addiction. Once addicted, pregnancy was not enough motivation to break cocaine's hold. Although these women tended to have healthy babies, they regretted that prior drug use had forced their babies to go through withdrawal. Medical experts worried about the babies' longer-term problems.

Next came the poor women of color, residents of America's chaotic inner cities, the crack mothers who activated the crusade. Physically addicted, these women were shown by the networks as indifferent or hostile to the plight of their drug-exposed infants. According to news accounts, crack-exposed infants had high mortality rates. They also underwent withdrawal, suffered severe congenital defects, and faced life with grave mental impairments. Later, the networks humanized crack mothers and even normalized the babies. Like the earlier wave of cocaine mothers, rehabilitated crack mothers recounted their tales of addiction from the safety of drug treatment facilities—though in many cases it had taken legal intervention to force them into treatment. Some crack mothers were angry about being sentenced to prison on drug charges, but these "survivors of the crack 'epidemic'" were prepared to take advantage of treatment to regain custody of their children and to rebuild their lives.

In chapter 2, the focus is on the period leading up to the panic, looking in particular at discrepancies between the news images of actively addicted crack mothers and the much less alarming scientific findings about the problem. Using a variety of documentary sources, I review trends in cocaine and crack use, profiles of crack and cocaine users, and the prevalence of maternal cocaine use. This chapter looks at medical research on the prenatal effects of cocaine and on the controversies surrounding the research cited. I argue that network images, if not most media claims, were based on misinformation, half-truths, exaggeration, and distortion.

The criminal prosecution of crack mothers is the subject of chapter 3. County prosecutors, affected by media stereotypes, invented new crimes. Using manslaughter statutes, laws against child abuse, and even drug-trafficking laws, prosecutors presented charges to grand juries or filed them in court. Timely prosecution would, according to county attorneys, discourage drug use among pregnant women and save babies. To do otherwise bordered on barbarism.

While the war on drugs encouraged such prosecutions, frustration with its failures led some prosecutors to questionable legal theories. Political opportunism cannot be overlooked as a motive. The crusade against crack mothers was also a crusade to protect smaller cities from big-city problems. The goals of the pro-life movement were also embedded in the prosecutions. The failure of prosecutors' attempts to criminalize drug use during pregnancy meant that the problem would have to be addressed in other political arenas.

Chapter 4 provides an understanding of women who used crack, the nature of their addiction, and expansion of the drug treatment network to address their needs. Using ethnographies based on the lives of desperate street addicts, I attempt to place crack mothers in the broader context of economic marginalization, the concentration of poverty, and Republican cutbacks in social services. As crack transformed neighborhoods into drug markets, women as well as men smoked, sacrificing everything in a compulsive effort to purchase the drug. Under these circumstances, mothers sent their children to relatives; but because pregnancy remained valued even among crack smokers, women who understood the effects of crack on the unborn tried, but often failed, in their efforts to cut back or stop drug use entirely.

Understanding this behavior means understanding addiction, including the cultural context that idealized the high and provided settings that encouraged binge behavior. It also means understanding that stopping drug use requires professional intervention. In reality, women struggled to stop or reduce their drug use, but most were unsuccessful (Murphy and Rosenbaum, 1999). The networks used a few success stories, replacing images of renegade mothers with recovering addicts. They also highlighted a few rehabilitation centers to replace images of treatment as questionable endeavors with images of effective, community-based interventions. But bringing drug treatment programs into line with women's needs and expanding the treatment network's capacity to deliver services were difficult, expensive tasks. Women's needs for housing, food, job skills, child care, and transportation continued to go unmet. And the unmet need for drug treatment was even greater in 1994 than it was in 1985.

Shifting from the mothers to the children, chapter 5 profiles the problems children faced as wards of the state and as learning-disabled school children. Because child protective services tended to place in foster care children labeled as drug-exposed, these children disappeared into the increasing population of abused and neglected children. When crack hit the drug markets, child welfare services were already in crisis. Because the federal government sets policy and has a hand in funding child welfare services, the children's fate depended on how Congress resolved differences over the mission of and funding for child protective services. Educators, drawing on questionable clinical studies that defined drug-exposed children as learning disabled, tailored programs to their needs. Statewide plans implemented some of these programs and placed significant new burdens on district administrations and classroom teachers. As special education services geared up to meet the needs of students protected under federal entitlement, Congress capped the increasing costs and provided districts with greater flexibility in disciplining disruptive and potentially violent students with learning disabilities.

Chapter 6 stands back from the details of the crack mother episode to answer questions about its origins and consequences. Under what circumstances and with what effect did possibly the most powerless group of American women become the symbol of all that distressed the nation? This chapter frames the emergence of the crack mother panic against the background of the 1980s and 1990s. Political conservatives and Republicans redefined poverty and the public's responsibility for it. Racial fears renewed by debates about affirmative action policies found expression in the crusade against crack mothers. Moral conservatives, evangelical Christians, and the New Right opposed women's political gains, especially in the arena of reproductive liberty, and saw the crusade against crack mothers as an opportunity to raise, if not extend, fetal rights. Fiscal conservatism fueled by racist and sexist images of poor women of color justified cutbacks in social services in the 1980s. In the 1990s, the problem of maternal drug use was institutionalized in the drug treatment network, child protective services, and special education, and it continued to affect the lives of women and children. Reflecting on the federal response to maternal drug use, the chapter concludes that despite the impression created by the news, the response clearly falls short of the demand for services for women and their children.

The News about Crack Mothers

"Crack mothers," a term coined by the media, referred primarily to women who used cocaine or crack during pregnancy. Socially constructed as black and urban, this group of women became a threatening symbol of everything that was wrong with America. Its cities, its poverty, and its welfare dependency were laid at the feet of crack mothers, who were also blamed for undermining the family and driving up the rates of infant mortality and morbidity. This view of crack mothers, however, is a snapshot in time. Other images existed, some before and others that followed, each uniquely complex and rich.

This chapter sets out to understand the origin of, and the changes in, images associated with crack mothers. My primary source for such images is national network television news—ABC, CBS, and NBC evening news shows—aired between 1983 and 1994. News segments were selected because they mentioned women and crack or cocaine, although not all the women fit the widely recognized "crack mother" image. In all, 84 news segments met these criteria, the universe of prime-time news devoted to this issue. Altogether, the videotapes run 5½ hours; individual segments have a mean running time of 2 minutes, ranging from 20 seconds to 6 minutes.

Analysis of coverage of drug scares and moral panics reveals a typical news-coverage pattern: volume increases, reaches a peak, and then trails off because of decline in the story's news value. The news segments about crack mothers followed a similar pattern (see figure 1.1).

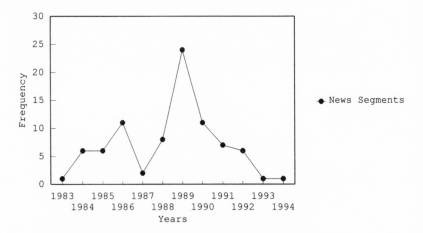

Figure 1.1 Trends in Network News: Women and Crack or Cocaine

Their frequency increased from 1983, peaked in 1989—the height of moral panic—and dropped off after 1991. Because their frequency distribution is bimodal, I have divided coverage into four stages. The networks' discovery of crack revised previous images of drug addicts, and this key event in December 1985 separates the period of increasing news coverage into stage 1 (1983–85) and stage 2 (1985–87), as shown in table 1.1. In 1987, unrest in the Soviet Bloc, Irangate, and the Tawana Brawley story left little time for the news about drugs. This natural break marks off the period of increasing news volume from the panic, stage 3 (1988–90), which begins when the networks broadcast images of crack mothers in 1988. Following the panic, the networks reduced coverage, moving onto more newsworthy stories by 1994. Stage 4 runs from 1991 to 1994.

Features that run through the news coverage about crack mothers are summarized in table 1.1. "Main story line" refers to whether a news segment focused on the spread of drugs or drug use by pregnant women. The spread of cocaine and crack from one group to another was the main story line in the first two stages of news coverage. In the second two stages, drug use by pregnant women defined the story line. Turning to the people depicted as addicts, table 1.1 shows that men

Table 1.1 Network News Images: Women and Crack or Cocaine

	Stages of News Coverage							
	1		2		3		4	
	1983–85[a]		1985–87		1988–90		1991–94	
Measures and Variables	n	%[b]	n	%	n	%	n	%
No. news segments	10	12	16	19	43	51	15	18
Main story line								
Spread of drugs	7	70	10	63	13	30	2	
Mothers/babies	2		3		29	67	13	86
No. crack/cocaine addicts								
Women	16	42	18	34	89	63	19	76
Men	22	58	35	66	53	37	6	24
Total	38	100	5	10	142	100	25	100
No. drug-exposed babies	3		11		93		31	
Race/ethnicity — women								
White	12	75	13	72	28	31	3	
Black	3		2		49	55	16	84
Hispanic	1		3		3		3	
Unknown	0		0		10	11	0	
Context — women								
Civil society[c]	6	37	1		7	8	3	
Drug life[d]	2		5	28	23	26	4	
Drug treatment	5	31	8	44	35	39	5	26
Criminal justice	1		0		15	17	3	
Social services	0		0		0		4	
Other	2		4		9	10	0	
Total women	16	100	18	100	89	100	19	100

Note: Table is based on 84 news segments about women and crack or cocaine aired on ABC, CBS, and NBC from 1983 to 1994. News segments are the unit of analysis for "main story line"; persons are the unit of analysis for remaining variables.
[a]The first stage of coverage ends in November 1985; the second stage begins in December 1985, when the networks discovered crack.
[b]Percentages are rounded off to the nearest whole number.
[c]"Civil society" refers to conventional settings, e.g., the home, restaurants, and television studios.
[d]"Drug life" refers to settings in which illicit drugs are used, e.g., parties, street corners, and crack houses.

outnumbered women in the first two stages of news coverage and that in the last two stages, the pattern was reversed. All but a few of the drug-exposed babies appeared on camera during the second two stages of news coverage, underscoring the news value of maternal drug use.

In the section focusing on the race of female addicts, the table indicates that they were white in the first two stages of coverage and black in the last two stages. The last variable described in table 1.1 is labeled "Context," and it refers to the social settings in which female addicts were interviewed or filmed. In stage 1, conventional settings or "civil society," including homes, restaurants, or television studios, provided a background for female addicts. While most female addicts shown in stages 2 and 3 were filmed or interviewed in drug rehabilitation centers, a quarter were filmed on street corners, at parties, or in crack houses. Some 17 percent of the female addicts shown in stage 3 were filmed in the context of law enforcement, criminal courts, or prison. In stage 4, female addicts were interviewed in drug rehabilitation or social service centers.

This chapter places in relief the events surrounding the social construction of crack mothers, and the progression of the panic can be discerned in the accounts described. Organized according to the four-stage model illustrated in table 1.1, the chapter traces the rise and fall of crack mothers as a news story. And while other news lines initially overshadowed the women who used drugs during pregnancy, their portrayal provided the framework for the later emergence of race- and class-specific images of crack mothers.

Stage 1: Recreational Cocaine Use (1983–1985)

Cindy, a white middle-class housewife, was the first "cocaine mother" to appear on network news, but she was the third woman interviewed for a 1984 NBC report on the cocaine epidemic (August 9 and 10). Like the other women, Cindy had been introduced to cocaine by the man in her life. The women had not understood cocaine's addictive potential; each had been assured that the drug was safe—that is, non-

THE NEWS ABOUT CRACK MOTHERS

addicting—and could be used recreationally. Dr. Josette Mondonaro, a drug expert interviewed at a California treatment center, explained that women used cocaine to "pump up [their] low self-esteem." Cindy and other women used it to cope with personal problems, to feel better, to gain a competitive edge. But they became addicted. Even when Cindy realized she was pregnant, she continued to use cocaine. Interviewed in her home after the baby was born, Cindy was shown bathing a healthy infant. An NBC correspondent, however, put the maternal scene in darker context: when a woman uses cocaine during pregnancy, the fetus suffers from oxygen deprivation. Normal-looking babies like Cindy's could as a result still suffer from the longer-term effects of cocaine.

Linda, another white middle-class mother, interviewed on CBS, stopped using cocaine when she found out she was pregnant. She avoided miscarriage and premature labor but failed to protect her baby from withdrawal (1985, September 11). Babies exposed to cocaine during pregnancy go through withdrawal, showing signs of jitteriness and tremulousness, said Dr. Ira Chasnoff of the National Association for Perinatal Addiction Research and Education. Other dangers existed, too. Sudden infant death syndrome and birth defects were linked to maternal cocaine use. Relieved to have avoided these dangers, Linda admitted that her daughter had at birth exhibited the telltale signs of withdrawal—nervousness, tremulousness, and irritability. She was remorseful for having put her daughter through the ordeal.

Still, two cocaine mothers hardly stood out when 7 out of 10 news stories aired from 1983 to December 1985 tracked the spread of cocaine. The networks reported staggering estimates for cocaine use: In the early 1980s, 20 to 22 million people had tried cocaine (CBS, 1983, February 7; NBC, 1984, August 9 and 10). Four to five million people used it regularly (CBS, 1984, May 31; NBC, 1984, August 9; ABC, 1985, July 16). Of the regular users, 20 to 50 percent were expected to become addicted (CBS, 1984, May 30). Cocaine users included heirs to industrial fortunes, members of the House of Representatives, and Hollywood stars.[1] Ongoing investigations conducted by the

23

major sports leagues produced a continuing source for stories about sports heroes and cocaine. The Vikings, the Saints, the Broncos, the Dodgers, the Cowboys, and the Royals were among the teams investigated between 1980 and 1983. Blue-collar workers emulated the rich and famous, though technicians interviewed for a segment on cocaine use among defense-plant workers noted that most dealers and users were to be found at managerial levels (CBS, 1983, February 7). Network reports also chronicled cocaine use by nuclear-power-plant workers and, following air crashes, by transportation workers.

Women were a concern in the spread of cocaine. As a vulnerable group, they illustrated dangers of middle-class cocaine use. In February 1983, CBS correspondent Jerry Bowen interviewed middle-class cocaine users at a treatment facility in California (February 7). Jennifer, 14 years old and white, said that she began snorting cocaine because "everyone was doing it." Like many others, she thought cocaine was harmless. Bennet, a 23-year-old white businessman, became a dealer to support his cocaine habit. Another man squandered his inheritance on cocaine. Cocaine reached into the heartland of America, too, corrupting unlikely groups. In 1984, NBC broadcast a segment on teenage cocaine use in Driggs, Idaho, population 727 (August 9). Chuck, the son of a Mormon bishop, grew up in a bucolic farming community, yet he described having had a $500-a-day cocaine habit. Lori, blond and blue-eyed, swallowed hard as she recalled exchanging sex for cocaine.

The on-site correspondent cited statistics from the National Institute on Drug Abuse: 22 million people had tried cocaine, 4 million used cocaine regularly, and each day 5,000 people tried cocaine for the first time. The number of young people using cocaine had tripled between 1979 and 1984. Teenagers freebased cocaine, smoking more concentrated doses and engaging in riskier behavior, according to a 1984 CBS report (November 27 and 28). Chas, who was interviewed in his middle-class home, explained that he started to sniff and freebase cocaine in response to pressures to do well in school. Tina, a white 19 year old, regularly freebased cocaine. And a shrouded figure, seen only in outline, explained that freebasing produced an exhilarating experience and an uncontrollable desire for more cocaine. Teens, not realizing that snorting cocaine only once could produce addiction, were in danger of ruining their lives, said William Pollen, spokesperson for the National Institute on Drug Abuse. Dr. Mark Gold, director of the Cocaine Hotline in New Jersey, noted that most adolescents wanted to get off drugs but did not know how (CBS, 1984, November 28).

Once thought safe, cocaine was redefined as dangerously addictive. It was considered psychologically addicting;[2] that is, people who used it liked its effects on their mental state and wanted to use the drug repeatedly (CBS, 1984, May 30). Most addicts had started as recreational cocaine users, but soon some lost control (CBS, 1983, February 7; see also NBC, 1984, August 9 and 10). Dr. Gold of the Cocaine Hotline estimated that 25 to 50 percent of the people who used cocaine would fall victim to addiction (CBS, 1984, May 30). Cocaine was reported to produce intense cravings (CBS, 1984, November 27). One user described his exhilarating first experience with cocaine and then recalled thinking, "God! Where am I going to get some more?" Kim started with a $10 bag of cocaine and then wanted more, too. Within a single week cocaine had taken over the life of Chuck, an IV cocaine user. He would get high, the effects would subside, and then the craving would "get bad" and he would want more and more cocaine (NBC, 1984, August 9).

According to animal research, cocaine use could prove fatal (CBS, 1984, May 30). In one experiment, monkeys were able to push a button, releasing different drugs via an IV lead into the bloodstream. Cocaine was the only drug monkeys ingested to the point of seizure and death. This deadly progression was masked, Dr. Gold explained, by the euphoric feelings produced by cocaine. The consequences were no less deadly for humans (CBS, 1984, May 30). Kathryn, a recovering addict, recalled becoming addicted to cocaine from the first moment she tried it. For five years she was an active addict. Motivated to achieve the ultimate high, she could not live without cocaine. She lost the desire to eat, to engage in sex, and to survive. Dr. Gold noted that because people like Kathryn think drug use is normal, it takes near-death experiences to make them realize the extent of their addictions. Arnold Washton, a noted drug researcher, added that cocaine gives the illusion of control when in fact addicts cannot stop using the drug (CBS, 1984, May 31).

For a largely middle-class client population, recovery programs were abundant. CBS examined several of these (1983, February 7). Co-kenders of San Francisco ran a one-week residential program that catered to an affluent clientele. A more traditional program run by Beverly Glenn Hospital required a three-week stay in the hospital followed by counseling for one year. At a cost of $400 per day, however, hospital programs were not within the reach of blue-collar addicts. Perhaps this is why, CBS noted, Hollywood studios and large companies like Lockheed had started to put drug awareness information in employees' pay envelopes.

The Cocaine Hotline, a New Jersey answering service staffed by ex-cocaine addicts, counseled callers.[3] In New York, established treatment centers like Phoenix House geared up to deal with cocaine addicts, requiring abstinence, using ex-addicts in support groups, and working to prevent relapse (CBS, 1984, May 30 and 31). A Santa Cruz, California, treatment facility designed specifically for women cocaine users, some of whom had children, was the focus of a 1984 NBC report (August 9 and 10). The correspondent remarked that feelings of guilt over failing their children explained why some women avoided treatment. To make treatment more attractive to women, men had to be excluded, added Josette Mondonaro, one of the facility's doctors. Even so, recovery was difficult. One woman at the California center said she was so distraught at defining herself as an addict that she cried every day for a year.

Stage 2: The Discovery of Crack (1985–1987)

In December 1985, NBC announced that crack, a new form of cocaine, had taken the drug markets by storm (December 1). The first sketchy estimates of crack use came from New York City. CBS reported that over a quarter of crack users there were under the age of 28 (1985, December 4). A year later, ABC noted that in New York City a third of the cocaine users smoked crack and that half the drug-related hospital admissions were for crack abuse (1986, May 27). Crack had spread from 19 cities in 1986 to 40 in 1987 (ABC, 1986, August 5; NBC, 1987, February 27). Crack produced the most powerful high experienced drug users had ever felt. It was so good, one user said, he could do anything (NBC, 1985, December 1). Another described an intensely vivid high just five seconds after smoking crack pellets (CBS, 1985, December 4). A young man said the drug put him on top of the world (NBC, 1986, May 23); and a teenager who claimed to have smoked two rocks within the previous 30 minutes said he wished he had two more just like them (ABC, 1986, May 27).

In addition to the euphoria it produced, the drug had a darker side. Michael, a crack cook and dealer, said he got hooked the first or second time he tried crack. He lost weight, became suicidal, and almost died (ABC, 1986, July 15). And an increasing range of violent behavior was reported. When the money runs out, crack addicts turn into violent criminals, said one experienced drug user (ABC, 1986, July 15). They would do anything, including robbing, beating, and killing people, to get money for the drug (ABC, 1986, July 28).

Experts were called in to explain the addiction (NBC, 1985, December 1; CBS, 1985, December 4). Mitchell Rosenthal, Phoenix House Foundation president, described crack as causing secondary dependence.[4] The drug produced a short high, followed by a depression. To alleviate the depression, the user smoked more crack. Dr. Rosenthal predicted more people would become addicted. Interviewed by CBS, Arnold Washton, spokesperson for the Cocaine Helpline in New Jersey, noted that addiction could set in within two to three months (CBS, 1985, December 4). A year later, Dr. Washton likened crack to fast food: it's cheap, consumed immediately, and leaves the user wanting more (ABC, 1986, May 27). He also reported that its effects included intense paranoia, violent behavior, extreme depression, and suicide. In treatment, Dr. Washton noted, crack addicts were prone to sudden unexplained relapses (ABC, 1986, July 15).

ABC reported that crack could be purchased anywhere from the ghetto to suburbia (1986, May 27). In one Westchester County high school, 25 to 30 percent of the students had tried crack, and a school counselor predicted that curiosity about crack would lead to an increase in use among teenagers. In Miami, crack smokers included people from all backgrounds—one South Florida entrepreneur shown had a $1,000-a-day habit (ABC, 1986, July 15). And the networks followed the crackdown. In one litter-filled crack house, police arrested black users, while in a major move against dealers, the New York Police Department impounded 27 cars belonging to buyers from New Jersey suburbs who had driven into northern Manhattan (NBC, 1986, August 4).

Crack was labeled an inner-city problem in a pivotal 1987 news segment that changed stereotypes. NBC reported that crack use had spread, but, said Robert Stutman, spokesperson for the Drug Enforcement Administration, there was some good news (February 27): Crack use had leveled off in the suburbs—although Stutman said he did not believe it had leveled off in the inner city. As he reported a rise in drug-related violence, the camera showed police surveillance tapes. Black and Hispanic Americans furtively bought and sold crack on chaotic inner-city street corners. In like manner, the camera panned a treatment center in which all the clients were Hispanic or black. Drug therapist Arnold Washton noted that admissions to drug treatment centers for crack addiction were on the rise.

In contrast with the interest they showed in crack, the networks paid limited attention to cocaine. As table 1.1 shows, only 6 of 16 news segments covered the cocaine story, although the plight of cocaine babies, the "newest victims" of the drug epidemic, occasioned dramatic coverage (CBS, 1985, December 30; ABC, 1986, July 11; CBS, 1986, August 29). In a Los Angeles hospital, a premature baby whose mother had snorted two lines of cocaine before delivery trembled in an incubator (CBS, 1985, December 30). The reporter explained that the baby was on life-support systems, did not move, made no sound, and had gone through withdrawal. This baby was the tip of the iceberg: half the babies in one Los Angeles hospital tested positive for cocaine.

Moreover, the effects of maternal cocaine use were serious. Judy Howard, a UCLA pediatrician, said that babies exposed to cocaine in the womb had fluctuations in blood pressure, showed physical abnormalities including kidney and facial deformities, and faced later problems in development. Symptoms varied, said the CBS correspondent (1985, December 30). Angela, a three year old, had been prenatally exposed to cocaine, and she had no visible defects, although her symptoms included hyperactivity and jitteriness. Another toddler, however, could not sit up, crawl, or feed herself. The correspondent announced, "At 21, the child will have an IQ of 50. She will be unable to dress herself or live alone."

In ABC's report, cocaine babies were considered to risk such serious problems as strokes and heart attacks (1986, July 11). And the incidence of cerebral palsy and mental retardation was said to be higher than normal among these babies. Because so many babies at the hospital featured had been exposed to cocaine—from 20 to 50 percent—the staff had to be prepared at each birth to counteract the effects of withdrawal. As one doctor spoke, the camera panned the neonatal unit, showing row upon row of incubators, in each presumably lying a cocaine baby.

The mothers were portrayed to be at fault. Jane, who had a $500-a-day freebase habit, had given birth prematurely to twins each weighing 2 pounds 3 ounces. Although she had believed cocaine would not affect the pregnancy or her babies, she had tried but been unable to stop. The twins were jittery and tremulous, revealing the signs of cocaine withdrawal. Expressing the same guilt that other white middle-class cocaine users had, Jane regretted her choices. "Innocent children," she said, "had to go through withdrawal because I wanted to use these drugs" (ABC, 1986, July 11).

ABC reported an enormous demand for treatment: 14 million of the 21 million Americans who used drugs and alcohol needed treatment (1986, September 17). Most Americans thought addicts should be treated, but most treatment programs had relapse rates of 70 percent, and successful treatments came at a high price. Lifeline, a Washington, D.C., residential treatment program, claimed a 60 percent success rate. Patients were prescribed antidepressants to relieve cocaine cravings; they attended meetings and counseling; and upon discharge patients entered a two-year follow-up program. Lifeline cost $15,000, while other programs' fees varied from $3,000 per year for outpatient treatment to $12,000 per month for inpatient programs.

Medical insurance covered the fees and financed significant growth in the so-called "treatment industry." The ABC news report noted that not all programs were as concerned with patient follow-up as Dr. Herb Klebber, a Yale University psychiatrist, would have liked to see. Dr. Klebber warned against the "dreadful" practice of releasing patients with only a telephone number as follow-up. The ABC correspondent, however, reminded the audience of the real problem: 180,000 treatment places existed to serve 7 million drug abusers.

Stage 3: The Crusade against Crack Mothers (1988–1990)

The American public was introduced to crack mothers by NBC in the 1988 report that featured Tracy Watson, Erocelia Fandino, and Stephanie (October 24 and 25). A pregnant Tracy Watson smoked crack on national television; Erocelia Fandino was shown recovering after giving birth to her premature, cocaine-exposed baby; a street addict named Stephanie, headed for a crack house, told of leaving her baby in the hospital because she had no housing or money. All three were active drug users, although they were filmed at home, in the hospital, and on the street.

They were also women of color: black women represented 55 percent of the women shown as drug users on television from 1988 to 1990 (see table 1.1).[5] And Tracy, Erocelia, and Stephanie belonged to the inner city, a turbulent, drug-infested world set apart from the circumstances of middle-class news audiences. NBC reported that middle-class Americans had stopped using crack (1988, January 13). The middle class, according to a recovering crack addict, had "too much to lose not to give up drugs" (NBC, 1988, May 16 and 17). On the other hand, drugs were "a way of life in the city," noted another

NBC report (1988, May 16 and 17). That the inner city had crack addicts, added David Musto of Yale University, was understandable. There were no jobs, the schools were inferior, the future bleak.

Crack mothers, like other inner-city residents, were caught in the grip of a powerful physical addiction, according to a 1988 ABC report (July 13).[6] Crack caused a change across the brain said noted drug researchers Dr. Anna Rose Childress and Dr. Charles O'Brien, both of the Philadelphia Veterans Medical Center. The rapid, intense euphoria—the rush—produced by smoking crack was permanently encoded in the brain. Dr. Childress explained that the change accounted for the quick compulsive addiction associated with crack use. And according to Dr. Jerome Jaffe, director of the Addiction Research Center, the rush helped explain the sudden relapses of people who had completed treatment. External triggers reactivated the memory, and with it, the craving.

Interviewed again later by ABC, Dr. Childress related what crack addicts had told her (1989, February 28). Addicts, she said, likened cravings to something that washed over them—as if someone had emptied a pail of water on their heads. From that moment on, addicts thought only about crack. They were powerless to resist it (CBS, 1990, December 17). For women, crack became more important than their children: They did not think about pregnancy. They abandoned infants in their pursuit of crack. When irritable, they abused or neglected children (CBS, 1989, June 20). The compulsion was so great that it drove some white middle-class women to high-risk behaviors. And in urban centers like Harlem, a few risked death and injury (NBC, 1990, January 3).

Cocaine-exposed babies emerged as a news story in their own right. In Florida, health workers were required to report suspected cocaine use by pregnant women to social services. From these numbers ABC projected that 10,000 cocaine babies would be born in Florida in 1988 (1988, October 13).[7] NBC showed a Florida hospital where 1 in 10 delivering women used cocaine within hours of childbirth, and the report said drug use had become so common among pregnant women in Chicago that routine obstetrics included drug treatment (1988, October 24 and 25). CBS and NBC reported the results of a 40-hospital survey conducted by Dr. Chasnoff of the National Association for Perinatal Addiction Research and Education: His conclusion was that women gave birth to 375,000 cocaine babies a year (CBS, 1989, January 9; NBC, 1989, July 7). CBS used this same figure to describe both crack and cocaine babies (1990, April 5; 1990, December 17). In New York and Kansas City, cocaine babies represented 15 percent of the births (CBS, 1989, May 10; NBC, 1989, November 7). ABC reported a lower estimate: 100,000 babies had been prenatally exposed to cocaine in 1990 (1990, March 7).

Prenatal cocaine exposure was linked to infant mortality. In Washington, D.C., infant mortality rates were reported to have increased by 50 percent (NBC, 1989, September, 30; ABC, 1990, January 13). ABC, however, provided background, indicating that Washington, D.C., already had the highest rates of infant mortality, which was also related to poverty, unemployment, and lack of prenatal care (1990, January 13).

Birth or congenital defects were reported, too. A study conducted by the Centers for Disease Control in Atlanta showed that babies exposed to cocaine were five times more likely to suffer serious birth defects than were other babies (NBC, 1989, August 10). Babies born to cocaine users had three times the normal risk of birth defects (ABC, 1989, November 14). This was the first study, ABC news anchor Peter Jennings said, that linked cocaine to specific defects; previous studies had only linked cocaine to withdrawal (1989, November 14). In a CBS news story, Dr. Avery, a physician at Children's National Medical Center, said he had examined hundreds of crack babies and that many were premature and underweight and some had suffered brain damage (1990, April 5). To demonstrate, Dr. Avery held up a cross-sectional image of a child's brain, pointed to the dark spots on the film, and said that the shadows represented brain tissue destroyed by cocaine.

Although cocaine use during pregnancy was also linked to miscarriage and premature birth, low birth weight epitomized cocaine babies. In one case, a premature baby weighing 15 ounces was shown on television and described as a cocaine baby (ABC, 1990, January 13). Tubes connected him to life support. He struggled in his incubator as a nurse took his minuscule hand in hers, offering comfort while he endured withdrawal. The camera panned the hospital unit showing dozens of incubators; each held a very small, one assumes cocaine-exposed, baby.

In addition, cocaine was linked to neurobehavioral problems in infants. Withdrawal made the babies irritable, and offsetting possible lifelong consequences required special care, according to Dr. Chasnoff (ABC, 1988, October 13). ABC reported more severe difficulties: "cocaine syndrome" was described as neurological damage that created lifelong problems for the children—hyperactivity, poor concentration, and a limited attention span (1988, October 13). The impact of prenatal exposure, explained an ABC correspondent, was worse in the ghetto (1990, January 13).

At Hale House in Harlem, a home for abused and abandoned children, six or seven crack-exposed children were shown playing games. Dr. Lorraine Hale, the director, said they were not retarded but slow learners (NBC, 1988, October 25). In a Los Angeles school, teachers described drug-exposed toddlers as forgetful, unable to perform tasks they had learned the day before (NBC, 1988, October 25). School-aged children were expected to have problems, too. Edward, a seven year old who had been exposed to crack during his mother's pregnancy, pushed and shoved his classmates (CBS, 1990, April 5). His foster mother described the disruptive activities that got him suspended from school: fighting, destroying property, and hitting his teacher. He had wide mood swings. He could not concentrate. His behavior was unpredictable and impulsive.

In 1990, Dr. Reed Tuckerson, the U.S. public health commissioner, called for the inclusion of drug treatment in routine prenatal care; later he resigned his post for lack of support (ABC, 1990, January 13). At Harlem Hospital, more social workers were needed to track down crack mothers who had abandoned their infants (NBC, 1988, October 25). Hale House was one of the few places that took the abandoned babies (NBC, 1988, October 24). In Philadelphia, the Children of

Light Mission ran a 24-hour-a-day emergency placement service for children whose families had been disrupted by drugs and alcohol. The welfare department in Philadelphia had certified nurses as foster care parents to provide enough placements for abandoned crack babies (CBS, 1990, June 13).

Across the country the numbers were climbing: 500,000 children were wards of the state in 1989, and the figure was expected to increase to 850,000 by 1995 (CBS, 1989, January 9). In 1990, NBC attributed the increases in children in foster care to abuse by drug- or alcohol-impaired caretakers (1990, October 4). The cost of the various associated services—drug treatment and child protective services—was staggering: Government estimates reported by ABC and CBS placed the cost at $5 billion over five years (ABC, 1990, March 7; CBS, 1990, April 5).

Reports of criminal cases against cocaine mothers announced the panic. CBS reported in 1989 that Toni Hudson—a black woman filmed standing before the court—had used cocaine during pregnancy and delivered a cocaine-addicted baby. Florida prosecutors arraigned her on criminal charges of delivering a controlled substance to a minor (January 9). In May of the same year, CBS reported that after Melanie Green's newborn died of cocaine-related complications, Illinois prosecutors took a charge of manslaughter to the grand jury (May 10). The grand jury refused to indict Green, a decision that cleared her of all charges in the death of her son, but that did not resolve the growing controversy (CBS, 1989, May 26).

The networks reported the cases of other black women who had been charged (NBC, 1989, July 7). Jennifer Johnson was indicted in Florida for delivering a controlled substance to her newborn. Cassandra Gethers was awaiting trial on charges of child abuse for having delivered a second "cocaine-addicted baby." In Washington, D.C., Brenda Vaughan, pregnant and found to be using cocaine, was arrested for forging a check. For an offense that usually drew probation, the judge sentenced Vaughan to four months in jail, in an effort to protect the baby from its mother's drug use.

Two prosecutors, Paul Logli from Winnebago County, Illinois, and

Jeff Deen from Seminole County, Florida, took center stage in the networks' coverage of the crack mother trials. Logli, who had charged Melanie Green with manslaughter, said in a CBS interview that he saw no difference between "an adult giving a child cocaine and a pregnant woman ingesting the drug to the detriment of the unborn child" (1989, May 10). If an adult who gives a child cocaine acts with criminal disregard, then by the prosecutor's analogy, the same intent would apply to the pregnant woman. On NBC news, Logli explained further. "There is nothing more wanton," he said, "than to voluntarily ingest illegal drugs when that person knows she's pregnant and that person knows she is doing irreversible harm and sometimes fatal harm to that child" (1989, July 7). The well-being of unborn babies weighed heavily on court officers. In Washington, D.C., Judge Peter Wolf, who sentenced Brenda Vaughan, noted, "Maybe sending a woman to jail is like killing a fly with a shotgun, but I had other concerns. I had concerns about an unborn helpless child to be" (NBC, 1989, July 7).

Lynn Paltrow, staff attorney for the American Civil Liberties Union, defended or assisted in the defense of several women charged with crimes for using cocaine during pregnancy. Interviewed widely, Paltrow and her clients focused their comments on four issues. The first was intent: there was none. Even though traces of cocaine were found in the urine of her baby, Jennifer Johnson had not intended harm to the baby (ABC, 1989, July 12). The second issue was bad precedent. "When prosecutors go after women for this kind of behavior," Paltrow said, "there is no stopping the state. . . . We will see the formation of prenatal police" (CBS, 1989, May 10). The third issue was deterrence. Prosecutors' charges were intended to discourage drug use among pregnant women. But Paltrow and others argued that the threat of prosecution would backfire, encouraging pregnant drug users to stay away from treatment and to avoid prenatal care, get abortions, or deliver at home (ABC, 1989, July 12). The fourth was lack of treatment programs. Incarcerated women reported they had tried to get drug treatment, but programs had turned them away (NBC, 1989, July 7).

In the "first trial of its kind," Jennifer Johnson was found guilty on two charges of delivering drugs to a minor, her two cocaine-exposed babies (ABC, 1989, July 13). According to the judge, the verdict gave notice to women to seek treatment before giving birth. Afterward, networks framed matters as a conflict between treatment and punishment. ABC, for example, began its segment on the Johnson trial by asking, "What would you do with pregnant women who use drugs and pass those drugs on to their babies?" The correspondent continued, "You should know that some law enforcement authorities think it's time to prosecute, to consider those mothers as criminals" (1989, July 12). NBC blurred the lines between treatment and punishment in its report on a court program in Miami that gave first-time offenders the choice of going to jail or getting treatment (1989, September 12).

CBS compared treatment and punishment approaches, finding a get-tough approach more effective (1990, December 17). A young mother in Minneapolis was described as being one of the lucky ones. A public health nurse advised the young woman on parenting, and she attended group therapy and went for drug treatment, including acupuncture. She had been moved into affordable housing. But a county health official said programs like hers seldom worked. On the other hand, coercive programs seemed to be effective, according to CBS. Another young mother said that the humane approach had not worked with her. She smoked more crack when social workers brought her baby to the crack house hoping to persuade her to come home. What got her to stop was the threat of jail. The tougher the program, she said, the better.

Stage 4: Recovering Mothers and Resilient Children (1991–1994)

Still, recovery was portrayed as possible for some mothers. A young black woman enrolled in a New Orleans drug treatment program recalled she had first used crack after her brother's death in a drug deal gone bad (NBC, 1992, December 29). Addiction followed. If she had crack or the money to buy it, she was fine. If not, she had only the pain of her brother's loss and her mother's anger. She consistently chose the drug over the pain. And even when the son of another woman, Charron Gaines, told her he feared she would die from drugs, Gaines did not stop (ABC, 1993, June 10). For many addicted mothers, it took legal intervention to force them into treatment, although a few got help on their own. Once in treatment, the young women expressed remorse at having hurt their families and children, and they looked forward to rebuilding their lives and their families.

Some former addicts featured credited their recovery to the Christian Community Youth Against Drugs Foundation that operated a therapeutic community in New Orleans (NBC, 1992, December 30). The program treated addiction as a physical and a spiritual condition. Spiritual renewal through religious practice and companionship was as important to recovery as rebuilding the body through medical care and good food. The program turned no one away. It served the poor and the uninsured. It was free and permitted addicts to stay as long as they wanted. The program, according to independent evaluators, worked: it had a 70 percent success rate.

Outreach programs were shown that catered to women, offering "a second chance" (ABC, 1993, June 10). Sisters, an outreach program in Nashville staffed by counselors and former addicts, went door-to-door in six public housing projects, getting drug-using women into a 30-day outpatient treatment program. Sisters picked up the women, transported them to treatment, and afterward returned them home. If the women needed child care, Sisters provided it. When the women completed the program, Sisters provided 24-hour support, including counseling, group therapy, and recreational activity—especially in the evenings, when the temptation to use drugs was the strongest.

Women who abused or neglected older children began to be included in definitions of crack mothers. Maggie Baily, for instance, was charged with cocaine possession in Houston after her three-year-old grandchild sold the drug to an undercover police officer (NBC, 1991, September 17). ABC noted that another crack mother, Joyce Howard, was turned in to police by her frightened 11-year-old daughter—the oldest of six children. The tape of the daughter's 911 call from the family home on Long Island was played repeatedly on television (1992, September 10).

It was increasingly plain that crack destroyed whole families. As a result the epidemic put social workers in the position of making critical decisions about babies and children of drug-using parents (ABC, 1992, May 20). According to David Liederman, executive director of the Child Welfare League of America, social workers—not police— were the real frontline troops in the war on drugs; but without more social workers and smaller caseloads, child welfare services could do little to protect the children. The recession had driven up caseloads, while funding for child protective services had been reduced. The stress of trying to do more with less when children's lives were at stake pushed experienced social workers into early retirement.

In June 1991, the U.S. Commission on Children published its report on the status of children in America. CBS and NBC both aired segments on a "lost generation," attributing the deterioration of life for children to drugs, homelessness, and poverty (CBS, 1991, June 24; NBC, 1991, June 24). CBS interviewed Dr. Houchang Modanlou, director of newborn services at a Long Beach, California, hospital, who said many young lives are impaired from birth by a mother's drug and alcohol use (1991, June 24). The camera focused on a four-day-old premature infant, a "cocaine baby." Dr. Modanlou said 375,000 babies a year were threatened by prenatal exposure to drugs—the figure that had been widely reported. The segment included an interview with a homeless woman who said that when her welfare check ran out she lived on the street, taking her son with her. It also included an interview with a grandmother who stretched meager resources to take in the children of her daughter, who had been jailed on drug charges.

Signaling a broadening perspective, a 1991 ABC report indicated that while falling victim to their parents' drug abuse, crack-exposed children were also the victims of three myths (July 24). First, there may be no such thing as a crack child, said an ABC reporter. Most youngsters had been exposed in utero to a variety of drugs. Another myth was that crack-exposed children were "minorities and city kids":

"Surveys . . . show that most are white, and they are in school yards everywhere." Third, crack kids "are not monsters," said the correspondent. "Some are severely impaired, some not at all; most are somewhere in between, with a wide variety of problems."

The ABC report followed two crack-exposed youngsters, a white brother and sister, enrolled in special education classes in an undisclosed location. The brother, aware that he was a drug-exposed baby, said crack made him "hyper, a lot hyper." His struggle to gain a measure of self-control was a precondition for learning. The elementary school staff helped with behavioral and academic trouble, focusing on difficulties in learning basic skills like reading. His younger sister had also been exposed to drugs in the womb, although she had benefited from three years of preparation for kindergarten. But most schools were ill equipped to meet the needs of students like these youngsters.

In addition the ABC report examined an experimental approach taken by a predominately black elementary school in St. Louis. Alma Grimes, a case manager for kids with problems, coordinated an outreach program that identified drug-using parents and brought them into the schools, where she mobilized services to help them and their children. But most schools, noted the ABC correspondent, could not afford this level of service. "America," she said, "is now faced with an inescapable choice: watch its growing numbers of drug-exposed children become more lost and confused, posing an even bigger problem for the country. Or it can go to the trouble and expense of helping them."

ABC also reported two studies challenging the notion of "crack babies" as premature, underweight, trembling infants headed for developmental problems (1992, July 2). The first study, by Dr. Jane Ellis at the Yerkes Primate Center in Atlanta, found that baby monkeys prenatally exposed to cocaine were as healthy as those not exposed. In a human study conducted by Claire Coles at Grady Hospital in Atlanta, babies born to women both who had and who had not used cocaine were all found behaviorally normal. It was not cocaine exposure but lifestyle that made the difference: If the mother used alcohol, smoked, abused drugs, and had no prenatal care, then the outcomes were poor.

Cocaine was not, therefore, the single cause, said Dr. Coles. No one involved with either study, ABC's correspondent said, thought cocaine was harmless. Its long-term effects had to be examined. But most researchers would be happy to see the term "crack baby" disappear, because "it is impossible to single out one factor—crack—among so many that posed grave risks to a newborn's health and future."

However, prosecuting crack mothers still attracted media attention. In Greenville, South Carolina, prosecutors used criminal negligence statutes to arrest drug-using pregnant women (ABC, 1991, September 17). Once arrested, the women were given the choice of treatment or jail. Proponents claimed that the program made women seek treatment before delivering babies. Critics said the threat of jail drove women away from the hospital and that it fell more heavily on the poor. ABC represented the Greenville program as one that appeared to work, although the news segment raised questions about fairness (1991, September 17).

In Charleston, a CBS correspondent described a controversial program at the Medical University of South Carolina (1994, March 10). It too gave women a choice of treatment or jail. Pregnant women who tested positive for drugs were ordered into drug treatment, and if they refused or did not attend, then the police were brought in and the women threatened with jail. Charles Condon, attorney for the county, defended the program: "They had a neonatal unit filled with crack babies, and the question became how to stop that." Condon explained, "It's medicine that cares about children. Would you let people come into this hospital year after year after year with drugs, cocaine, with crack-affected babies?"

According to the correspondent, critics complained that success came at the expense of violating mothers' civil rights. Betty Collins, a 24-year-old black woman, was sent to prison following a conviction on child endangerment charges. Collins's three-week-old daughter was taken from her after cocaine was found in the child's stool. "Nobody," she said, "should have to go through this just to get off drugs. It doesn't take jail." But despite Collins's efforts to get off drugs, she was charged with child endangerment. "They did not consider my efforts to improve myself," she said. "They just threw me in jail. I think that is very unfair."

Collins's attorney, Rauch Wise, denied his client intended to harm her child. His client had "abused her body in taking cocaine"; she had "not abused her child." Wise also believed South Carolina was playing a racist game. "Of all the women I've represented, only two have been white. The vast majority of them are black. And all of them are poor," said Wise.

The Center for Reproductive Law and Policy, Lynn Paltrow's group, announced plans to sue Medical University of South Carolina on behalf of women like Betty Collins to end South Carolina's punitive approach and to replace it with drug treatment programs designed for pregnant addicts. But while giving air time to the critics, CBS did not endorse their position. Standing outside the courthouse in Charleston, the correspondent said, "Both sides say they want to protect children. Both sides say they want to help mothers kick drugs. So which side is right? Like a modern-day Solomon, this court is being asked to decide" (1994, March 10).

Realities and Images

At the height of the crusade against crack mothers, network news defined crack mothers as criminals and focused on the harmful effects of
prenatal cocaine exposure. In the crusade's concluding phases, the networks tempered their portrait of crack mothers and scaled back on
their estimates of cocaine-related harm. That the news assessments
changed suggests that the problem rested on less firm ground than the
American public had been led to believe. This chapter tests that basic
insight by comparing news images and documentary evidence. The
news images are those described in the last chapter; the documentary
evidence consists of drug surveys, research on the prevalence of maternal drug use, and medical findings on the effects of prenatal exposure
to cocaine or crack.

According to the best national surveys available, had drug use actually reached epidemic levels in the late 1980s? To what extent did
survey evidence support news claims about women's crack or cocaine
use? Could maternal drug use be measured accurately? What was the
nature of harm that crack mothers inflicted on their babies? The
answers to these questions fit into the broader inquiry concerning
moral panic.

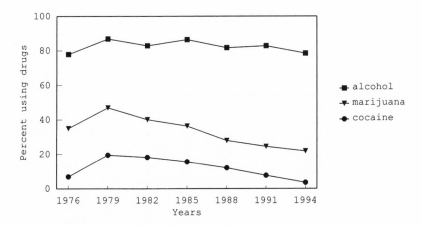

Figure 2.1 Trends in Past-Year Drug Use in the U.S., 18–25 Year Olds
Source: **SAMHSA, 1993a, 1995b.**

Cocaine and Crack "Epidemics"

The National Institute on Drug Abuse's (NIDA) *National Household Survey* and its *National High School Senior Survey*, conducted annually since 1972 and 1975, respectively, provide the most reliable and widely used estimates of drug use and trends in the United States. Based on probability and representative samples, the results can be generalized to the larger population.

Since 1979, the downward direction in drug use, including cocaine, is one of the most widely accepted general findings in drug studies (NIDA, 1988, 1992; and see figure 2.1). The surveys do have shortcomings: the absolute numbers are open to question because drug use is measured by self-reports—that is, asking respondents to recall past drug use—and unknown differences in recall may skew results. Moreover, the omission of groups believed to use drugs heavily means that NIDA and other surveys underestimate drug use.[1]

Still, for cocaine users, the profile was remarkably consistent throughout the 1980s: cocaine use was common among males, whites, young adults (ages 18–25), and adults (26–34) (NIDA, 1988, 1990; Substance Abuse and Mental Health Services Administration

[SAMHSA], 1993a). With respect to lifetime cocaine use in the 1980s, the difference between males and females had narrowed, especially among teenagers (12–17) and young adults (18–25) (NIDA, 1988, 1990; SAMHSA, 1993a). White females were "significantly more likely than black females to have ever used cocaine" (NIDA, 1990, 49; see also SAMHSA, 1993a, 1995b). As the 1993 NIDA report explained, higher lifetime rates for white than for black and Hispanic females might reflect youthful "experimental" use (SAMHSA, 1995b, 56–57). On the other hand, increasingly similar rates of cocaine use among whites, blacks, and Hispanics might also reflect underreporting by blacks (SAMHSA, 1995b, 56–57).

Regular crack use was apparently stable between 1988, the year NIDA first distinguished it from cocaine, and 1994. (See figure 2.2.) Contemporaneous sources reported otherwise, however. The U.S. General Accounting Office had issued findings showing that while cocaine use had declined, the prevalence for frequent crack and cocaine use had increased (U.S. General Accounting Office, 1991).[2] Short-term changes like this are difficult to interpret because the sample sizes for weekly and daily drug use are too small to yield reliable estimates.[3] Critics questioned the increase, wondering about the so-called epidemic, but crack had already attracted the attention of the media and policy makers. It took some time before Substance Abuse and Mental Health Services Administration set the record straight: while weekly estimates for cocaine (and crack) were too unreliable between 1988 and 1993 to report, the important point was that there were no significant differences in the rates over the survey years (SAMHSA, 1995b, 59). (See figure 2.2.)

The user profile was stable as well. Over the 1988–93 period, crack was a common drug among males, blacks and Hispanics, and the unemployed.[4] Male-female differences in the prevalence of lifetime crack use diverged, although young adult women reported higher lifetime crack use than young adult men (NIDA, 1989, 1990; SAMHSA, 1995c). Black females were more likely to have ever used crack than white or Hispanic women, but the differences were not significant (NIDA, 1989, SAMHSA, 1995c).

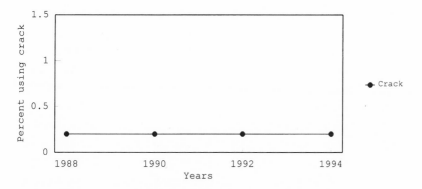

Figure 2.2 Trends in Past-Month Crack Use in the U.S., All Groups
Source: NIDA, 1989, 1991; SAMHSA, 1995b, 1995c.

The media either neglected to report the decline in drug use, or only mentioned the trend as preliminary to the real news: the frighteningly high, and misleading, estimates of drug use. In a segment aired in 1984, NBC reported that from 4 to 5 million people regularly used cocaine (August 9). The 5 million figure was true to NIDA's *National Household Survey*, but the network distorted the problem in another way: its filmed interviews with recovering cocaine addicts seemed to equate "regular use" with severe drug addiction. "Regular use" refers to past-month drug use; so the impression conveyed by the report that hopelessly addicted persons numbered in the millions was completely wrong.

The networks at first covered cocaine use among women by turning their attention to a group they viewed as vulnerable, white affluent women. Using traditional gender stereotypes, NBC and CBS developed news stories about the "myth of recreational drug use." Women had been taken in, believing that cocaine was a drug without addictive potential (CBS, 1983, February 7; NBC, 1984, August 10). And once addicted, the desire for cocaine impelled women to sell their jewelry, exhaust their funds, and finally exchange sex for the drug. The news stories also raised questions about the ability of drug-addicted women to mother: this aspect of coverage is discussed below.

In contrast with what they did with cocaine, the networks turned a small but enigmatic increase in weekly crack use into a clear epidemic. Technically, an epidemic refers to a cluster of cases that is greater than the background noise level: thus, if the background is zero, the appearance of any cases at all would equal an epidemic (Nelkin, 1987, 178). If the background is declining drug use, then even a questionable increase in frequent crack use fits the metaphor. To the lay public, however, the term *epidemic* conveys something much more serious than the small countertendencies in drug use and, as detailed below, the equivocal estimates of maternal drug use found by NIDA. "Epidemic" describes the rapid, perhaps deadly, spread of disease. It implies a multiplying risk of infection. Any increase in the rates of morbidity or mortality is ominous proof that things are getting worse.

The networks applied the metaphor as they covered the new drug. On the ABC evening news, Robert Stutman, a spokesperson for the Drug Enforcement Administration, offered personal testimony on crack's rapid spread in New York City: "I've been a federal agent for twenty-one years, and I've never seen a drug phenomenon like this. Three months ago you could only buy crack in two or three areas. Ninety days later, you can buy it in almost any area of the city" (1986, May 27). Crack had already spread to vulnerable groups, from New York City to the suburbs, where "25 to 30 percent of the students in some high schools used it" (ABC, 1986, May 27). And the epidemic had national implications. The ABC report said that 15 major cities had reported "dramatic increases" in crack use. As in an epidemic, new cases of the disease added to the potential of infection throughout the population. The ABC segment quoted unnamed sources as saying, "fifteen hundred Americans will try crack today" (1986, May 27). Finally, the infection was serious enough to require medical attention. Back in New York City, ABC reported 50 percent of emergency room admissions in some hospitals were for crack.[5]

The networks interviewed young black and Hispanic men, linking crack to minorities against an urban landscape. Cities were portrayed as war zones where police teams rounded up drug dealers, drug dealers battled for turf, and customers came and went. Into the war zone came middle-class consumers searching out drugs.[6] But by 1987, NBC announced a racial shift: the DEA's Robert Stutman reported that in the suburbs crack use had leveled off but that he did not believe the same held true for the inner city (1987, February 27). Stutman's impression was based on reports from the National Institute of Justice's *Drug Use Forecasting* showing that crack had spread from 7 to 40 cities in the previous eighteen months.[7] What the networks did not explain, however, was that the *Drug Use Forecasting* surveys were based on arrestees who had voluntarily submitted to drug tests and that the results did not apply to the larger population.

The *National Household Survey* showed that by 1988 women were less likely to use crack than men, a pattern that would continue (NIDA, 1990; SAMHSA, 1993a, 1995b). Network news, however, featured women in their coverage of crack without differentiating them from the men who peopled the scenes of urban chaos: blacks and Hispanics of both sexes were filmed on the street, in crack houses, in court, and in drug treatment centers. For network news teams they described their drug: crack created the most intense high, and by implication the most intense depression, including unrelenting cravings that propelled periodic binge behavior and sabotaged recovery. Under its influence people would commit every conceivable act of violence or theft. Weight loss, suicidal thoughts, and death were what awaited crack users.[8] From these images of urban disorder, spreading drug use among minorities, and the specter of mindless addiction emerged the group known as crack mothers.

Maternal Drug Use

Unfortunately, there are no satisfactory estimates of drug use by pregnant women available. Fifteen separate studies attempted to establish such estimates between 1982 and 1994, but their results were inconsistent and ambiguous (see Norton-Hawk, 1997; NIDA, 1996; Chasnoff, 1989). The first national, and perhaps the most widely cited, study was conducted by Dr. Ira Chasnoff, director of the National

47

Association for Perinatal Addiction Research and Education. Based on discharge records from 40 hospitals, the Chasnoff study projected a national estimate of 375,000 drug-exposed babies, or 11 percent of the live births in 1988 (1989). Surveys of this type were important in identifying high-risk patients and designing appropriate interventions, but for reasons discussed below, their results should not have been generalized.

Another authoritative number was introduced by the National Drug Control Strategy Report: 100,000 crack/cocaine babies a year were delivered (Office of the Inspector General, 1990a). The original survey, designed to judge the impact of crack/cocaine use on the child welfare system, was based on the number of drug-exposed babies referred to child welfare in eight cities in 1989.[9] Even the studies designed specifically to estimate maternal drug use failed to provide clear results. NIDA's National Pregnancy and Health Survey was prospective, used a national probability sample, and found that in 1992, 1.1 percent of, or 45,000, women had used cocaine during pregnancy (NIDA, 1996). Because it relied on self-reported drug use, a measurement procedure known to underestimate drug use, the survey failed to clear up the ambiguities that have plagued this area of research. It offered numbers, however, far, far below the Office of the Inspector General's 1990 estimate of 100,000 crack/cocaine babies.

Published articles made clear that methods used by these and other studies to detect maternal drug use biased the estimates. While self-reported drug use yielded low estimates, urine tests given to new mothers overselected for heavy drug use. Drug screens were limited in several different ways. Tests were drug-specific: a single test did not reveal the battery of drugs a woman may have consumed. Instead, if cocaine was suspected, the sample was tested, producing either a negative or positive result for cocaine. In addition, researchers were concerned about false negatives, misclassifying active cocaine users who tested negative for the drug as drug-free individuals. On the other hand, defense lawyers complained that drug screens generated false positives, exposing drug-free women who tested positive to the threat of legal sanctions. Moreover, a positive drug screen showed only that the patient had ingested a drug within the last few days. It did not identify the frequency or duration of drug use.

A wide array of other circumstances affected estimates of maternal drug use. More than one study found that hospitals that had formal protocols produced higher estimates than those hospitals lacking protocols. Even with formal protocols, the choice of drug tested for was discretionary. When attention focused on cocaine, health workers may have screened more frequently for cocaine, producing higher estimates. Moreover, discretion extended to the choice of which patients to test. Even among patients in a single clinic, stereotypes about who used drugs influenced that decision, producing higher estimates for groups perceived as drug users. Public hospitals screened more frequently, producing higher rates of maternal cocaine use. But at least one study found comparable drug use rates among public and private hospitals (Chasnoff, Landress, and Barrett, 1990).

In covering maternal drug use, the networks quoted figures, but not once did they question the numbers on cocaine-exposed babies. Instead, the networks made authoritative assertions about prevalence, giving far more validity to the suspect estimates than they deserved. Reporters did not question local figures on the numbers of cocaine-exposed babies supplied by hospitals. ABC reported in 1988, for example, that in Florida, recent increases in the number of cocaine-exposed babies justified a statewide projection that 10,000 such infants would be born in the coming year (October 13). Despite error and bias, that projection was low, amounting to 0.25 percent of the approximately 4 million live births in 1988.

The scientific studies placed estimates even higher. A study in Dallas placed the percentage of cocaine-exposed infants at 9.8 percent (Little et al., 1988). NBC's claim that 1 in 10 women who had given birth in a Miami hospital were crack users came closer to the Dallas figure (1988, October 25). Yet in 1988, NBC would have found support for an even higher estimate: a Boston study found that 17 percent of the babies in a hospital sample had been prenatally exposed to cocaine (Frank et al., 1988).

Once national estimates were available, the networks seized on them—375,000 drug-exposed babies and 100,000 cocaine-exposed babies. They did not, however, always report these figures correctly. The networks asserted or implied that the 375,000 figure referred to infants who had been exposed to cocaine or crack (see, e.g., CBS, 1989, January 9; NBC, 1989, July 7). And this sort of error was not confined to the networks. Most news organizations confused drug exposure and cocaine exposure, and for a while it was difficult to associate the numbers with the appropriate problem. CBS showed the most erratic pattern. It apparently rounded off the 375,000 figure to report 370,000 cocaine babies in January 1989, then the network used 100,000 in April 1990, and 375,000 in June 1990. It cited 100,000 again in December 1990 and repeated the 375,000 figure in June 1991.[10] The obvious puzzlement of network news writers matched researchers' frustration with ambiguous or inconsistent findings (Norton-Hawk, 1997).

Cocaine and Crack Mothers

The sociodemographic profile of maternal drug use raised difficult questions. Virtually every source consulted repeated the following description: women who used crack or cocaine during pregnancy were black, in their midtwenties or older, came from large cities, were admitted to public hospitals, and paid for the delivery of their babies through Medicaid (see NIDA, 1996).

On the one hand, the profile may reflect the involvement of black women of childbearing age in using cocaine and crack. The consistency of findings on this question is persuasive. NIDA's *National Pregnancy and Health Survey*, for instance, showed that during pregnancy black women used cocaine at significantly higher rates than did white or Hispanic women: 4.5 percent of the black women (30,000), 0.4 percent of the white women (9,200), and 0.7 percent of the Hispanic women (4,400). In addition, the study showed that black women preferred crack: 4.1 percent or 27,700 had used crack at least once during pregnancy (NIDA, 1996). Other studies confirmed the tie between black women, pregnancy, and crack or cocaine. An important Florida study found that among women entering prenatal care, 3.4 percent had used cocaine. Black women used it at significantly higher rates than whites: 7.5 percent of the black women and 1.8 percent of the white women had used cocaine before visiting the clinic, hospital, or doctor for prenatal care (Chasnoff, Landress, and Barrett, 1990).

On the other hand, racial and ethnic discrimination cannot be ruled out in the interpretation of this sociodemographic profile. While the Florida study found that black women were more likely to have used cocaine, results also showed racial bias in drug testing: black women were significantly more likely than white women to be tested for drugs at the time of delivery (Chasnoff, Landress, and Barrett, 1990). If black women were overselected for drug testing, then there was every reason to believe that white women were underselected. Whites did not fit the prevailing stereotypes about who used drugs. Moreover, private physicians would have hesitated to alienate their patients—who were disproportionately white—by reporting their drug use to health authorities. With so much bias in the measurements, it was difficult to know who among pregnant women actually used crack or cocaine.

The networks constructed a portrait of crack mothers based on race, by showing film footage of black women, without ever addressing troubling questions about racism. A racial breakdown of the women who appeared on camera in the news segments shown in table 1.1 shows the shift from white to black (Humphries, 1998). White women were associated with cocaine use during the first two stages of coverage (though only a few of these women were cocaine mothers). Black women came to be identified with maternal drug use in the last two stages: 55 percent and 84 percent of the women in stages 3 and 4, respectively, were black.[11] The construction was consistent with other news: network news teams had interviewed minorities; crack, according to a Drug Enforcement Administration spokesperson, had not leveled off in the inner cities; crack, according to one correspondent, could be found wherever poverty, despair, and drugs coincided. And it was consistent with NIDA reports showing that crack was common among blacks and Hispanics.

Not only were their racial constructions an issue; the networks' construction of crack mothers revealed a deeply embedded moralism about women and drugs. But to understand this requires a second look at cocaine mothers. The networks had shown an unusual degree of tolerance toward white middle-class women, filming them in conventional maternal poses, bathing and caring for their babies. As former addicts, these cocaine mothers expressed an appropriate level of remorse, appearing on television to warn other women about the dangers of cocaine use during pregnancy. In the war against cocaine, their conformity to recovery—the final stages in the moral career of an addict—was more important than were their infractions as bad mothers. Similar to that used in the nineteenth century to describe the moral career of drunks, this tale of addiction traced the same path: from drugs, to the loss of control, recognition of a disease state, to cure—abstinence and the burden of redemption (Levine, 1978).

Recounted by recovering cocaine and crack addicts, the moral tale began with an expression of relief. The patient was glad to be alive and restored to a normal life. The tale went on to describe addiction. The addiction had taken hold rapidly, and once it did, finding and using the drug became all-consuming. The addict was willing to sacrifice anything to get money to maintain use, squandering the family's paycheck, selling personal items, exchanging sex, and stealing. Hitting bottom generated insight. Realizing that he or she had to change or face death, the patient entered a drug rehabilitation program and headed toward recovery. The patient expressed regret and made efforts to recover the good opinion of family and friends. The moral tale, however, concluded on a cautionary note: sobriety was a difficult and lifelong struggle.

Cocaine mothers who told this tale—expressing appropriate emotion—had greater worth in the public's eyes. Crack mothers who violated its dictates were designated as renegades. Tracy Watson, Erocelia Fandino, and Stephanie, the crack mothers introduced earlier and shown in the active stage of addiction, were renegades (NBC, 1988, October 24). Instead of showing shame, Tracy was defiant in the face of obvious censure. Instead of revealing remorse, Stephanie was indifferent to the baby she had left in the hospital. If anything, Erocelia registered surprise that smoking crack had brought on premature labor and delivery. And networks' coverage framed crack mothers as violating the standards of motherhood. In a world of surrogate mothers, successful mothering depended on a woman's capacity to provide a healthy environment, a nontoxic womb, for the developing fetus. "Capacity" encompassed self-sacrifice—putting fetal needs first. Crack mothers lacked this capacity. For them, drug use came first. And on this basis the networks castigated them.

Prenatal Cocaine Exposure

The prognosis for cocaine babies was far from good. Cocaine had been associated with premature labor and other complications of pregnancy. While the majority of babies had no symptoms, some did. Low-birthweight babies, their size attributed to cocaine, were at higher risk for mortality and morbidity. Kidney damage and malformation of other parts of the urinary tract were tied to prenatal cocaine exposure. Cocaine babies were also at risk for cardiovascular accidents—of stroke, aneurism, and infarction—and although the record indicated that these were rare events, the consequences would have been lethal. In babies without obvious defects, developmental delay remained a question, albeit an unresolved one.

Although the foregoing results are based on studies that withstood criticism, not all of the medical claims about prenatal cocaine exposure did withstand critique. Generally speaking, methodological and other criticisms were an increasing concern in medical reviews published after 1990, casting doubt on earlier studies that had shown the significant adverse effects so interesting to news organizations.

Infant Mortality

Infant mortality showed promise as a reliable index of just how serious maternal cocaine use was. The collection of these data was independent: the war on drugs had not affected collection procedures, and the data series provided a basis for evaluating trends, although maternal drug use was not listed among the causes of death. Nonetheless, if the problem of maternal drug use had been as bad as the media suggested, its effects would have shown up in infant mortality rates. This was not the case on the national level: infant mortality rates for the U.S. declined in the 1980s and 1990s (National Center for Health Statistics, 1994, 1996). U.S. infant mortality rates were higher for babies born to black mothers, but from 1983 to 1992 the rates for these babies declined from 20 to 17 per 1,000 live births. In 1989, NBC reported that infant mortality rates had doubled over the past six months in Washington, D.C. (1989, September 30). The report failed to mention well-documented declines, seizing on short-term dramatic jumps in the District of Columbia, the city with the highest infant mortality rates in the nation.

Congenital Defects

Case reports that cocaine caused birth defects sparked a contentious debate about whether cocaine was a teratogenic drug, one that produced physical defects in the fetus. Teratogenesis can occur when a drug interferes with the growth process, resulting in arrested or distorted development of an organ or of tissue or skeletal structure. The vulnerability of the fetus to teratogenesis depends on its stage of development. The first trimester of pregnancy is the time of greatest vulnerability. Some drugs are established teratogens. Thalidomide, a tranquilizer once thought safe enough for pregnant women, interrupted the development of limbs, so that hands, for example, grew attached directly to the trunk of the body. Alcohol is another teratogenic drug, producing in exposed infants mental retardation and characteristic facial features.

Two different theories had been advanced to explain cocaine teratogenesis (Lissauer, Ghaus, and Rivers, 1994). Cocaine may have direct toxic effects, especially on the central nervous system, where it alters the production of neurotransmitters, which in turn may interfere with tissue growth in the fetal central nervous system. Alternatively, any interference with processes essential to fetal growth may result indirectly from vasoconstriction. Cocaine, a known vasoconstrictor, reduces the flow of oxygen and nutrients to the placenta; and once the drug crosses the placenta, it constricts the fetal vascular system, cutting off oxygen, nutrients, and blood supply necessary for the normal development of organs and tissue. In addition, constriction induced by cocaine increases fetal blood pressure and with it risk of internal bleeding or infarction, which also destroys tissue.

Animal research provided the strongest evidence that cocaine was a teratogen, but researchers recognized that the most convincing evidence would have to come from human studies. And results from human studies were far from conclusive, even though a high number examined an array of defects—some down to the molecular level. The literature reviews tended to concentrate on four malformations: those affecting the genitourinary tract, the heart, the gastrointestinal tract, and skeletal development.

Early reviews (1989–90) concluded that organ malformation was a rare event, although it remained a risk for babies whose mothers had continued to use cocaine during pregnancy. Genitourinary-tract abnormalities were confirmed, although abnormalities were confined to the urinary tract. Reviewers agreed that urinary-tract malformation was the most likely teratogenic effect; other literature reviews, however, continued to include defects in the central nervous system and heart and gastrointestinal-tract malformations (Roland and Volpe, 1989; Doering et al., 1989; Pitts and Weinstein, 1990).

After 1991, reviewers began to apply stricter standards for identifying teratogenic effects and to treat findings as more equivocal. The finding for urinary-tract abnormality stood up to the higher standard, but for other abnormalities there was no agreement (Zimmerman, 1991; Slutsker, 1992; Chasnoff, 1992; Holtzman and Nigel, 1994).[12] Two major reviews concluded that for most effects the evidence was too equivocal to sustain any conclusions at all (Richardson, Day, and McGauhey, 1993; Holtzman and Nigel, 1994).

Neurobehavioral Consequences

Withdrawal and impairments in motor skills, emotional stability, and orientation were among the problems identified as neurobehavioral consequences of prenatal exposure to cocaine. Within medical circles disparate views on the severity and duration of symptoms drove much of this research. A central question was whether symptoms disappeared or whether they signaled lifelong impairment.

Withdrawal in newborns was marked by tremors, irritability, and jitteriness, among other symptoms, and was a serious consequence of cocaine exposure, according to the medical literature surveyed (Roland and Volpe, 1989; Rosenak et al., 1990; Chasnoff, 1992). During the crack mother episode, the degree of seriousness of withdrawal's effects was a matter of controversy, but as panic wound down, the weight of medical opinion tended toward moderation. Cocaine withdrawal in infants, according to a 1990 review, was less severe than withdrawal from heroin, which was life-threatening and required special treatment (Rosenak et al., 1990).

Subsequent reviews acknowledged widespread reports of withdrawal in cocaine-exposed babies, but after surveying a broad spectrum of studies, one review found "no aberrant behavior" associated with cocaine withdrawal (Singer, Garber, and Kliegman, 1991). Another concluded that symptoms attributed to cocaine deprivation were not unique to that drug (Richardson, Day, and McGauhey, 1993). Researchers were also divided over whether the symptoms were temporary or permanent. One review asked whether symptoms were due to withdrawal or to cocaine's direct toxic effects on the central nervous system, citing evidence that symptoms persisted for at least six months (Richardson, Day, and McGauhey, 1993). Another posed the same question about central nervous system effects, citing evidence that the symptoms dissipated over time, and concluding that the withdrawal symptoms were transitory (Roland and Volpe, 1989).

Dr. Chasnoff of the National Association for Perinatal Addiction Research and Education conducted some of the first clinical studies on the development of cocaine babies. According to Chasnoff, cocaine accounted for the greatest amount of dysfunction in infant behavior (Chasnoff, 1991). Infants in the study were assessed using the Neonatal Behavior Assessment Scale for motor skill, emotional control (state organization), and orientation. Motor behavior concerned reflexes, motor control, and the coordination of motor activities. State organization involved an infant's response to stimulation or other demands in the environment. Orientation concerned an infant's ability to respond to visual and auditory stimulation.

Clinical results suggested that the effects of cocaine were not uniform. Motor deficits varied: some babies showed abnormal increases in muscle tone and abnormal reflexes; others were lethargic at birth and showed abnormal decreases in muscle tone. State organization varied, as well. One group of cocaine-exposed infants slept in response to stimulation. Another group slept but whimpered, breathed irregularly, and thrashed about. A third group alternated between sleeping and crying. The largest group slept and cried, but when carefully managed they could be aroused for brief periods of alertness. And finally, cocaine-exposed infants had difficulty tracking stimuli either visually or aurally, because they could not maintain an alert state or because they were easily distressed by stimuli.

Chasnoff attributed neurobehavioral changes to cocaine's direct toxic effect on the central nervous system, concluding that the changes persisted over a long period of time (1991). At one month infants showed improvement in state orientation but still performed below the level of normal two-day-old babies. Subsequent development was assessed, but small head size—attributed to the effects of cocaine on slowing fetal growth—was related to poor infant outcomes at 12 and 24 months. Group differences were not significant at 12 or 24 months, but Chasnoff reported as noteworthy that cocaine-exposed infants had performed below the level of infants in the comparison group. At three years no group differences were found when children were assessed for IQ, although Chasnoff pointed out that drug-exposed children had delayed language acquisition and problems with attention and self-regulation.

Second Thoughts

The conclusion that cocaine-exposed babies exhibited serious neuro-behavioral deficits, discernible from infancy through the toddler stage, was subjected to serious criticism (Singer, Garber, and Kliegman, 1991; Slutsker, 1992; Richardson, Day, and McGauhey, 1993; Kain, Kain, and Scarpelli, 1992; Holtzman and Nigel, 1994).[13] The samples in clinical studies were too small to rule out confounding variables; as a result, researchers had no way to eliminate alternative explanations for observed differences. For example, differences attributed to cocaine could have reflected differences in infant age or health status at the time of testing, differences in the drugs or drug combinations used by the mothers, or differences in the methods used for ascertaining the mother's drug status. Without a design powerful enough to rule out confounding factors, the results would be ambiguous.

Even as new studies remedied some design flaws, however, the results remained cloudy (Singer, Garber, and Kliegman, 1991; Holtzman and Nigel, 1994). One study found that cocaine-exposed babies had difficulty in adapting or shutting out aversive or redundant stimulation in the first week of life (Eisen et al., 1991). But according to a review, the sample size was too small to test habituation, as the adaptation is called (Singer, Garber, and Kliegman, 1991). Two other studies failed to confirm similar deficits during the first week (Neuspiel et al., 1991; Coles et al., 1992). But according to another review, they failed to rule out alternative explanations for null findings (Holtzman and Nigel, 1994). In one case, the infants were tested at three days. The absence of findings might have been due to the lingering effects of analgesic and anesthesia on babies in all groups. In the other case, the comparison group of mothers was not screened for drugs, raising the possibility that not all were drug free.

Even at the height of the panic over crack/cocaine mothers, Gideon Koren and his colleagues at the University of Toronto posed basic questions about the research cited. In an influential article, "Bias against the Null Hypothesis," they documented a publication bias against research that failed to show detrimental effects for prenatal co-caine exposure (Koren et al., 1989). The project reviewed all the abstracts on prenatal cocaine exposure submitted to the Society of Pediatric Research for presentation at its meetings between 1980 and 1989. While 57 percent of the abstracts reporting adverse effects were accepted, only 11 percent not showing adverse effects were accepted. The studies that found no adverse effects had actually verified cocaine use more often and used control cases more frequently.

Controlled studies were essential for accurate findings, but they were difficult to conduct because, as, Koren noted, women dependent on cocaine also had a "cluster of risk factors, including the use of other illicit drugs, heavy alcohol and cigarette consumption, and poor medical follow-up" (1989, 1441). Uncontrolled studies, especially those using high-risk populations, not only increased the perceived risk of cocaine use but generated inappropriate warnings. As for medical warnings against a single dose of cocaine, Koren wrote, "Counseling women exposed to cocaine in early pregnancy in Greater Toronto led us to suspect that there is a substantial distortion of medical information, which has led many women to terminations even when they were exposed briefly and mildly in early pregnancy" (1989, 1441).

The article's critical edge was, however, aimed at the scientific community's failure of objectivity. Koren wrote:

> Bias by journals, scientific societies, and funding agencies against negative results may have far-reaching detrimental effects: scientists, realizing their slim chance of having such data acknowledged, may be thus discouraged from submitting negative results [results showing no adverse consequences for cocaine]. . . . It is the duty of editorial boards, scientific committees, and funding agencies to acknowledge this serious bias and to indicate clearly that research results are not more important if they are positive. Rather importance should be dictated by the relevance of the scientific questions and by the ways they are answered. (Koren et al., 1989, 1442)

But scientific questions can be distorted, especially when perceptions are driven by misinformation about cocaine's effects (Koren et al., 1992).

In another study conducted by Koren and his colleagues, researchers asked physicians and lay people to assess the relative risks of cocaine and thalidomide to a hypothetical pregnancy. Thalidomide was a known teratogenic drug; cocaine was not—it did not cause a homogeneous pattern of malformations. Doctors and lay people alike had a distorted view of the risks associated with these drugs: both believed that cocaine was as damaging to the fetus as thalidomide (Koren et al., 1992).

In 1991, Beatrix Lutiger and her Canadian colleagues reassessed many adverse effects that clinical studies had attributed to cocaine, finding fault with the choice of comparison groups (Lutiger, Graham, and Einarson, 1991). Lutiger's team had pooled data from 20 comparable studies in order to conduct a meta-analysis. Meta-analysis cannot compensate for the shortcomings of the studies reviewed, but because random errors are assumed to cancel one another out, it gives a clearer picture of effects. In explaining the meta-analysis, the adverse effects of cocaine were "mainly" linked to the selection of comparison groups. "If the control group consists of middle-class women then cocaine could appear to be associated with many adverse effects; conversely, if the control group is addicted women, using other drugs but no cocaine, then the apparent adverse effect of cocaine cannot be documented" (Koren et al., 1992, 567–71; see also Hutchings, 1993). By selecting appropriate control groups, the resulting comparisons would, according to Lutiger, clarify the prenatal effects of cocaine (1991).

The first comparison involved groups of women who had used only cocaine and women who were drug free. The second comparison involved women who used cocaine along with other drugs and women who were drug free. And the last comparison involved women whose drug use included cocaine and women whose drug use did not include cocaine. In all three comparisons, genitourinary-tract malformation in the babies was associated with cocaine use, leading Lutiger to conclude that the drug was a risk factor. The comparisons ruled out a link between cocaine and cardiac malformations, sudden infant death syndrome, and abruptio placentae (placental bleeding after the twenty-eighth week of pregnancy that may result in detachment of the placenta from the wall of the uterus).

The comparisons supported a link between cocaine and small head circumference, gestational age, and low birth weight and length, although the size of the effect depended on the nature of the comparison. When the control groups were drug free, cocaine appeared to have a medium-sized effect on reducing head circumference, gestational age, and birth weight and length. When polydrug users were compared (one group used cocaine, the other did not), cocaine appeared to have little or no effect on these physical outcomes.

The shortcomings of the clinical studies were further summarized by Dr. Linda Mayes of the Yale Study Center and her colleagues, writing in the *Journal of the American Medical Association* (Mayes et al., 1992). First, the samples had either been poorly defined or highly selective, making them inappropriate bases from which to generalize to the larger population. This was Koren's point in advising against issuing medical warnings based on a highly selective sample—the cluster of risk factors shared by women dependent on cocaine (1989). Poorly defined samples posed dangers, too. When researchers select subjects on the basis of convenience, for example, when a doctor studies the patients who happen to come to a particular clinic, the resulting group is called a convenience sample. Such samples are easily assembled, but because they are unrepresentative of the larger population, generalizations cannot be drawn from them. Based on a convenience sample, the initial strong link between sudden infant death syndrome and cocaine was widely publicized despite studies, based on better sampling techniques, that showed a modest and then a questionable link.

Second, the methods for ascertaining drug status had thrown much of the research into question. Third, no study identified the timing, quantity, and duration of prenatal exposure to cocaine. It was generally assumed that first-trimester fetuses were more vulnerable to the effects of cocaine; but without comparison groups, the relative risk of second- and third-trimester exposure was difficult to ascertain.

61

Women's drug use varied in quantity and frequency, but in studies that have attempted to control for these factors, available measures— weekly or past-month use—were still too crude to determine dose- related effects. Determining the nature of cocaine exposure is com- plicated by polydrug use, lack of medical care, and unhealthy lifestyle, including exposure to sexually transmitted diseases.

Fourth, no study had successfully disentangled the unique effects of cocaine from confounding variables that themselves adversely af- fect pre- and postnatal development. The factors include not only use of other drugs but environmental factors such as poverty, violence, abandonment, homelessness, short-term foster placements, and inad- equate or abusive parenting. Fifth, no study had unambiguously iden- tified the specific functions in children who were said to be impaired by prenatal exposure to cocaine. Research suggesting that cocaine al- tered the neurotransmitter activity in the brain, which in turn ex- plained infants' difficulties with arousal or toddlers' impulsiveness and mood swings, required replication. Given these problems, Mayes and her colleagues concluded, "Our review indicates that available evi- dence from the newborn period is far too slim and fragmented to allow any clear prediction about the effects of intrauterine exposure to cocaine on the course and outcome of child growth and development" (1992, 406).

In an open peer commentary in *Neurotoxicology and Teratology,* Donald Hutchings of the New York State Psychiatric Institute attempted to ex- plain physicians' collective loss of critical judgment (1993). Doctors, he wrote, may have reasoned backward from the severe toxic effects of cocaine on adults. If adults were so affected, then fetuses would have to be even more seriously affected. Also, as crack hit the streets, doctors were as influenced as the general public by anecdotal news reports about the mothers of the babies reported to be so damaged by a drug perceived as more toxic even than cocaine (or thalidomide, for that matter—see Koren et al., 1992). Finally, it was a confusing time for substance abuse researchers, Hutchings wrote. On the one hand, "all [researchers] were acutely aware of the published reports citing seri- ous developmental effects reported for cocaine use during pregnancy and could hardly escape the daily deluge of anecdotal reports from the press" (1993, 283). On the other hand,

> many of these researchers were not confirming these observa-
> tions in their own hospital units. Many substance abuse prac-
> titioners and scientists at major metropolitan hospitals were
> seeing large numbers of neonates who tested positive for co-
> caine but were not observing the more serious toxic effects
> [malformation, withdrawal] that had been given such promi-
> nence in the first reports. Though there seemed to be an associ-
> ation of cocaine use in the third trimester with premature
> labor, most exposed infants presented in the nursery as remark-
> ably normal and asymptomatic. (283)

Network News

The network news called crack/cocaine babies the newest, most innocent victims in the crack epidemic, and for most Americans the phrase
appropriately described irreparable harm visited upon babies by their
mothers. What the news reports failed to tell the American public,
however, was that the medical research was too limited or poorly conducted to yield any reliable results. When the networks covered the
story, they simplified, overstated and mystified harm, creating the dis-
tortions that escalated concerns about maternal cocaine use to the level
of legal threat.

Shocking news reports about congenital defects, such as deformities at birth, lent credence to claims that cocaine was a potent
teratogenic drug. But by blending questionable claims, fragmentary
evidence, and misstatements, the networks made it difficult for viewers
to know what cocaine actually caused. Organ abnormalities, including
kidney deformity and facial defects, were reported by CBS (1985, December 30). While the former had been accepted by the scientific
community as teratogenic effects, facial defects, such as those that
characterize fetal alcohol syndrome, had not. Other defects recalled
thalidomide. An ABC report announced that a study had linked cocaine

to malformed arms (1989, November 14).

The babies were said to suffer heart attacks and strokes, cerebral palsy and mental retardation (ABC, 1986, July 11). Prenatal exposure to cocaine did increase blood pressure and the risk of cardiac problems, but cerebral palsy had not been linked directly to cocaine, and although medical attention was focused on developmental delay, the claim of mental retardation overstated the concerns. While CBS said the babies were at risk for sudden infant death syndrome and unspecified defects, their link with cocaine was highly questionable (1985, September 11).

NBC reported a study conducted by the Centers for Disease Control showing that cocaine babies were five times more likely than other babies to suffer serious birth defects (1989, August 10). ABC reported that cocaine babies were three times more likely to suffer other defects (1989, November 14); but despite every effort, I was unable to identify the specific defects. CBS reported that brain tissue damaged by cocaine accounted for behavior problems observed in cocaine-exposed babies (1990, April 5). In ignoring how cocaine might bring about this result, CBS missed the debate over whether teratogenesis occurred by cocaine's direct effects on the central nervous system, as its report seemed to suggest, or whether it occurred indirectly by way of cocaine's vasoconstrictive effects, as an NBC report suggested (1984, August 9).

As evidence mounted that cocaine was not a potent teratogen, network news shifted ground: perhaps defects were uncommon, but there were still problems. Normal-looking babies suffered from the delayed effects of cocaine (NBC, 1984, August 9). Experts confirmed that withdrawal was serious, and because the condition was visible, film crews were able to exploit it. A tiny trembling newborn, incubated and attached to monitors, was one of the most enduring images of the crack mother episode. Irrespective of its accuracy—many crack babies had no symptoms—the image was shown until the jittery, withdrawing newborn became the icon for the crusade against crack mothers.[14]

As such, withdrawal eclipsed developmental problems. The neurobehavioral research conducted by Chasnoff and others had pointed

64

to subtle deficiencies; motor skills, arousal states, imaginative play were all areas in which clinical studies had shown problems. Irritable babies tested parents' patience, but aside from caregivers in the act of soothing and swaddling, there was nothing to film (CBS, 1985, September 11).

Dr. Lorraine Hale of the Hale House in Harlem, a center for drug-exposed children, said in an interview that the children in her care were slow, but the toddlers-engaged-in-play scenes revealed nothing troubling (NBC, 1988, October 25). Children attending a Los Angeles school were also drug-impaired, but nothing in the scenes of children at play conveyed that they were forgetful or unable to perform tasks they had learned the day before (NBC, 1988, October 25). The older children were said to present disciplinary problems, to have difficulty with concentration, and to have mood swings that made their behavior unpredictable, but hyperactive, aggressive, or violent conduct was not to be captured on film (CBS, 1990, April 5).

• • •

In sum, despite widely accepted findings that drug use was on the decline, the networks in the mid-1980s declared an epidemic of middle-class cocaine use. It did this by ignoring trends and sensationalizing raw numbers (for example, that 20 million people had tried cocaine in 1983), linking them to images of severe addiction. According to the National Household Survey, cocaine use was common among whites, males, and young adults; but the networks developed a handful of news stories about white women, a vulnerable middle-class group, ensnared by cocaine.

While this was not the major trend in cocaine use, the stories employed traditional stereotypes of sexuality and motherhood. The desire for cocaine had led young women to trade sex for the drug. Still, while cocaine mothers raised concerns about their unborn children, the networks took a tolerant attitude: The women appeared remorseful, they warned others to stay away from drugs, and thus their transgressions as mothers were less important than their role in educating others about the dangers of drugs.

With respect to crack, the networks declared an epidemic of underclass drug use. They did this by amplifying crack's reputation as a dangerous drug and by exploiting a questionable if not fabricated increase in frequent crack use. The networks illustrated their stories with images of urban chaos and poverty. This was an epidemic, they implied, that affected the poor, black, and Hispanic sections of big cities, into which went network news teams to cover the desperation of the crack houses, the madness of street arrests, and their mindlessly addicted residents.

The networks' stories employed a broad range of stereotypes to frame crack mothers as a threatening presence. Building on images of urban chaos, the networks linked prenatal crack use with poor, minority women and questioned the capacity of black women to mother. As addicts, crack mothers openly defied the prohibitionist stance taken by policy makers, in a climate of zero toleration. As crack mothers, the women violated emerging expectations about self-sacrifice and motherhood. They had given no thought to who would shoulder the long-term costs of caring for defective children.

The networks distorted the record on crack babies, representing the worst possible outcomes as the norm. Infant mortality rates in Washington, D.C., hardly generalized to the rest of country, but news about these rates dramatized the deadly effects of prenatal cocaine exposure. In addition, the networks' coverage was decidedly partial. It stressed congenital defects even as researchers argued over cocaine's role as a teratogenic drug. It stressed neurobehavioral effects of crack, omitting reference to the limitations of the studies on which the findings were based. The networks ignored entirely the gathering voices of dissent, beginning in 1989 with publication of Koren's article on publication bias against research that tended to disprove the dire news about crack. The prevailing wisdom, then, held that prenatal cocaine exposure risked the life or health of the newborn, that crack-addicted women who used drugs during pregnancy should be prevented from inflicting avoidable harm to the fetus and newborn, and that someone should take action.

CHAPTER 3

The Point of Moral Panic

In any moral panic the decisive moment arrives when moral entrepreneurs—experts, spokespeople, officials—determine that disapproved conduct exceeds the boundaries of permissible behavior. In this case, too many cocaine mothers had harmed their babies, or a few cocaine mothers had inflicted too great a harm on their babies. However overstated such claims might be, the point is that moral entrepreneurs came to believe that existing systems of social control no longer sufficed. Pregnant drug users were perceived as ignoring medical warnings, physician advice, and referrals to drug treatment or prenatal care. Termination of parental rights, a sanction available through social services, was not seen as a severe enough penalty to force drug users to halt maternal cocaine use. Firmer action was required.

Reacting to these perceptions, a handful of county prosecutors took the step that triggered the panic: treating cocaine mothers as criminals. Across the nation prosecutors brought over 160 criminal cases against women who used crack or cocaine during pregnancy. Although most cases were dismissed or overturned on appeal, the county prosecutors profiled in this chapter pursued the high-publicity cases that defined the issues and turned the crack mothers episode into a classic case of moral panic.

Consider what the prosecutions were not. They did not arise in America's big cities, nor did they necessarily reflect local epidemics of crack babies. The communities that generated them were like many other small- and medium-sized towns and cities. They ran the gamut from wealthy suburb to worn-out industrial center. They were overwhelmingly white; minority populations did not exceed the national average. So, many of the explanations developing from the symbolic implications of the prosecutions are ill suited to actual circumstances. The prosecutions did not arise in communities where affluent white groups felt threatened by unemployment, poverty, or minorities.

The prosecutions were localized responses to national priorities. Crack was the drug targeted by federal authorities. Any politically astute, ambitious, or ideologically inclined prosecutor understood that crack was also the target drug at the local level. At this level crack was a powerful symbol. It epitomized all the ills associated with America's urban centers. County prosecutors—white professionals occupying positions of power and privilege in small cities and medium-sized towns—labored to keep crack and big cities' problems out. As the suburbs turned against the big cities, prosecutors turned against cocaine mothers. The highly publicized cases that resulted galvanized hostility, directing it against some of the most vulnerable women in America.

It can be said that county prosecutors brought the cases in part because they could. Prosecutors have far-reaching latitude in how they conduct the business of prosecution (Jacoby, 1979): County prosecutors decide whether to prosecute a case. They make decisions that affect who is prosecuted, the charges that are to be filed, and the kinds of plea bargains that are struck. They decide which cases are to be pursued more aggressively than others. In this chapter, we will see how reports of crack mothers reached prosecutors, and we will examine some of the factors that influenced the decision to prosecute in the first place, to charge at the high end of the penalty spectrum, and to prosecute aggressively. The kind of power held over defendants, even before a judge gets involved, reflects the unparalleled role prosecutors play in the criminal justice system.

Across the country most prosecutors declined to prosecute women who had used drugs during pregnancy. States like Florida and California limited or declined to authorize criminal prosecution in cases of cocaine-exposed infants under the child abuse and neglect laws (Spitzer, 1987; Gomez, 1997).[1] Alternatives existed. The statutes on possession and distribution of drugs applied to women, pregnant or not. Child protective services investigated cocaine-exposed newborns and, where warranted, brought abusive or negligent parents into family or juvenile court to terminate parental rights. And the federal Ad Hoc Drug Policy Group had by 1991 recommended prevention and treatment for the mothers as well as shifts in the mission of child welfare services to cope with maternal drug use and drug-exposed children. The group's recommendations reflected a broader, but less visible, consensus about the efficacy of services over prosecution (U.S. Department of Health and Human Services, 1992).

Legal precedents made it unlikely that any attempt to criminally prosecute cocaine mothers would be successful. A fetus is not, legally speaking, a person. The state may act to protect fetal life, and often it imposes criminal sanctions for intentionally harming a fetus—but typically only someone else's fetus. In Roe v. Wade (1973) and later in Webster v. Reproductive Health Services (1989), the Supreme Court left no doubt that the state's interest in protecting fetal life is outweighed by a woman's interest in controlling her own reproductive life. Thus, a woman's fetus may be protected from other people, but not really from herself.

The fetal-rights advocates have never accepted this, asking, if a third party can be punished for harming a fetus, why can't the mother be punished, too? For years they have pushed at the limits of Roe v. Wade (1973), trying to read much into the "important and legitimate interest" the Supreme Court Justices said the state may have in a first- or second-trimester fetus. Knowing a declaration that legal life begins at conception is beyond them, right-to-life jurists have tried to work around the edges, using related issues like maternal drug use to advance their cause.

In no state was there a criminal statute in place applying to the specific circumstances of cocaine-exposed newborns. This meant that prosecutors drew from the statutes available, stretching the meaning of their provisions beyond the legislature's original intentions (Maschke, 1995).[2] A 1986 case in San Diego shows the lengths to which prosecutors went in finding applicable statutes (Moss, 1988).[3] Pamela Rae Stewart was charged with child abuse for failing to provide "medical attendance" for her unborn child. Stewart had disregarded doctor's instructions to avoid cocaine and other illicit drugs and to avoid sexual intercourse. And she delayed getting help when she started to hemorrhage. When she reached the hospital, the infant she delivered tested positive for cocaine, and it died of brain damage. The statute used to charge Stewart had been designed to force fathers to provide for the women they had impregnated. It had been amended, however, to require mothers to support their children as well. The prosecutors seized on this later provision to charge Stewart, but because the legislature had not intended it to penalize conduct during pregnancy, the case was dismissed.[4]

A few years later, riding a wave of anti-drug hysteria, county prosecutors in a handful of other states acted. Karen Maschke suggests that these prosecutors had a "conviction psychology" (1995). Some had prosecuted child abuse cases; others were strong advocates of victims' rights. They all believed that babies had a right to be born free of defect—a variant of the defeated fetal-rights argument. They all believed that the mothers should be held responsible.

But the county prosecutors who tried the cocaine mother cases shared other things as well. As elected officials, they identified voters as their primary constituency (Jacoby, 1979), and their need to remain visible led them to make politically popular decisions. The early Stewart case had set off a national controversy without settling the issues; other statutes remained to be tested. Publicity earned by prosecuting a high-profile case had carryover value in winning higher office or attracting the attention of national decision makers. Indeed, their need to remain visible led prosecutors to legally questionable decisions. Paul Logli, the state's attorney from Rockford, Illinois, said the plight of cocaine-exposed babies was so severe in Winnebago County that one could do no less than to exploit all avenues of the law. Other prosecutors were every bit as adamant and inventive. Using manslaughter, drug-trafficking, and child-abuse statutes, they applied existing laws to a situation never envisaged by the legislature: a mother and her cocaine-exposed newborn.

Irrespective of how individual prosecutors justified their action, the decision to prosecute reflects the isolation of public prosecutors as a group of privileged white professionals. Dwight Greene, who wrote about Tony Tague, the Michigan county prosecutor discussed below, calls this isolation "pluralistic ignorance" (Greene, 1991). Tague made his decisions about the case, said Greene, on the basis of "false knowledge"—misconceptions about women, race, and poverty that he shared with other attorneys. It's hard to know whether any of the prosecutors reviewed in this chapter saw the women they prosecuted as real people; they apparently saw them as symbolic targets in a battle to save children. What they did not see or would not admit were the increasing depth of urban poverty, the desperation of the people burdened by it, and the impact of crack on the lives of people, especially of young women. Prosecutors instead saw women who had refused to help themselves, who had used up all their chances, and who required the full impact of the criminal sanction to get them to carry out their duties as mothers.

Here, then, are the highly publicized cases that signaled the moral panic. The defendants were for the most part poor, single mothers who had succumbed to crack because it defined the social worlds in which they lived. Two defendants were white. The case against Lynn Bremer, a white attorney, helped county prosecutor Tony Tague fend off accusations of racism for having charged Kimberly Hardy, a black single mother whose baby tested positive for cocaine. Josephine Pelligrini, the other white defendant, came from a middle-class family in Brockton, Massachusetts, but the father of her infant was black. The remaining defendants were poor, black, single mothers: Melanie Green in Illinois, Jennifer Johnson in Florida, and Kimberly Hardy in Michigan. Several additional cases grew out of a program in Charleston, South Carolina; defendants in these cases were almost all black, too. Charges filed against these women included involuntary manslaughter, delivery of a controlled substance to a minor, and child abuse or neglect.

The cases were filed in Illinois, Florida, Michigan, Massachusetts, and South Carolina. Paul Logli, state's attorney for Winnebago County; Jeffrey Deen, assistant state attorney in Seminole County; Anthony Tague, county attorney for Muskegon County; William O'Malley, district attorney in Plymouth County; and Charles M. Condon, ninth circuit solicitor in Charleston prosecuted the cases.

Melanie Green and Involuntary Manslaughter

Melanie Green, 24, was the first cocaine mother in the country to be charged with manslaughter in the death of her baby. She was as unlikely as any other poor, single mother to find herself at the center of a national debate about women's rights and drug abuse. Raised in a large working-class black family in Rockford, Illinois, she had dropped out of high school before drifting into drug use. When she was 17, she pleaded guilty to shoplifting charges; later she attributed her problems to having got involved with the wrong people. She gave birth to her son, Damen, in 1983.

Green was pregnant with her second child in September of 1988. Back in Illinois from an extended stay in Iowa, she was on welfare and had sought help for a drug problem, but the waiting list was too long, so she tried on her own to cut back. Six months later, Green gave birth to a daughter, Bianca, and both tested positive for cocaine. Bianca was underweight, had suffered brain damage, and she died within days of her birth. Later Melanie described the loss of her daughter as the most difficult days of her life. When another close family member died in April, Melanie Green was emotionally less prepared than ever for what was to come. Three months after the death of her daughter, she was arrested at her home as she waited for her son Damen to return from school.

The state's attorney for Winnebago County, Paul Logli, had in the meantime been pondering the legal situation presented by the death of Bianca Green. "It was a living, breathing baby that died, for no other reason, we believe, than that cocaine was ingested by the mother," Logli said. "To ignore that is unconscionable. It borders on barbarism"

(Stein, 1989). His frustrations were with the law. If a living infant was prenatally exposed to cocaine, an Illinois prosecutor can bring the mother before the juvenile court for a hearing to determine custody. If, on the other hand, the cocaine-exposed infant dies, the Illinois law provides no remedy. "The statutes of this state," Logli said in a published interview, "specifically exempt mothers from the aggravated battery or manslaughter of a fetus." He went on to explain, "That's so prosecutors like me can't use that to get around the [U.S. Supreme Court abortion] decision [in *Roe v. Wade*]" (Reardon, 1989, May 14).

Logli disputed suggestions that his Roman Catholic background— he attended Catholic high school and a Catholic-affiliated college— had any bearing on his decision in the Green case (Stein, 1989). As for the legal test that he proposed and later wrote about, Logli reported finding precedent for filing criminal charges against Melanie Green in a 1982 Illinois reckless homicide case (Logli, 1992). The facts were straightforward: a car driven by the drunken defendant collided with another car in which a pregnant woman rode as a passenger. Within hours of the collision, the woman delivered a baby who died a few minutes later. The injury to the baby was prenatal. But because the baby was born alive—like Bianca Green—Logli hoped this could be the precedent for holding Melanie Green responsible for her own child's death. Thus, the Rockford office of the state's attorney presented to the grand jury one charge of involuntary manslaughter in the death of Green's daughter and one count of delivering drugs to a minor.

The obstacles to the involuntary manslaughter charge were serious (Reardon, 1989, May 28). The American Civil Liberties Union (ACLU) had entered the case, pointing out that the injury was prenatal. In attempting to hold a mother criminally responsible for prenatal injury to her own child, the ACLU argued, Logli ran afoul of the U.S. Supreme Court ruling in *Roe v. Wade*: the fetus is not a person with protectable rights (Kreiter, 1989, May 10). Prosecuting a woman for acts to her own body is an unconstitutional intrusion into the right to privacy (Kreiter, 1989, May 27). Harvey Grossman, legal director of the ACLU in Chicago, defended Melanie Green and said of the case, "It's a question of how society related to women, period. She is not simply a vessel for carrying a fetus. She doesn't lose her rights to personal autonomy because of pregnancy" (Parson, 1993).

The eight women and four men on the grand jury agreed and chose not to indict Green on either the manslaughter or the drug delivery charge.[5] Bowing to defeat, Logli admitted that manslaughter may not have been the best mechanism for charging women who used drugs during pregnancy (Lamb, 1989). Questions asked by the grand jurors, he conceded, showed that they had concerns about Green's right to privacy, that is, her right to make decisions about her body free from government interference. There were also some risks, Logli admitted, in criminalizing the behavior in question (Reardon, 1989, May 28).

From where did this high-profile prosecution come? Logli cited the local epidemic of crack babies, although Winnebago County, Illinois, was not the most likely place for a prosecutorial campaign (Logli, 1990). While 27 babies born to women allegedly using cocaine had been identified in the hospitals between the summer of 1988 and May of 1989, this figure is small in contrast with the much larger estimates from urban centers like New York City or Los Angeles (Stein, 1989).

Logli may have been more concerned with keeping big-city problems, including crack babies, from taking hold in the smaller community of Rockford. And Logli was frustrated with the war on drugs (Logli, 1990). "We undertook this prosecution in an effort to find one more way to fight a cocaine war that all society is presently losing," Logli wrote in a 1990 law journal article (Logli, 1990). "Concerned citizens and child welfare authorities" who wanted to remedy the problem of substance-abused infants had asked him to step in, he said (Logli, 1992). Criminal sanctions, Logli maintained, remained an effective remedy. They "raised the consequences of maternal drug use to a tough enough position that these persons . . . might be encouraged to seek the treatment, the help they need" (Primetime Live, 1989).

The Green case gave Paul Logli national exposure. On the day he filed charges against Green, he flew to New York City to appear on two national television shows (Reardon, 1989, May 11), and television talk show hosts continued to provide a forum for him to express his prosecutorial views. Reports circulating in the late 1980s had it that Paul Logli was considering a run for Congress, but he remained state's attorney for Winnebago County well into the 1990s (Stein, 1989). He became president of the Illinois State's Attorney Association in 1996.

Melanie Green, on the other hand, tried to escape the publicity that surrounded her case. Even though she was unavailable for interviews, the troubles she experienced in 1989 were played out on national television. As she mourned the death of her daughter and an aunt, she faced very serious criminal charges: the drug distribution charge carried a sentence of 15 years in prison, the manslaughter charge, of 5. And had Logli tacked on the drug possession charge he threatened to file after the grand jury dismissed the others, Green would have faced 3 years in prison. After the grand jury dismissed charges against her, Green left Rockford to enter a three-week day-treatment program. To avoid the permanent stigma of being Rockford's most infamous crack mother, she announced plans to relocate.

Jennifer Johnson and Delivery of Drugs to a Minor

Jennifer Clarise Johnson was the first woman ever to be convicted of delivering a controlled substance to her unborn child. At the time she was 23 years old and the mother of four children (Davidson, 1989). She had grown up on the fringes of an all-black, desperately poor section of Altamonte Springs, Florida. Raised by a religious mother, Johnson completed high school, but soon succumbed to crack, the neighborhood's major industry and recreation. She married a drug dealer and began using drugs. In an interview Johnson said that for the first two years of her marriage she used drugs recreationally, but later she could not stop—drugs were all around her. She said she had not used drugs during her first pregnancy, but she admitted to being addicted during her third and fourth pregnancies. At birth, both those children tested positive for cocaine; neither showed signs of drug impairment.

During her fourth pregnancy, Johnson was admitted twice to emergency medical care, each time telling the physician that she had used crack. She was treated and sent home on both occasions. When Johnson delivered Jessica in January 1989, the baby tested positive for cocaine. Florida's Department of Health and Rehabilitative Services investigated, and, according to the court decision in her case, Johnson told investigators that "she had smoked pot and crack cocaine three to four times every-other-day throughout the duration of her pregnancy with her daughter" (State v. Johnson, 1991; Johnson v. State, 1992).

According to an account given by Lynn Paltrow, staff attorney for the ACLU, a social worker had violated patient confidentiality and turned over Johnson's medical file to Seminole County prosecutors (O'Neal, 1992). In March 1989, Johnson's file came as a suspected child abuse case to Jeffrey Deen, assistant state's attorney for Seminole County, Florida (Davidson, 1989). Deen, who had grounded his career in child abuse litigation, was the chief child abuse and sexual assault prosecutor for the county. He had worked with the Florida Department of Health and Rehabilitative Services and served on the Committee on Legal Needs of Children for the Florida Bar Association.

In a 1989 interview on ABC, he talked about the Johnson case in terms of child abuse. "There is such a lack of regard for the baby," Deen said (1989, July 12). He dismissed Johnson's addiction as an excuse, describing her as someone who had used up all of her chances. The second cocaine baby exceeded the limit. The community, Deen said, could not afford to have her deliver a third (Curriden, 1990). "You've got to fix it so this person who's abusing doesn't come back out and continue abusing" by having more crack babies (Vielmetti, 1990).

Even before the Johnson file crossed his desk, Deen had been searching for a way to prosecute drug-addicted mothers (Davidson, 1989). Florida officials had estimated that 10,000 cocaine-exposed babies would be born in 1989, four times more cocaine babies than had been born in Florida the previous year (Davidson, 1989). Miami had the highest number of cocaine babies, with about 500 born that same year ("Cocaine Babies," 1989). In Seminole County, officials placed the 1989 estimate at over 200 drug-exposed babies, double the number from 1988 (Davidson, 1989).

The numbers pressed for a response, but prosecutors like Deen were frustrated by restrictions. Florida's child abuse and neglect statutes had been amended in 1985 to include drug-exposed babies, but the Florida legislature rejected a proposal to authorize criminal penalties in those cases (Spitzer, 1987). Deen believed that he could get around the prohibition on abuse cases like Johnson's by using a law that barred delivery of controlled substances to a minor. He intended to argue that drugs could be "delivered" from mother to child through the umbilical cord (Davidson, 1989). As a first-degree felony designed to deter the sale of drugs to school children, delivery to a minor carried a prison sentence of 15 to 30 years.

In looking for a cocaine mother case, assistant state attorney Deen had in mind a specific defendant: "a woman who is likely to continue using drugs, is not seeking treatment, and is not a classic victim of poverty-and-addiction since birth" (Vielmetti, 1990). Johnson, who had come from a stable but poor family and who had finished high school, barely met the not-poor-from-birth standard. Married to a drug dealer, she may have had more income than her background would suggest, but soon after her husband's arrest, she found herself addicted and out on the streets (Sharp, 1989). In April 1989, three months after the birth of her fourth child, Jennifer Johnson was arrested in a crack house (Logli, 1990). She admitted to being an addict—someone who is likely to continue using drugs—but once arrested, she sought drug treatment. Deen believed, however, that Johnson would not have sought help without the arrest, meaning that Johnson fit the not-seeking-treatment standard of the profile, too (Curriden, 1990).

The prosecution's theory of the case was unorthodox: cocaine ingested by the mother crossed the placenta and flowed via the umbilical cord to the baby; more critical, however, was the claim that the cocaine continued to flow to the baby after it had passed through the birth canal but before the umbilical cord was cut. The drug was delivered to a live baby—in other words, a person, rather than a fetus, under the law.

James Sweeting, who represented Jennifer Johnson at her trial, argued that his client should not have been tried under a drug-delivery statute intended to apply to traffickers, not mothers and children ("Cocaine Mother," 1989). He also argued that it was medically impossible to determine whether the drugs passed to the infants after or before birth, when as fetuses they had no legal rights (Davidson, 1989). In a two-day bench trial in Seminole County Circuit Court, Jennifer Johnson was nonetheless convicted on two counts of delivering cocaine to a minor, one count for each of her two drug-exposed babies. In August 1989 she was sentenced to 15 years' probation, including one year of strict supervision by probation officers during her drug rehabilitation program, monthly random drug testing for one year, educational and vocational training, and an intensive prenatal care program if she became pregnant again. The conviction gave the case its landmark status.

ACLU attorneys led by Lynn Paltrow joined Sweeting in appealing Johnson's conviction, asking the court to determine whether the drug-trafficking statute had been appropriately applied.[6] The Fifth District Court of Appeals upheld the conviction, ruling that the drug had passed through the babies' umbilical cords, thereby accomplishing the "delivery" (State v. Johnson, 1991). Citing its "great public importance," however, the appellate court asked the Florida Supreme Court to review the case (Shillington, 1991). Lynn Paltrow argued the appeal, asking again whether the circuit court had applied the appropriate statute, whether the convictions violated Johnson's constitutional rights to due process and privacy, and whether the state failed to present sufficient evidence to show she intentionally delivered cocaine to a minor. The supreme court, adopting the dissenting opinion in the lower court, found in favor of Johnson (Johnson v. State, 1992).

In what it considered the primary question in the case, the supreme court ruled that the drug-trafficking statute was inappropriately applied to the state's theory of the case, namely, that Johnson delivered cocaine to her babies via the umbilical cord. No other case had ever construed "delivery" to apply to an involuntary act, such as blood flow. That application, the court concluded, was contrary to legislative intent: it noted the Florida legislature's rejection of criminal penalties in the area of child abuse and maternal drug use. The court also said that the threat of prosecution drove women away from needed prenatal care and drug treatment.

"This is just an example of a higher-level appeals court not knowing what is going on in the streets," said Deen ("Mother's Cocaine Conviction," 1992). But the ruling ended cocaine baby cases in Florida. Its effects on Deen were ambiguous. He left the Seminole County Prosecutor's Office in 1989 for private practice, returned briefly, and then resigned in 1990 to run for circuit court judge. The recognition he achieved by prosecuting Jennifer Johnson, however, did not translate into votes. Defeated by a wide margin, he returned once again to the prosecutor's office and then moved to criminal defense work with a firm in Altamonte Springs.

The ruling did not lead to Jennifer Johnson's immediate freedom. After her conviction Jennifer Johnson completed a one-year stay at a residential treatment facility in Apopka, Florida. She worked in the program's office for about six months, but in 1992 she violated probation by using drugs and by not maintaining contact with the court. Back in circuit court, Johnson got one last chance. The judge sentenced her to at least 18 months in a treatment center for women, Operation Parental Awareness and Responsibility, or Operation PAR, in St. Petersburg. Despite the Florida Supreme Court's decision to reverse her conviction, she still had to serve out her sentence for violating her probation. Her four children remained in the custody of relatives.

The Prosecution of Josephine Pelligrini

When William C. O'Malley, district attorney for Plymouth County, Massachusetts, decided to prosecute Josephine Pelligrini for delivering cocaine to her baby, he turned a social service matter into a crime and made national headlines. Pelligrini first came to the attention of the Department of Social Services when her two-year-old son, Ernest, tested positive for lead poisoning (Scaglione, 1989). The department arranged to have a visiting nurse help Pelligrini, who because she was pregnant also received classes in baby care; but she missed prenatal checkups with the doctor (Coakley and Richard, 1989; Scaglione and Cahill, 1989, August 21). On July 2, 1989, Pelligrini gave birth to a son, Nathan, who exhibited symptoms of drug exposure. He was tested for drugs; the positive finding for cocaine was reported as child abuse to the Department of Social Services (Scaglione, 1989). Many hospitals filed such reports with the Department of Social Services, and in processing them the department's policy was to keep families together (Townsend, 1991). The department was not required to refer cocaine-exposed infants to the police or prosecutors (Cahill and Scaglione, 1989).

The next encounter Pelligrini had with the Department of Social Services occurred six weeks later, in August 1989. The caseworker assigned to the family noticed burns on Nathan's toes and ordered the family to take Nathan to the hospital, but the family refused (Coakley and Richard, 1989). The social worker decided to take Ernest, Nathan, and their sister, Melissa, into state custody (Scaglione and Cahill, 1989, September 28). She summoned the Brockton police to remove the children and to take Nathan to the hospital, where his burns were attributed to a lit cigarette (Coakley and Richard, 1989).

The medical assessment of Nathan's burns led police to file a separate child abuse report, which brought Nathan's case to the attention of Geline Williams, supervising attorney for child abuse prosecution for Plymouth County (Coakley and Richard, 1989). In investigating the child abuse report, the district attorney's office also discovered that Nathan had tested positive for cocaine at birth. Multiple charges were drawn up. Pelligrini pleaded not guilty to drug possession and to felony charges that she delivered cocaine to a minor, a charge that in Massachusetts carried a 3- to 15-year sentence. Pelligrini and Aaron Jackson, the children's father, also pleaded not guilty to charges of assault and battery with a dangerous weapon, brought in connection with Nathan's burns (Coakley and Richard, 1989).

Whether a drug-trafficking statute applied to cases of cocaine-exposed babies in Massachusetts remained an open question, although the chances for a successful prosecution were remote. Alan Dershowitz, Harvard law professor, accused O'Malley of usurping legislative prerogatives (Kennedy, 1989). Critics argued that even when a woman's decisions during pregnancy were "fraught with harm," her right to privacy prevents the government from interfering, even to protect the fetus (Kennedy, 1989). O'Malley attempted to reassure critics that a woman's use of illegal drugs, not potential harm to the fetus, was the focus of his case, but he insisted throughout that children have a right to be born without defect (Kennedy, 1989).

Following Pelligrini's arraignment, in September 1989 district attorney O'Malley presented multiple charges to the grand jury (Scaglione and Cahill, 1989, September 28). On the assault and battery charge, the grand jury returned an indictment against Nathan's father, Aaron Jackson, but not against Pelligrini.[7] On the delivery and possession charges, the grand jury found sufficient evidence to hold Pelligrini over for trial in superior court, but superior court judge Suzanne DelVecchio granted the defense's pretrial motion to dismiss them (Coakley, 1990). Judge DelVecchio held that the statute on delivering illicit drugs to a minor was never intended to apply to the diffusion of cocaine through an umbilical cord. She also said that since Nathan was not harmed by the drugs his mother took, the state did not have the compelling interest it would have needed to justify intervening. Criminal sanctions, DelVecchio agreed, were not an effective means of protecting potential life; they drove women away from needed prenatal care and undermined the state's interest in potential life.

DelVecchio's decision did not end the case, however. O'Malley appealed the court's dismissal of the possession charge, won, and reinstated it, based on hospital records showing the presence of cocaine in Nathan's system. Attorneys for Pelligrini argued unsuccessfully that she had a privacy interest in the hospital records and that Nathan's positive drug test could not be used as evidence of cocaine possession by the mother. In 1993 the state supreme judicial court ruled that Nathan Pelligrini's hospital records could be used as evidence against his mother (Commonwealth v. Pelligrini, 1993). Josephine Pelligrini was later convicted in superior court and placed on probation for six months.

The Pelligrini case may have reflected cocaine problems in the community. In addition to recorded increases in the number of cocaine babies statewide, Brockton's figures—350 cocaine babies in 1989—had prompted the Department of Social Services to review all reports of cocaine babies and to respond with appropriate actions including termination of parental rights. But other factors were at play in the district attorney's decision. William O'Malley, who died in 1995, was known as a tough prosecutor and strong champion of victims' rights. In deference to victims, he refused to bargain many cases. And victims' rights meant recommending harsh penalties for convicted offenders. So even though the Department of Social Services had taken custody of Pelligrini's children and even though the state had convicted their father of assault, O'Malley believed that "a serious form of child abuse" such as prenatal drug exposure warranted a harsher penalty, a deterrent sentence in addition to loss of custody (Thompson and Reardon, 1995; Hancock and Thompson, 1995).

O'Malley continued to insist that the unborn needed legal protection and urged legislation to that effect (Scaglione, 1989). He also entered the national arena (Hoey, 1993). Elected president of the National District Attorneys Association in 1993, he was asked by President Bill Clinton to take part in key negotiations with the Senate Judiciary Committee on the 1993 crime bill. His endorsement helped enact the bill, preempting possible criticism from prosecutors who had killed a previous crime bill Clinton sponsored.

Pelligrini served out her probation, but aside from disclosures made by her parents that she feared her boyfriend, Aaron Jackson, who they said beat her and ruined her life, the public record ends.

The Cases against Kimberly Hardy and Lynn Bremer

Anthony D. Tague, the prosecutor in Muskegon County, Michigan, filed charges in two high-profile cases against mothers who had used drugs: Kimberly Hardy, a young black woman living on the poor side of town, and Lynn Bremer, a white Muskegon attorney, who lived in more affluent circumstances. They were twin cases in all respects save race; critics said Tague prosecuted Bremer to take the sting out of accusations that racism had motivated his charges against Hardy.

Kimberly Hardy, 23, of Muskegon Heights—a poor, black, and crack-infested section of the run-down factory town—became Michigan's test case on crack mothers (Hoffman, 1990). Raised in a religious, working-class, black family in Mississippi, Hardy had an early pregnancy but got her high school diploma before moving north with her son, Darius. In Muskegon, where she had relatives, she worked on an assembly line and met and formed an intimate relationship with Ronald, a man with long-standing drug and alcohol problems.

Pregnant with her second child, Hardy quit her job, going on assistance until after the baby was born. Within months of Nyseassa's birth, she was pregnant again, and by this time Hardy too had a serious crack problem, and her relationship with Ronald had deteriorated. She returned with her two children to Mississippi for the duration of her third pregnancy. By moving she had lost welfare and medical benefits, including prenatal care, so she returned to Muskegon to give birth. She and her children moved back in with Ronald. One night she accepted the offer of crack from one of Ronald's friends. She thought the drug would help her relax and go into labor. It did.

Meanwhile, the Muskegon County prosecutor, Anthony Tague, the son of a retired local police chief, had launched a high-profile, anti-drug crusade aimed at keeping big-city drugs like crack out of Muskegon. The cases produced clogged the courts and jails and overwhelmed Tague's office. Still, Kimberly Hardy represented another new front for the prosecutor.

In August 1989 Hardy gave birth to a baby boy, Areanis, at Muskegon General Hospital. The baby's premature birth, jaundice, and distended abdomen led the attending physician to test the baby's urine for drugs. The test revealed cocaine in the baby's system, which the hospital reported to state social service workers and law enforcement personnel (Medendorp and Walsh, 1989; Walsh, 1990, February 2). Ten days later, a child protective service worker and a police sergeant told Hardy that her newborn son and two other children would be put in a foster home (Beachum, 1989). About the same time, the sheriff's department looked into the report from Muskegon General Hospital. The narcotics unit found that child protective services already had a case against Hardy. So with the aid of a search warrant, the sergeant in charge of the case obtained Hardy's hospital records (Medendorp and Walsh, 1989).

Charges were filed against Hardy in mid-October accusing her of delivering a drug to her infant—a felony in Michigan—and of second-degree child abuse. The penalty for conviction on the delivery charge included a 20-year sentence and a $25,000 fine. Upon conviction the child abuse charge carried a sentence of four years (Medendorp and Walsh, 1989). Authorities, unable at first to locate Hardy, discovered she had enrolled in a substance abuse program in Lansing. Police waited until she had completed the two-week program before arresting her (Medendorp and Walsh, 1989). She surrendered to authorities at the end of October and was arraigned in district court, where, in addition to the child abuse and delivery charges, she was charged with a two-year-old misdemeanor, a theft of first-aid materials from a Muskegon drugstore.

The district court judge found sufficient evidence to bind Hardy over to circuit court on cocaine delivery and child abuse charges (Walsh, 1989, November 13). At the arraignment, Judge Frederic Grimm Jr. found basis for the delivery charge in that delivery continued until the umbilical cord was cut. The judge also found basis for the child abuse charge in the medical testimony that the infant's defects were caused by the reckless act of the mother—her ingestion of cocaine (Walsh, 1989, November 13). However, the circuit court trial, originally scheduled for June 1990, was postponed when the Michigan Court of Appeals agreed to review the charge of delivering a controlled substance to a minor (Burns, 1990). When the child abuse charge was dismissed by the circuit court in April 1991, the case depended on the status of the delivery charge (Walsh, 1991, April 2). But the court of appeals dismissed the delivery charge, the opinion reflecting a growing consensus that the legislature never intended the drug-trafficking statute to apply to the transfer of drugs via the umbilical cord (*Michigan v. Hardy*, 1991).

In the midst of the Hardy case, Tague arranged with the Department of Social Services to be notified of cocaine- or alcohol-related births (Walsh, 1990, June 27). A central record-keeping system in place together with the department's obligation to report suspected births meant it was not long before another potentially high-profile cocaine mother came to the attention of the county prosecutor. That mother was a lawyer herself, a 36-year-old white woman named Lynn Bremer. The day after she gave birth to a healthy daughter in April 1989, mother and daughter tested positive for cocaine (Walsh, 1990, April 16 and 19). Bremer admitted using cocaine throughout her pregnancy (Hoffman, 1990). She had gone to her doctor but refused his advice to go into a residential treatment program.

Bremer, who had recently joined a law firm, felt that any leave would jeopardize her job. The demands of her job, she said, did not permit time for day treatment. She saw a drug counselor and managed to cut down on her cocaine use, but despite warnings from her boyfriend, who also used cocaine, she still flunked drug tests administered by her doctor. She had also ignored warnings from her doctor that continued cocaine use would place her at risk for intervention by child protective services (Walsh, 1990, April 16 and 19). When Bremer's baby tested positive for cocaine, child protective services took custody, placing the infant in a foster home pending further probate court action (Walsh, 1990, April 16 and 19).

Law enforcement officials reviewed the Bremer case, and in May 1989 prosecutors charged her with delivering cocaine to her newborn daughter (Walsh, 1990, April 16 and 20). Arrest was postponed until after Bremer had completed a 28-day treatment program. If convicted on the delivery charge, Bremer faced a mandatory one-year prison term with a maximum penalty of 20 years' incarceration. She also faced suspension of her law license or disbarment (Walsh, 1990, April 20). A district judge reviewed the evidence at a preliminary hearing, and finding it sufficient for the charge, ordered Bremer bound over for trial in district court (Walsh, 1990, July 19).

Because Bremer had practiced law in the fourteenth circuit, her case was reassigned in October 1990 to a judge from another county (Hogan, 1991). In February 1991, Eaton County Circuit judge Thomas Eveland threw out the felony charge against Bremer on the ground that

Michigan's drug laws were not intended to apply to the delivery of controlled substances through the umbilical cord—the same conclusion the court of appeals would reach several months later in the Hardy case. He went further, citing the district court judge for abusing his discretion in requiring Bremer to stand trial on the charge. Moreover, Judge Eveland held, Bremer could not have anticipated that the statute would be applied in the way it was (Walsh, 1991, February 4).

Stepping back for a moment to consider the origins of the cases against both Hardy and Bremer, it is clear that the cocaine baby crisis Tague cited never existed (Wilkerson, 1991). The Department of Social Services identified only six cases of cocaine-related births in Muskegon between 1989 and June 1990 (Walsh, 1990, June 27; Walsh and Medendorp, 1989). Instead, the cases reflect the ambitions of a newly elected prosecutor who was both tough and politically astute.

He began his term with a high-profile anti-drug campaign that made him a local celebrity. He invited television camera crews to film drug raids, and then, in an unusual move, he led the raids himself (MacNeil/Lehrer, 1990). Anti-drug stickers and pins were stamped with his message: "Help Tony Tague Fight Drugs!" (Hoffman, 1990). High visibility, Tague believed, got the message across. "People know in my community," said Tague, "that if you're dealing crack cocaine, you're going to go to prison" (MacNeil/Lehrer, 1990).

But when the problem proved intractable, he turned his anti-drug crusade into a campaign he might win—one to save the children, the smallest victims of the crack epidemic (Pluta, 1991). The crusade was ready-made. Cocaine mother cases had already created a national controversy. The Muskegon cases, like those against Johnson and Pelligrini, were intended to send a "strong message that mothers, if they learn they're pregnant, shall immediately seek some type of treatment if they're using cocaine at the time" (Walsh, 1990, June 20). And he meant immediate treatment, for neither Hardy's nor Bremer's enrollment in substance abuse programs after giving birth led Tague to withdraw charges (Walsh, 1990, April 20). Criticizing the social service agencies for ineffectively addressing the problem, Tague summed up the prosecutorial approach: "We are providing the incentive by the strong arm of the law" (Walsh, 1990, July 19).

Not everyone agreed. Tague's anti-drug crusade, said Alan Rapoport, attorney for Kimberly Hardy, was a witch-hunt ("Trial to Start," 1990). Feeding on the anti-drug hysteria Tague had cultivated in Muskegon, when Tague and other prosecutors targeted pregnant women, they had turned the war on drugs into a "war on women," according to Rapoport (Stone, 1990). Lynn Bremer's attorney, Norman Halbower, raised questions about Tague's tactics after court employees overheard prosecutors say they had no case against Bremer (Warren, 1990).

Anthony Tague continued as the county prosecutor for Muskegon County; apparently his defeat in court did not destroy his appeal to voters. A year later Bremer pleaded no contest to child neglect in probate court and was allowed increasing visitation, pending reunification with her child in September 1990 (Walsh, 1990, August 10). Kimberly Hardy finished drug treatment, enrolled in a community college, and hoped to become a drug counselor. When interviewed by Dwight Greene for a law review article on prosecutorial discretion, Hardy described her experience as a defendant: "It's been a nightmare! . . . My baby was taken away from his mother for the first ten months of his life: there was no bonding with his mother. If this was to protect my baby [taking him away] was more damaging. . . . And what about my other children?" (Greene, 1991). Hardy saw racism in Tague's actions, noting that "after all the publicity in my case, the prosecutor later prosecuted a thirty-six-year-old white woman lawyer to show he wasn't prejudiced; but the judge dismissed her case quick" (Greene, 1991).

Crack Mothers in Charleston, South Carolina

Charles Malony Condon, South Carolina's ninth circuit solicitor from 1980 to 1991, served both Charleston and Berkeley Counties. One of the things that attracted Condon to the job of solicitor was its promise of autonomy and discretion. In an article profiling his career, he told interviewers that the job allowed him to pick his cases, discarding bad ones to concentrate on good ones: "I think the prosecutor should always wear the white hat. And if you don't wear the white hat, you're not doing your job" (MacDougall, 1991).

In the late 1990s, now state attorney general for South Carolina, Charles Condon looks back on a career that includes developing the program he says reduced the number of cocaine-addicted babies in Charleston (MacDougall, 1991). Hospital officials from the Medical University of South Carolina (MUSC) had originally called in the Circuit Solicitor's Office when nurses and doctors began seeing five or six pregnant women a week who had used cocaine or crack, some with hemorrhaging or other complications related to pregnancy (Lewin, 1990). Physicians linked the symptoms to cocaine, and because they felt they were witnessing a crime, went to the circuit solicitor (Siegel, 1994).

Condon had already enlisted in the war on drugs, and with a politician's eye to a winning issue, agreed that the hospital had an obligation to report such cases (Siegel, 1994). In a *Los Angeles Times* article, Condon is reported to have admonished hospital officials, "It's nice you came in. . . . But the fact is, you have to come in. There's no patient-doctor privilege on this. If you don't report it, it's a crime" (Siegel, 1994). In response, Dr. Edgar Horger and nurse Shirley Brown, both from MUSC, joined Condon in developing a program for drug-using pregnant women that sent a deterrent message: Seek drug treatment or face arrest and jail time (Condon, 1995).

The program developed in three stages.[8] From October 1988 to September 1989, during clinic visits urine drug tests were administered to pregnant women suspected of using cocaine or other illicit drugs. The testing program identified 119 cases of cocaine use among pregnant women. For most, the drug test coincided with the delivery of their babies. Referrals for drug rehabilitation were made for 15 women tested for drugs early in their pregnancies, but their babies tested positive for cocaine when they returned to the hospital for delivery.

In the program's shock stage, arrests were made. In October, November, and December 1989, patients were arrested if they or their newborns tested positive for cocaine. Ten women were arrested, their babies turned over to foster care. In a final stage, beginning in January 1990, the program modified its procedures so that patients could avoid arrest by successfully completing drug counseling. The threat of arrest, made real by the program's shock period, was thereafter used to "leverage" women into treatment. Over the program's five-year life, 42 women were arrested, some of whom avoided charges by agreeing to drug treatment (Associated Press, 1994).

Following an investigation in January 1990, the ACLU and the Center for Reproductive Law and Policy pointed to serious deficiencies in the MUSC program (Goetz, Fox, and Bates, 1990). Screening procedures were discriminatory. Doctors began by screening patients on a discretionary basis, but implementation of a nine-point protocol intended to reduce bias still permitted selective drug screening. Combined with the fact that MUSC served poor patients, this meant that poor women, the majority of whom were black, were singled out as drug-abusing mothers.

The MUSC program was also punitive. Once the hospital identified drug-using women, the circuit solicitor recommended against releasing them on their own recognizance, insisting instead on bail. The judge set bail, which had the effect of keeping cash-strapped, postpartum women in jail and away from adequate medical attention or drug treatment. The MUSC program purported to give mothers a choice between treatment and jail, but treatment was either nonexistent or inappropriate. Initially, the hospital had not developed treatment options for women, but when it did, the program did not work well for most. This population needed day treatment, child care, and transportation, or residential facilities with accommodations for children—none of which existed in Charleston.

Still, Condon defended the program as effective in reducing the number of cocaine babies (MacDougall, 1991). The program's evaluation reportedly showed that MUSC had reduced the number of drug-using women coming to the hospital for delivery, but a flawed methodology made it a poor demonstration of effectiveness (Horger,

Brown, and Condon, 1990). Nonetheless, in a 1990 interview on *Nightline*, Condon summed up the MUSC experience: "We have been able to demonstrate quite clearly that with an effective prosecution program available as a last resort and the women knowing that something will in fact happen to them eventually, they [the women] have simply stopped using cocaine" (1990). And because there had been growing criticism that prosecutions like those in South Carolina frightened women away from needed prenatal care, he added, "And there's absolutely no evidence here locally that the women are not seeking prenatal care. . . . They go to the same hospitals as before."

His experience in South Carolina, Condon said, showed that without the threat of prosecution, women who used cocaine during pregnancy would do nothing to help themselves or their future children: "When the women have been coming into the hospital and have been told simply and educated simply that cocaine use is bad, it can hurt you or your fetus and can cause great damage, many women continue to use cocaine" (Nightline, 1990). In a different context, Condon predicted, "Until they [cocaine mothers] suffer sanctions, . . . you're going to see the problem increase" (Sataline, 1991). Moreover, he argued, if it is against the law in South Carolina to use cocaine, then it is against the law for pregnant women to use it, too. If the law applies to pregnant women, then no woman has the right to bear a drug-affected baby (Sataline, 1991).

In the midst of what was shaping up as a major debate on public health policy, the ACLU and the Center for Reproductive Law and Policy publicized details about the women who had been jailed because of the MUSC program (Siegel, 1994). They were black, poor, and as single mothers in their late twenties and thirties, they had used crack or cocaine, and they had several children. On the basis of a positive drug screen, they were arrested on charges of possession and delivery of drugs to a minor.

One example, Theresa Joseph, 35, was the mother of several children, only one of whom lived with her. Although she avoided the hospital throughout her pregnancy for fear of prosecution—she had seen Condon's public service announcement threatening jail for pregnant substance abusers—an infection brought her to MUSC. There the staff told her to get drug treatment, but fearing prosecution, she fled. She returned for further medical care but did not keep the appointment for drug treatment. Back at the hospital for the birth of her baby, she was arrested and taken to jail after the baby tested positive for cocaine.

In addition to fear, the lack of appropriate options in the MUSC program kept women away from treatment. Crystal Ferguson, 31 years old and the mother of three children, was referred late in her pregnancy to MUSC, where she tested positive for cocaine. She was given the option of getting treatment or going to jail, but she felt she could not leave her children, and treatment facilities had no room for children. Ferguson returned to her children, rejecting the offer of treatment, and tried to stop on her own. When she went to the hospital to give birth to her daughter, she tested positive for drugs, and Ferguson was arrested and jailed.

Defense attorneys easily got the charges (drug possession and drug delivery to a minor) against Ferguson and Joseph dismissed (Siegel, 1994). In 1992 an appellate court overturned the child-neglect conviction of a pregnant substance abuser, holding that the law had been misapplied. So when Lynn Paltrow of the Center for Reproductive Law and Policy and the ACLU and Charleston public defender Ted Phillips moved to quash the distribution charges against Joseph and Ferguson, the new ninth circuit solicitor, David Schwacke, who replaced Condon when Condon became state attorney general, did not put up a fight. Schwacke dismissed the charges and rescinded the bench warrants on five other women also charged with possession and delivery of drugs to a minor, hoping to avoid a ruling that the drug delivery charge was misapplied as well.

The Center for Reproductive Law and Policy assembled an impressive array of experts and public health organizations (Siegel, 1994). All had gone on record opposing the MUSC program on public health grounds: prosecution was the least effective way to deal with maternal drug use. Dr. Barry Zuckerman, chairman of the department of pediatrics at the Boston University School of Medicine and Boston City Hospital, and Dr. Jay Katz, professor emeritus of law, medicine, and

91

psychiatry at the Yale University, raised objections to the MUSC program. The American Medical Association, American Academy of Pediatrics, American Public Health Association, American Nurses Association, March of Dimes, and other groups opposed the threat of arrest to force pregnant women into drug treatment programs. Women's groups, including the National Organization for Women, opposed prosecution for public health reasons and because it threatened women's right to make reproductive decisions free of government interference. They were also concerned because prosecution might give anti-abortion advocates grounds for expanding fetal rights.

The Center for Reproductive Law and Policy devised a two-pronged strategy in South Carolina (Siegel, 1994). It first complained to the National Institutes of Health that the evaluation of the MUSC program had not met federal guidelines requiring the consent of human subjects in research. Subjects had not consented to participate in the evaluation research that was later published in a medical journal. MUSC and the study's authors (Dr. Edgar Horger, nurse Shirley Brown, and circuit solicitor Charles Condon) stood accused of conducting unethical experiments on African American women. The U.S. Department of Health and Human Services reviewed the charges and threatened to cut off federal funding unless MUSC corrected its procedures. To avoid losing federal funding, MUSC shut down the program in 1994.

Second, the Center for Reproductive Law and Policy filed a $3-million class-action suit against MUSC, the city of Charleston, and local law enforcement officials and agencies (Siegel, 1994). The suit asked for compensatory and punitive damages for 10 women whose civil rights had been violated by MUSC's arrest-and-jail policy. In January 1997 a federal jury decided, however, that the choice between drug treatment or jail was not racially motivated, nor did the conduct of the hospital in turning over the results of drug tests to prosecutors amount to an illegal search. The U.S. district judge, Westin Houck, had six months to determine whether the search itself was unconstitutional, whether MUSC violated confidentiality of medical information, women's right to procreate, and the Federal Civil Rights Act (Baxley, 1997).

Although Lynn Paltrow did not believe that the case was over, the judge failed to act within the time limit, and the issues remain unresolved.

The federal suit in Charleston stirred up local prejudices against the outsiders who defended cocaine mothers (Siegel, 1994). The ACLU, feminists, and "California-type liberals" were rebuked by officials for moralizing and interfering with the way things were done in Charleston. "The left-wing ACLU doesn't represent the American people," said Condon at a press conference during a break in the federal class-action suit. "MUSC deserves an award. If the plaintiff [the women jailed by MUSC] prevails, in effect we'd be legalizing the use of crack cocaine during pregnancy" (Siegel, 1994). As Condon turned back to his private conversation, *Los Angeles Times* correspondent Barry Siegel recorded his comments: "Tell Lynn [Paltrow] thanks for suing me. Running in South Carolina for attorney general, the best thing you can have happen is to be sued by the ACLU" (1994).

• • •

With the 1996 federal court decision in South Carolina, the moral panic ground to a halt. One by one, the cases built by prosecutors had unraveled. While the media and the public understood the prosecutions as legitimate attempts to deal with the problem, the judiciary cast a more critical eye.[9] The Rockford grand jury doubted the wisdom of Logli's manslaughter strategy, and in an unusual move for any grand jury, refused to indict Melanie Green. The grand jury in Brockton, less suspicious of O'Malley's drug-delivery strategy, indicted Josephine Pelligrini, and O'Malley managed to get the case to court, but the judge quickly dismissed it and effectively ended such prosecutions in Massachusetts. Tague took advantage of sympathetic lower-court judges to get both his cases bound over for trial, but the Michigan Court of Appeals threw out the charges. The prosecutor in Florida managed to convict Jennifer Johnson, but the Supreme Court of Florida refused to uphold it and ended the cocaine baby cases there.

The five prosecutors had surprisingly little support within their own professional circles. In the National District Attorneys Association (NDAA), one subcommittee, Substance Abused Infants and Children, strongly endorsed their efforts. But most other NDAA sections were less enthusiastic, including the American Prosecutors Research Institute (APRI), the research arm of the association ("Substance Abused Infants," 1990). Charles Condon, Anthony Tague, and Jeffrey Deen figured prominently in an APRI conference, "Substance Abused Infants: A Prosecutor's Dilemma," held in Chicago in July 1990. But the conference failed to endorse the high-profile prosecutions. Jill Hiatt and Janet Dinsmore, spokespeople for the National Center for Prosecution of Child Abuse, distanced APRI and NDAA from the "very few but highly publicized cases, involving novel use of laws to prosecute women who have given birth to drug-affected babies" ("Pregnant Addicts," 1990).[10]

Prosecutors made it easier both morally and politically to cut social service spending, to push fetal rights, and to attack racial preferences. Their crusade appealed to the prejudices of white audiences who watched the panic unfold on the nightly news, but their limited racial experience blinded them to the racial implications of the prosecutions (Greene, 1991). Misconceptions fit into a long line of stereotypes about black sexuality and incompetent mothering (Roberts, 1991). As another dehumanizing wave of restrictions on reproduction, the prosecutions showed that state officials were all too willing to punish black women for having babies. Under slavery, an owner's profit dictated the reproductive choices of black women. Later, involuntary sterilization eliminated the choices arising from fertility. Pronatalist attitudes combined with restrictions on Medicaid abortions made termination unlikely. The crusade against crack mothers, consequently, served as punishment for women who carried their pregnancies to term and delivered babies (Roberts, 1991).

Women, Addiction, and Drug Treatment

Equally important to looking at the development of a moral panic is reviewing how matters are resolved, or, more precisely, how they appear to be resolved. In the concluding phases of the anti-crack crusade, the networks' dwindling interest can be measured by the precipitous drop-off in the number of news segments about crack mothers (as illustrated in figure 1.1). A sense of closure emerged, centering around humanized crack mothers, a less threatening concept of addiction, and a drug treatment network designed to address their problems.[1] Crack mothers were portrayed in a more sympathetic light, although not all of them fit into the middle-class model of redemption required by the moral career of an addict.

This chapter contrasts the media portrait with the external forces that shaped the lives of women who became crack mothers. In addition, it looks closely at the concept of addiction—both its realities and media representations thereof. Generally speaking, a sense of closure on the question of maternal drug use depended on the development of a drug treatment network that addressed the needs of addicted women. Whether the problem had been solved or not, new programs brought into being by the crack mother episode were made by the networks to appear as effective solutions.

Drug Realities and News Images

After 1991 the general decline in drug use, including cocaine use, continued (see figure 2.1).[2] Among young adults (ages 18–25), monthly cocaine use was still more common among males, blacks, and the unemployed, but in the 1990s, full-time workers were less likely to use cocaine regularly (SAMHSA, 1993a, 1995b). Declining cocaine use among men and blacks narrowed earlier gender and racial differences, but black females in comparison with white females were still more likely to use cocaine monthly. This race/gender difference was not significant, however.

Unaffected by the decline in drug use, the prevalence of crack remained unchanged and low: 0.5 percent of the sample reported past-year crack use in 1991 and 1993 (SAMHSA, 1993a, 1995b). Crack remained common among young adults, males, blacks, and the unemployed. Among young adults, females and blacks were both less likely to have used crack in 1993 than in 1991, establishing a trend that narrowed the gender and racial differences in past-year crack use (SAMHSA, 1993a, 1995b). Black females in comparison with white females reported slightly more past-month crack use in 1994 than in 1991, but differences in rates were small (NIDA, 1992; SAMHSA, 1994, 1995c).

Persistent difficulties in estimating the prevalence of maternal drug use made it certain that the actual extent of the problem would remain a mystery. Of the 15 separate studies that attempted to measure the phenomenon, 8 were published in the concluding phase of the anti-crack mother campaign. None of the studies, however, had adequately addressed bias in the measurement procedures, resulting in estimates for cocaine use among pregnant women that ranged from 0.6 percent to 7.1 percent (Norton-Hawk, 1997). The networks continued to seize on estimates in their stories about the high cost of maternal cocaine use. NBC reported that "158,000 babies [had been] born addicted at a cost of $500 million in annual hospital costs" (1991, September 17). And a CBS segment on drug testing in Georgia again used the two most commonly cited estimates: the 1989 federal estimate of 100,000 cocaine babies a year and the earlier estimate of 375,000 drug-exposed babies (1991, March 12).

The racial stereotypes associated with crack mothers were more troublesome than ever. The disproportionate percentage of black women who used cocaine during pregnancy was confirmed by clinical and epidemiological studies. One low estimate (0.6 percent), for instance, was based on a clinical sample of rural white women, but another study showed that 7.79 percent of the black women in a probability sample had used cocaine (Norton-Hawk, 1997). True, crack use was more common among black women than among white,[3] but the networks exaggerated this pattern out of all proportion, more so than ever before.[4] In the concluding phase of the anti-crack crusade, 84 percent of the women shown in the news segments were black, in contrast with 55 percent shown at the height of the panic (see table 1.1).

The racial profile of crack mothers emerging from documentary sources and network news was a matter of concern, especially among ethnographers whose work reached publication toward the end of the crack mother campaign. On the one hand, the National Household Survey, the National High School Senior Survey, and clinical and epidemiological studies of maternal drug use all suggested that black women did use cocaine and crack more frequently than white or Hispanic women. While ethnographers wanted no part in further racializing the drug problem, their convenience samples picked up minority women. For the studies designed to look at AIDS, convenience sampling identified a disproportionate number of minority women who had exchanged sex for crack (Ratner, 1993a; Mahan, 1996). Similarly, in the enthnographies designed to explore the role women played in the consumption of crack, convenience sampling brought researchers into contact with minority women (Maher, 1995, 1997; Murphy, 1992).

The women who because of greater resources avoided detection as crack or cocaine mothers were disproportionately white. In her book Women on Heroin, Marsha Rosenbaum outlined various pathways to drug use, showing that in the 1960s and 1970s, white middle-class teenagers who had made their way from suburban rings into the urban drug culture escaped arrest and prosecution (1981). Middle-class women in the late 1980s who snorted cocaine also had the resources to protect themselves from criminal liability, a factor in facilitating recovery. Poor women were generally more vulnerable to prosecution for illicit drug use, one among several factors that frustrated efforts at recovery (Murphy, 1981; Murphy and Rosenbaum, 1997). In their book on pregnancy and drug use, Murphy and Rosenbaum also noted that researchers by and large had been unable to penetrate the middle-class world of drug use (1999).

Despite such limitations, ethnographies provide the only accounts of the women who used crack. And because news stereotypes have so mystified crack mothers, little is known about their actual circumstances. In focusing on women, this chapter's objective is not to reinforce negative stereotypes, but rather to place the mothers in their communities, to look at the external forces that shaped their lives.

Crack Mothers in Context

This discussion draws on ethnographic studies that investigate the lives of women who used crack in the late 1980s and early 1990s. One collection on which I draw is entitled *Crack Pipe as Pimp: An Ethnographic Investigation of Sex-for-Crack Exchanges* (Ratner, 1993a). The research conducted in Chicago, Denver, Los Angeles, Miami, Newark and Philadelphia, New York, and San Francisco formed part of a larger investigation into AIDS and the exchange of sexual services for crack cocaine or for money to buy it, according to Mitchell Ratner, the volume's editor. In all, contributing ethnographers interviewed 340 respondents, all of whom had exchanged sex for crack or money to buy crack within the past 30 days. Just under three-quarters of the sample were black. Women made up about two-thirds of the respondents. The sample used crack heavily.

My research relies on a number of other studies as well. A Daytona Beach study conducted by Sue Mahan, similar in nature to those above, is based on interviews with 17 long-term crack addicts who exchanged sex for crack or for money to buy crack (1996). In another

San Francisco Bay Area study, Sheigla Murphy conducted 100 interviews with women who had used crack cocaine three or more days in the past month (1992). Two-thirds of the women in her study were black. Although Murphy wanted to restrict the sample to crack users, she included polydrug users—heroin addicts or women on methadone—to include white women in her study, entitled "It Takes Your Womanhood" (1992). Lisa Maher's study, described in *Dope Girls* (1995) and *Sexed Work* (1997), was conducted in Brooklyn, where she worked with a smaller sample: 45 women who actively used cocaine or heroin. Using a subsample of 13 women who got pregnant during her year of ethnographic work, Maher described their experiences of pregnancy and mothering in an unpublished piece of research, "Cocaine Mothers: (Re)constructing the Crack Mom" (n.d.).

In her ethnography Murphy described common threads in the backgrounds of women who used crack (1992). Born in the 1960s or earlier, the women began life in working-poor or welfare-dependent families in public housing or adjacent neighborhoods. These were among the children that the "war on poverty" was designed to protect. Launched in 1965, President Lyndon Johnson's poverty program provided income support (Aid to Dependent Families with Children), benefits in kind (food stamps), and human development programs (Head Start) to poor families. While it expressed the liberal optimism of the period, its premise, the existence of a deep-rooted culture of poverty, tended to reinforce older prejudices against the poor (Katz, 1989). The longer the poor endured poverty, said the theory, the more entrenched they became in a cycle of deprivation and degradation. Poor families socialized children into passivity and helplessness, transmitting poverty from one generation to the next. The Moynihan Report of 1965 came to a similar conclusion about the black family, making the black matriarch the principal character in discussions about welfare dependency. Poor school performance, juvenile delinquency, and drug use were evidence of the inadequate way in which she socialized her children.

The culture-of-poverty thesis tended to ignore the economic causes of concentrated poverty. Irrespective of cultural values or family organization, the possibilities of legitimate employment stemmed from shifts in the economy. And independent of economic shifts, racism excluded black workers. Roger Lane suggests that exclusion of black workers from the industrial labor force occurred in two stages (1992). At the beginning of industrial expansion, racism had kept black workers from entering manufacturing jobs; then, after World War II, economic shifts relocated manufacturing away from black workers. The relocation of jobs from once-prosperous city sites to suburban rings or to newer industrial sites in the South and the West placed jobs outside the reach of inner-city dwellers. The loss of manufacturing jobs hit the cities of the Northeast and Midwest hardest, creating zones of poverty that, despite anti-poverty programs, marked the early lives of the young women who succumbed to crack in the mid-1980s.

A new wave of research challenged the culture-of-poverty thesis.[5] It examined the adaptive strategies used by black families to survive poverty. Joyce Ladner's account of growing up poor, black, and female in a St. Louis housing project affirmed the resiliency of black families (1971). Ladner believed that inner strength was the most important resource a girl growing up in poverty could have, and she looked to the socialization agents and processes that might provide it (1971). The association of mothers, aunts, grandmothers, and friends inculcated values of self-reliance and equipped young black girls to deal with both worlds, black and white. Carol Stack's *All Our Kin* found "extensive networks of kin and friends supporting, reinforcing each other—devising schemes for self-help, strategies for survival in a community of severe economic deprivation" (1974, 28). Members exchanged goods, resources, and child care in a collective adaptation to poverty. Stack defined the extended family as "the smallest, organized durable network of kin and non-kin who interact daily, providing domestic needs of children and reassuring their survival" (31).

Some of the women interviewed by Murphy had been able as girls to rely on the extended-kin network for support (1992). Some of the women interviewed by Maher lived as children with single mothers or other female relatives (1995). However, situational factors isolated some young women from supportive kin networks (Murphy, 1992). Divorce, abandonment, or the death of a parent removed positive role models. Saddened by the death of her mother, one woman interviewed by Murphy said she just gave up (1992). She stopped trying to do well in school, and eventually took up drugs. Unstable living arrangements presented unknown difficulties. Another woman interviewed for the same study felt that in being shifted from one household to the next, she had missed the influence of permanent, caring adults who might have shown an interest in her.[6] Another who had lived with her mother as a child resented having to take on the household responsibilities of an adult, but she faced an even heavier work routine on entering foster care.

For many girls, the system of "other mothers" failed to protect them from physical or sexual abuse by male relatives, stepparents, family friends, or foster parents (Murphy, 1992). Sexually abused by her uncle, one girl had run away to a friend's house only to be abused by her friend's father. Another sought help from her mother after the mother's boyfriend abused her, but she was blamed for the incident by her mother and expelled from the house. Alcohol and drug abuse by parents contributed to the harm some women experienced, but with others, parents had shared drugs—cocaine and, in at least one instance, heroin.[7] Of the women who had shared drugs with parents, some saw this as the cause of later trouble with drugs; others treated it as a reflection of the permissive drug culture they passed through in the 1970s.

The women interviewed by Murphy had begun to use drugs—including alcohol, marijuana, powder cocaine, and some psychedelic drugs—as teenagers (1992). Heavier drug use, including IV cocaine and amphetamine use, led some to abandon high school. The time and energy it took for complete involvement in the drug culture, for finding and consuming drugs, ruled out finishing high school. Others left school because caretakers were unable or unwilling to provide the high-fashion clothes perceived as necessary in the high school social scene.

Pregnancy also led adolescent girls to leave school. Even under the best of circumstances, pregnancy carries high personal costs for women who have to sacrifice their own dreams to raise children. Under less auspicious circumstances, pregnancy may be a doubled-edged solution to immediate deprivations. Hurt and disappointed by her mother's indifference, one respondent got pregnant, moved in with her boyfriend's family, but was unable to return to high school (Murphy, 1992). Without a high school diploma, the young women were isolated from legitimate employment, leaving them eligible only for minimum-wage service-sector jobs, public assistance, and drug dealing, shoplifting, or prostitution as means for generating income.[8]

As young mothers, they were part of a larger trend. The proportion of black female-headed households had risen dramatically between 1970 and 1980 (Tucker and Mitchell-Kernan, 1995). While the origins of this trend are disputed, the trend itself left single women and their children with meager incomes and isolated them from kin networks.[9] According to a 1988 national survey of black Americans, female-headed households had lower family or household incomes than had male-headed households (Hatchett, Cochran, and Jackson, 1991). Low incomes could not always be offset by kin support. Because young mothers had set up independent households, adult relatives were not often in a position to provide economic assistance, emotional support, or help in child rearing (Sudarkasa, 1997). Informal support across households was contingent on feelings of family closeness and frequent contact between kin members (Hatchett, Cochran, and Jackson, 1991). Elderly women who headed households were even more isolated from kin and received less assistance than younger women, although the older women expressed feelings of being connected psychologically to their families. Younger female heads of households, while living closer to family networks and receiving more help, did not perceive as much family closeness. Both groups of women were especially vulnerable to fluctuations in informal and formal assistance.

By one estimate, the total number of people living in underclass neighborhoods—characterized by high dropout rates, joblessness, female-headed families, and welfare dependency—rose 230 percent from 1970 to 1980 (Peterson and Harrell, 1992). Race and class coincided. Some 70 percent of residents in these neighborhoods were black; 20 percent, Hispanic (Peterson and Harrell, 1992). Poor urban areas had become centers for a larger share of black families with children, and they were difficult places for adults to make income gains (Gramlich, Laren, and Sealand, 1992). Given the low quality of education in urban areas of poverty, and the high rates of violence and drug activity, the entrapment of black families there meant that their children grew up in settings that severely limited their opportunities (Peterson and Harrell, 1992). Just as poverty became even more grueling, federal policy changed, ushering in a new Republican approach to social spending. Poverty programs had erred by creating incentives for welfare dependency, the Reagan Republicans said, and the solution was simple: Cutting income supplements would give the poor incentive to work.

President Ronald Reagan's reductions in social spending were predicated on a distinction between the "deserving" and the "undeserving" poor (Katz, 1989). The "deserving," or working, poor eked out a living on minimum-wage jobs. They remained eligible for income supplements, but at reduced levels. Many of the "undeserving" poor were cut off entirely. The Omnibus Budget Reconciliation Act of 1981 reduced the number of families receiving AFDC (Aid to Families with Dependent Children) payments and cut benefits for those who continued to receive payments. Because 90 percent of the families who received AFDC benefits were headed by women, reductions hit these vulnerable families hardest. In the early 1980s, 408,000 families were eliminated from the rolls, and benefits for 299,000 more families were substantially reduced (Hill, 1997). Federal and state governments saved $1.1 billion in 1983, while the average family lost $1,555 per year in payments. The impact of these cuts was devastating. When interviewed in 1992, only a third of the women in Maher's ethnographic sample of crack-using women said that they had received family assistance, food stamps, or general disability payments (Maher, 1995, 1997). Two-thirds said they got by on money from prostitution, drug dealing, or working in crack houses, shoplifting, begging, or robbery (Maher, 1995). This, the informal economy—off-the-books work, prostitution, and small-time drug dealing—emerged as the most reliable source of income.

Crack made things even worse. By the late 1980s crack dominated the informal economy, and with it the character of social life, especially in key crack-dealing neighborhoods. The market peaked in 1989; thereafter a decline in the number of regular users, plus failure of crack to attract newcomers, led to the contraction of drug markets and concentration of drug activity in small geographical areas, a vortex where everyone was funneled and where drug activity was heightened (Maher and Curtis, 199_). Residents lived in terror, venturing out only in daylight hours, decrying the fate of their neighborhood (Bourgois and Dunlap, 1993). Although most drug dealers shared kin ties with the neighborhood, instabilities in the drug networks added to the potential for violence. Turf wars over retail drug markets drove up the homicide rate and spilled over, affecting innocent bystanders (Maher, 1995). The open availability of drugs, crack houses, and the proximity of prostitution strolls served as a magnet, attracting to the neighborhood markets a population of experienced polydrug users, including women.

Maher pointed out that the women she interviewed were experienced drug users who readily incorporated crack into a pattern of polydrug use (1995). This, however, did not mean that the incorporation was benign. When crack was attracting new users, the rules that normally regulate illicit drug consumption had yet to develop. Newcomers did not learn safe use and appropriate behavior; instead, more experienced users explained to novices how to maximize their high (Fagan and Chin, 1991). Curiosity and ready access to crack may have explained some women's initial attraction to the drug, and background factors like poverty and sexual abuse, according to Murphy, sabotaged their efforts to resist its appeal (Murphy, 1992; Mahan, 1996).

Maher put initial crack use in the context of emotional vulnerability: running away, homelessness, or the loss of children made some women susceptible to males who offered aid and introduced them to a steady supply of crack (1995). Philippe Bourgois and Eloise Dunlap, on the other hand, saw women's crack use as one of the tragic ironies of emancipation (1993, 89). Released from traditional gender roles to participate in street culture, women found crack, and engaged in sex work as a means for getting it.[10]

The high produced by crack reinforced a pattern of compulsive use—binges or missions that lasted up to 72 hours. That sex work funded or extended these binges allowed for "extreme degradation, especially for women," Bourgois and Dunlap said (1993, 89). "Novice crack smokers were often unable to pace their use, and they can fall apart rapidly, losing dozens of pounds of weight in a matter of weeks and/or spiraling into nervous breakdown. This is especially true for women exchanging sex for crack who have access to relatively large supplies of the drug and often lose control of their life-sustaining activities" (Bourgois and Dunlap, 1993, 103). Rapid physical and emotional decline was widely acknowledged as the major impact of crack on women (Ratner, 1993b; Maher, 1995; Murphy, 1992).

Women acquired crack through various exchanges, progressing from casual to heedless (Ratner, 1993b). Sexual exchanges could be quite informal, as when an acquaintance at a party made it known he had crack and was looking for a woman to share it. In explicit sex-for-crack exchanges, driven by intense drug cravings, the women traded sex directly for crack. Consuming it immediately, the women, who by then had neither money nor more drugs, were all the more desperate. Exchanges took place in crack houses, on the street, in cars, abandoned buildings, and alleys. Ethnographers agreed that oral sex, not vaginal intercourse, was the primary sexual service provided by the women they interviewed. Most women were of childbearing age, but in only two New York samples was the number of pregnancies noteworthy (Bourgois and Dunlap, 1993; Maher, 1995).

Patricia Hill Collins argued that the state of black motherhood reflects both the severity of oppression and the ability of black women to resist it (1990). The ability of black women to survive poverty has rested on collective arrangements for child rearing (1990; Stack, 1974; Ladner, 1971). The intensification of poverty, Republican cutbacks in social spending, and the rise of crack took a severe toll on the institutions of collective mothering. Having already taken in the off-spring of crack-addicted children, the grandmothers, aunts, and cousins had scant resources to provide for more.

Yet pronatalist values continued to make pregnancy a desirable state. Even among homeless crack addicts, Kathleen Boyle and M. Douglas Anglin found that pregnancy was symbolic of life, health, and hope (1993). Women in their sample did not try to prevent conception, but often attributed missed periods to menstrual irregularity. A woman might skip several periods, bringing her pregnancy into the second trimester before it was confirmed—a delay that then weighed against abortion. The lack of public funding represented another significant obstacle to terminating pregnancy. Add the tendency for drug users to delay, and many were left with only one option: carry the pregnancy to term.

Over the course of their pregnancies, women in Maher's sample experienced feelings of attachment and bonding (n.d.). The combination of attachment and crack addiction, however, produced high levels of denial. One study in Los Angeles found that homeless women discounted the impact of crack on the pregnancy (Boyle and Anglin, 1993). In another study, pregnant street prostitutes denied that smoking crack affected their babies; others, while recognizing potential harm to the fetus, understood that reducing their intake would protect the baby (Bourgois and Dunlap, 1993).

Pregnant women in Maher's sample wrestled with the incompatible demands of pregnancy and drug use (n.d.). They were aware of what crack might do to their babies, but only 2 of the 13 were able to stop using the drug. The other women who got pregnant during Maher's study attempted to moderate their drug use. One woman physically removed herself from the crack-dealing neighborhood and its stroll, but isolation in a shelter for pregnant women failed to stop her drug use. Her baby tested positive for cocaine at birth and was removed from her custody. Others stopped using crack in the weeks before delivery, used an herbal preparation to remove traces of cocaine from their blood, or avoided the hospital by giving birth in apartments or in vacant lots.

At the same time, pregnancy devalued the services of prostitutes.[11] Regular customers stayed away, leaving pregnant women to depend on the men in their lives for drugs. Living with someone who used drugs made cutting back more difficult, and sharing drugs with a partner increased the potential for violence. Once pregnant and unable to work, a woman's claim to a share of her partner's drugs was weak, and arguments about her right to share drugs turned violent. Perhaps this is why pregnant women in Maher's study spent their time on the street hustling men for money to buy crack (Maher, n.d.).

On the street, violence was a daily event. One woman was shot by a rejected date. Another suffered four miscarriages apparently brought about by her boyfriend's physical abuse. The women, pregnant or not, went on missions (drug binges) lasting several days, followed by collapse. Exhausted women slept in alleys or vacant lots, wherever they could find a place. Their diets were inadequate, consisting of potato chips, sodas, and occasionally fried chicken or pizza. Only a few women in the Maher sample got prenatal care (n.d.).

Most of the women in Maher's sample believed that crack shortened labor and eased delivery, but the mothers experienced a deep sense of guilt at the perceived effects of crack on their babies (n.d.). Babies born to women who used crack and heroin suffered low birth weight, premature birth, and the effects of withdrawal; one had intestinal-tract problems. Babies born to women who used only crack appeared to be unaffected, although women who had older crack-exposed children worried about developmental delay. In addition, the women were acutely aware that hospital staff perceived them as moral outlaws. And finally, crack mothers faced the loss of their babies. They knew that they had failed as mothers. They knew before going into the hospital that their mothering role would probably be terminated, although this knowledge did not prepare them for the actual loss of the infant.

Despite their own shortcomings, crack mothers tended to judge themselves and others by conventional standards of motherhood (Murphy, 1992). They held themselves accountable for providing basic necessities for their children, although poverty prevented them from taking food, shelter, or even safety for granted. The children's appearance and obedience to authority were the basis of any reputation they might have as adequate mothers. A mother's status also depended on her children's academic skills and on her ability to provide extra consumer goods. Shielding children from their crack use was another part of adequate mothering—for the most part women used crack only when baby-sitters, sleep, or television kept children occupied. When smoking, the women tried to stop early enough to be up in the morning with the children. And they planned ahead, paying bills and buying food at the beginning of the month, knowing full well that unspent money would be used for drugs.

The women themselves told tales of bad mothers that set the limits. Anecdotes reported by Murphy referred to inadequately supervised children, inadequate food and shelter, money squandered on drugs, using drugs or engaging in sexual activities in front of the children, and exchanging sex for crack (1992). Women who failed in this manner evoked scorn. To avoid derision mothers on the verge tried to cut back on their crack consumption. Failing this, they called on family and friends for child care. Drug use had already tested the limits of loyalty in this network. Addicted daughters had robbed family and friends. They had abandoned children, only to reappear, still drug impaired, to demand the children's return.

Meredith Minkler and Kathleen Roe looked closely at the grandmothers—elderly women on fixed incomes—who took up the burden of caring for the children of their offspring and other relatives (1993). Grandmothers often took full responsibility or provided regular baby-sitting for the children of kin, adding two or more children to their household or round of duties. Fixed incomes, already stretched to meet the needs of an adult, barely covered the costs of caring for additional children. In accepting this responsibility the women felt anger and resentment at kin for abandoning the children, and at the government for failing to provide adequate financial aid, child care, or other benefits. The grandmothers perceived the children as drug impaired, suffering the kinds of damage the media had associated with crack use:

hyperactivity, shortened attention span, and delayed development. While the children's problems made daily life quite difficult, many grandmothers felt rewarded for having made a difference in the lives of the children. Still, concerns about their own life expectancy raised disturbing questions about the eventual fate of the children. The grandmothers could only hold out hope that treatment would restore their crack-using kin.

Network news segments captured a few of these facts of life but missed the larger realities of crack and women altogether. Bourgois and Dunlap actually argued that the networks erred on the side of understatement. According to them, the plight of women was far worse than the media suggested (1993). There are good reasons for their criticism. Even at the height of the panic, the portrait of crack mothers rested on women who had been prepared for the camera. The circumstances that led to the filmed interview with Tracy Watson, for example, are difficult to imagine. Where did the news team find her? In whose possession was the crack? Given the laws on possession, why would anyone have violated drug statutes on national television? On the other hand, she was well groomed, spoke clearly, and aside from being pregnant and smoking crack on national television, her behavior was not aberrant. The same could be said of Erocelia Fandino, the woman who delivered a premature baby after smoking crack. She too was well groomed, spoke clearly, and behaved in a conventional manner.

The only portrait of a crack mother that came close to the women described by Bourgois and Dunlap was that of Stephanie. She was high, incoherent, pregnant for at least the third time, and headed for the crack house. Still, the coverage on Stephanie gave no inkling of what Bourgois and Dunlap described as the rapid descent into physical and emotional degradation, nor of the impoverished and desperate circumstances in which this occurred (1993).

Even if they did understate the ravages of crack, at the height of the panic the media still vilified crack mothers. Renegade "crack mothers" had emerged from urban chaos, the media's image linking poverty, race, and drugs to a threat posed by women to their babies. That image defined the social ills that most disturbed the New Right. In the concluding phase of the crusade against crack mothers, the networks finally began to humanize crack mothers. But until then neither spokesperson, expert, correspondent, nor recovering addict had been given the opportunity to explain why women used crack. True, the networks had earlier described the cocaine-induced boost in self-esteem that white middle-class women got from the drug; but until the concluding phase of the crack mother episode, no news account had broached the topic of motivation. What had driven women to use crack?

According to NBC, finally posing the question in 1992, it was despair. NBC aired an interview with a recovering woman who recalled how, after her brother was killed in a drug deal gone bad, she turned to crack (December 29). Recorded on camera, her obvious despair over her brother's death was the first hint that crack mothers had emotions. Recovery, the final phase in the moral career of an addict, had arrived, providing an appropriate narrative to humanize crack mothers.

Filmed in drug treatment centers, crack mothers recounted rapid addiction, bottoming out, and recovery (Levine, 1978). Like her white middle-class counterpart, however, the lower-class crack user quickly lost control of the drug. Crack became—to the exclusion of everything else—the single most important thing in her life. The woman interviewed by NBC, for example, said as long as she had money or crack, things were fine. Without either, the pain of having lost so much was overwhelming; to stop the pain, she would find a way to get more crack (1992, December 29).

Moreover, crack mothers had bottomed out like their middle-class counterparts but had not sought help. In an ABC segment, a recovering addict told how her son feared she would die from all the drugs she had taken, but still his admission had not led her to seek treatment (1993, June 10). Whatever help crack mothers got, at least according to network news, was due not to their own efforts but to legal intervention. ABC and NBC focused on the imprisonment of crack mothers in South Carolina, asserting that while the tough program may not have been fair, it appeared to work (ABC, 1991, September 17; NBC, 1991, September 17).

Some women seemed to concede that crack mothers needed prison in order to stop (ABC, 1991, September 17). Others denounced the prosecutions, indicating that county prosecutors had used them, turning them into scapegoats to scare others away from drugs (ABC, 1992, July 2). Most agreed, however, that treatment provided a better prognosis. In centers where they could bring their children, women who had used crack during pregnancy had a chance to rebuild their lives and reclaim their children. They regretted the suffering they had inflicted on their children and other family members, although most agreed it should not have taken prison to reach this end (NBC, 1992, December 30; ABC, 1993, June 10).

Addiction

Many people, including those in law enforcement, believe they know what an addict is; but addiction is hard to define. Its official definition has been modified many times. For most of this century, the understanding was that a pattern of tolerance and withdrawal established a physical condition called addiction. Tolerance refers to the body's ability to accommodate larger and larger quantities of drugs like heroin, barbiturates, or alcohol. Tolerance is also understood as the need for increasing doses of these drugs for the user to experience the heights of the initial euphoria. The buildup of tolerance is associated with the second feature of addiction, withdrawal. Withdrawal is the set of physical symptoms produced when someone abruptly stops taking a drug like heroin or alcohol. It varies by drug. Withdrawal can be unpleasant—chills, fever, vomiting, diarrhea, cramps, and body aches in the case of heroin. Alcohol withdrawal can be life-threatening. Some drugs, including cocaine, produce neither tolerance nor withdrawal symptoms.

Were we to consider these drugs less addictive? Obviously the answer was no, but amid competing definitions of addiction, it took the

World Health Organization to set a single worldwide standard (Eddy et al., 1965).[12] In its first attempt the World Health Organization distinguished between physical and psychological dependence. Physical dependence referred to classic addiction, marked by tolerance and withdrawal. Psychological dependence, on the other hand, referred to the positive mental effects of the drug. Heroin produces both forms of dependence. In the early stages, the euphoria motivates drug use (psychic drive), but once tolerance sets in, the desire to avoid withdrawal (physical dependence) was thought to be the overriding motivation. Other drugs—marijuana, cocaine, amphetamines—generate psychological dependence, but still seemed less dangerous than heroin. Renewed interest in psychological dependence, however, altered conceptions of what constituted an addictive drug.

Erich Goode, in his summary of the literature, made the case that psychological dependence is every bit as compelling as physical dependence (1989). Animal research, he noted, had demonstrated that the psychological dependence associated with cocaine was a force to be reckoned with. Cocaine had greater appeal than food, and it produced a longer-lasting dependency than heroin. The pattern of use was erratic, involving binges. In addition, the mortality rate for animals exposed to cocaine was higher than for heroin. What the animal research pointed to, according to Goode, was the powerful reinforcing effect of cocaine (1989). Intense pleasure was sufficient reward to sustain a single-minded desire for repetitive use and the willingness to make other sacrifices to use the drug.

Psychological dependence, however, was not understood as an automatic consequence of drug use, because drugs differed in their capacity to generate pleasure. According to Goode, cocaine ranked high on the pleasure scale, followed by heroin and amphetamines (1989). Marijuana ranked lowest; to enjoy marijuana, the novice had first to learn to recognize its effects and then to appreciate them as pleasurable. The effects of cocaine, in contrast, were immediately discernible and intensely pleasurable. Additionally, the route of administration affected the way a drug was experienced: the faster the delivery to target tissue and the larger the dose, the more pleasurable the drug's effects.

Intravenous injection and smoking delivered the largest doses rapidly to the brain. Intravenous drug use was limited only by the solubility of the drug in liquid and the body's capacity to absorb it. Injected directly into the bloodstream, the drug hit the brain within seconds. Inhalation, like IV drug delivery, enabled the user to maximize the dose—smoking exposed the entire surface area of the lungs to the drug—and to reduce to seconds the time it took to reach the brain. By contrast, snorting, chewing, or swallowing were less efficient. Most notably, the size of the nasal membranes regulated the amount of cocaine that could be snorted.

As psychological dependence—the reinforcing effects of the drug—came to be understood as the decisive factor in explaining cocaine use, several human studies raised questions about the inevitability of physical dependence. One study suggesting that alcoholics could engage in social drinking created quite a stir, since the prevailing wisdom required strict abstinence (Sobell and Sobell, 1978). What did it mean that a former addict could learn to manage drug use? If that were true, then addiction or physical dependence was not necessarily an all-or-nothing proposition. When the study proved to be flawed, the findings were dismissed, but questions about the certainty of addiction did not go away.

Another study involved heroin, the drug perceived in the 1970s as the most addicting. This study documented what most people considered impossible: the managed use of heroin, the drug on which modern notions of addiction rested (Zinberg, 1984). Heroin produces tolerance, and once tolerance sets in, addicts take the drug to avoid withdrawal—vomiting, chills, aching, and the secretion of bodily fluids. The addiction process was thought to be automatic and progressive: People who "chipped," that is, who tried to limit dose and intervals of use to avoid tolerance, would eventually succumb.

In finding a small number of people who managed dose and interval, Zinberg demonstrated that exposure to drugs like heroin did not automatically produce physical dependence (1984). Set and setting, he concluded, strongly influenced the outcome of drug use. Set referred to the user's expectations, which for managed heroin use would be recreational. Setting referred to the social and physical environment in which drug use took place. Managed heroin use depended on a particular setting—a gathering of friends reinforced rules about dose and interval, keeping use levels low. The same point has been made with regard to morphine. Patients whose expectations are of pain reduction and who receive morphine in a medical setting, titrated in carefully measured doses, do not experience euphoria, and they do not become addicted.

In its second attempt to define addiction, the World Health Organization developed the scheme that made psychological dependence a more important part of the definition. It recognized that different drugs produced distinctive patterns of dependence (Eddy et al., 1965). Dependence of the morphine type involved tolerance and withdrawal, but it also involved the psychic drive that defined psychological dependence. Because cocaine was classified as a stimulant, the dependence it produced had been equated with that of other stimulants: a high-energy euphoria followed by a "crash," depression, irritability, and drug cravings.

Research reported by the media at the height of the crack panic indicated that the brain encoded crack's rush. It was taken as documentation for a physiological adaptation that justified labeling cocaine's aftereffects as a withdrawal syndrome. That these effects were indeed withdrawal was a matter for debate in discussions of cocaine dependence, but the notion was institutionalized in treatment programs that prescribed tranquilizers, antidepressants, and drug antagonists for cocaine's aftereffects. Some textbooks now describe the irritability and depression that follows cocaine use as withdrawal.

The idea that different drugs produce different types of dependence shifted the focus of research from the intrinsic qualities of the drug to behavioral patterns of drug users. It had long been recognized that susceptibility to the pleasurable and reinforcing effects of drugs varied. Not everyone who used a drug was going to become psychologically dependent, and not all drug use resulted in chronic abuse. Any drug can produce a broad range of behaviors.

One widely adopted scheme includes experimenters, recreational drug users, regular drug users, and chronic drug abusers (Inciardi, 1986). Experimenters are the largest group. Given an appropriate setting, for example the company of friends and acquaintances, experimenters may try a drug, and thereafter use it only infrequently. Recreational drug use is more frequent, but it is still dependent on someone else's getting the drug. For regular or involved drug users, the drug itself does something important for them. A key distinction is between use and abuse, abuse being the point at which drug use interferes with one's life. Drug use might be controlled, but drug seeking begins to interfere with other areas of life, including school or work, family, and personal relationships. Chronic drug abuse is the least common pattern, but it means that other areas of one's life, whether personal, occupational, or family-related, are sacrificed to compulsive efforts to obtain and use the drug.

The capacity of a drug like crack to produce pleasure intense enough to reinforce chronic drug abuse is what made it problematic. Crack is produced by adding boiling water and baking soda to cocaine hydrochloride (Inciardi, 1997b). The result is a mixture that contains all the adulterants in cocaine hydrochloride, plus the baking soda and additives, like lidocaine, to increase bulk. The active ingredient is still cocaine, a fact that places crack at the high end of the pleasure continuum; that is, its effects are immediately pleasurable. Unlike powder cocaine, crack can be smoked, which further intensifies the drug's effect. Smoking crack or freebasing cocaine seems to be associated with a higher frequency of use. In several *National Household Surveys*, half those who had used cocaine once a month or more in the past year had smoked crack or freebase (NIDA, 1990; SAMHSA, 1995a, 1995b).

But if crack automatically produced chronic abuse, that would be reflected in the surveys on drug use: everyone who answered yes to the question "Have you used crack within the past year?" would also answer yes to the question "Have you used crack within the past month?" Survey results, however, show a different pattern. In surveys conducted from 1988 to 1993, each year about one million people said they had used crack in the past year, but the portion of people who said they had used crack in the past month was far lower, ranging from about 50 percent in 1988 to 40 percent in 1993 (NIDA, 1990; SAMHSA, 1994). The comparable figure for past-month marijuana use was about 45 percent in 1993 (SAMHSA, 1994).[13]

Legal drugs, by contrast, tended to sustain current use. About 80 percent of the people who had used alcohol in the past year reported past-month use. The equivalent figure for tobacco is 85 percent (SAMHSA, 1994). A related measure of chronic drug abuse is the percentage of people who report being drug dependent or having experienced withdrawal. Between 1988 and 1993, dependence or withdrawal symptoms were reported by 14 to 15 percent of the current marijuana smokers, by 15 to 17 percent of current cocaine users, by 19 to 23 percent of the drinkers who had had 5 consecutive drinks on 5 or more occasions within the past month, and by 78 to 83 percent of the cigarette smokers who had smoked a pack or more a day within the past month (NIDA, 1990; SAMHSA, 1994). With the exception of tobacco, many drugs, including cocaine, do not generate behaviors that fit the patterns of regular or chronic drug abuse.

Set and setting affect drug use, but when a new drug hits a population, special problems arise. LSD, newly marketed in the 1960s, caused occasional fatalities because novices did not know how to arrange set (a positive initial mood) and setting (the company of good friends) to avoid the paranoia or delusions of a bad acid trip. Similarly, the spread of crack in the mid-1980s caught even experienced drug users by surprise. Its reputation attracted new drug users, and the emergent ideal maximized the high. The crack smokers' phrase "beam me up" revealed an expectation that crack would transport the user to another dimension. Dealers prepared the settings—apartments, private homes, crack houses, and the like—where people gathered for extended drug use and sexual exchanges. The phrase "24-7" epitomized extended drug use—using crack 24 hours a day for 7 days a week. Whether consumption sites were indoors or outside, they became focal points for social life in communities hardest hit by crack.

The television networks presented a confused, often contradictory picture of addiction, hardening in response to the dictates of the war on drugs and then softening again as the problem lost value as a news story. The early reports on cocaine sent many messages: cocaine produced "psychological addiction" (CBS, 1983, February 7). The drug's effects were so pleasurable that they masked its deadly effects (CBS, 1984, November 28). Addiction, however, was not automatic: only 25 to 50 percent would fall victim (CBS, 1984, May 30). Addicted women found help in a variety of private treatment settings, including some designed especially for them (NBC, 1984, August 9 and 10).

Later, as the crack panic built, the media's interest turned to the physiology of addiction—reporting, for example, that the brain encoded cocaine's rush, a scientific finding that explained the high relapse rates (ABC, 1988, July 13). The networks, however, announced that there would be no magic bullet like methadone for crack or cocaine addiction. They focused on problems within the commercial treatment industry, on high fees and inadequate aftercare, and on the staggering costs to federal, state, and local governments of treating poor and uninsured addicts.

As the war on drugs wound down, the networks still maintained that crack was an extremely addictive drug, but in covering the success stories of treatment, they managed to convey a sense of closure to the problem that did not actually exist. In an upbeat two-part segment, NBC announced it had found a program that could bring back those who had once been consumed by crack (1992, December 29 and 30). It focused on the "survivors of the crack epidemic," a concept no one had previously thought possible. The profile began with an eye toward the severity of addiction. One crack smoker had been so addicted that he asked his roommate to shoot him; others had no control over the drug, either. Such addicts had their lives changed for the better by a New Orleans drug program run by the Christian Community Youth Against Drugs Foundation. As a last-resort sanctuary, it opened its doors, free of charge, to homeless and poor crack addicts for as long as they liked. The program turned no one away. It offered spiritual and physical renewal, and because its community of former addicts helped newcomers, it was judged uniquely effective by federal evaluators.

Six months later, ABC ran its last segment, an optimistic report on a program that gave women a second chance (1993, June 10). Noting that women were reluctant to go into treatment, ABC's anchor gave details about an outreach program in Nashville, Tennessee, saying that a lot can be accomplished when the right people come calling. In this case, the right people were "Sisters," drug counselors and former crack addicts who weekly went door-to-door in the city's housing projects. They looked for crack addicts, found them transportation and child care, and got them into treatment. Afterward, Sisters provided counseling, ran support groups, provided recreational activities, and kept the community drug free. ABC's correspondent boasted that three-quarters of the women in the experimental program were drug free. A few success stories were enough to suggest that an effective institutional structure had begun to emerge to manage the problem.

The Drug Treatment Network

The drug treatment network consists of drug and alcohol rehabilitation programs and state and federal agencies that fund, evaluate, and otherwise support drug treatment efforts. Developments within it are typically calculated by the number of drug treatment clients or the number of units providing treatment services. The National Drug and Alcoholism Treatment Unit Survey found that treatment units had increased from 5,900 in 1985 to 7,700 in 1990, although this does not adequately convey its increased capacity (Butynski et al., 1991). The *Sourcebook on Criminal Justice Statistics* reports that the number of people in correctional custody also in drug or alcohol treatment more than doubled from 478,000 in 1980 to 944,000 in 1990, leveling off at 945,000 in 1992 (McGuire and Pastore, 1995). According to the National Drug and Alcoholism Treatment Unit Survey, 1.1 million people were admitted to drug treatment units in 1985; this figure almost doubled to 1.9 million clients in 1990 (Butynski et al., 1991). While the Treatment Episode Data Set counts admissions differently, it shows that the number of drug clients leveled off at about 1.2 million after

1992, continuing to level until 1995 (SAMHSA, 1997). It is safe, then, to say that the drug treatment network had doubled its capacity since the 1980s and that it continued to serve a large client base through the 1990s.

Expanding the drug treatment network did not, however, happen automatically. The 1981 Budget Reconciliation Act, which transferred federal dollars to the states in the form of block grants, had left it up to the states whether to fully fund drug treatment programs (see Kandall, 1996; Katz, 1989). Cities and states had other demands: the state costs of imprisoning drug offenders and municipal expenses associated with aggressive enforcement of the drug laws. Kandall reports that by 1981 private methadone programs—the prototypical drug treatment program—had replaced federally funded ones (1996).

All this began to change in the late 1980s. AIDS and crack focused the nation's attention on the need to increase federal funding for drug treatment. The practice of exchanging sex for crack contributed to the spread of AIDS, so the babies born to crack users were at especially high risk. The pressure to authorize federal spending for drug treatment grew during the presidential campaign in 1988, resulting in the Anti-Drug Abuse Act of that year. Although President George Bush did not increase the amount available, which still represented only 30 percent of the budget for his war on drugs, the 1988 law allowed federal dollars to finance state treatment projects directly. A comparison of expenditures from 1985 to 1990 shows that federal dollars made the difference (Butynski et al., 1991). While states paid about half the cost of drug treatment in both years, the federal portion went up from 19 percent of $1.3 billion in 1985 treatment expenditures to 29 percent of $2.9 billion in 1990 expenditures.

Monies were earmarked for development of treatment programs for pregnant women and mothers with children (Feig, 1990; U.S. Department of Health and Human Services, 1992). Still, the drug treatment network was unprepared. An estimated 208,000 pregnant women were in need of drug treatment in 1989 (U.S. General Accounting Office, 1990). Some programs would not accept pregnant women at all. In New York City, a 1989 survey of 78 drug treatment programs showed that 54 percent refused admission to pregnant women, 67 percent refused to treat pregnant women on Medicaid, and 87 percent had no services available for Medicaid patients who were both pregnant and dependent on crack (Chavkin, 1989). Officials said obstetric care added unacceptable risks to drug treatment (McNulty, 1988; Moss and Crockett, 1990). The situation was similar in Michigan (McNulty, 1988). Only 9 of 13 programs that accepted women would consider a pregnant woman. Long waiting lists, delayed examinations, and restrictive admissions policies discouraged women from attempting to get help.

Before the mid-1980s, the systems for referring clients to treatment had focused on men (Humphries et al., 1992). Lower arrest rates kept women out of the criminal justice system and away from court-mandated drug treatment. Similarly, lower employment rates kept women out of employee-assistance programs for drug or alcohol abuse. Consequently, not much was known about women and drug treatment. If women were admitted to treatment, they were more likely than men to have been admitted on a voluntary basis (Anglin and Hser, 1990). If their drug use threatened to result in the loss of their children, women entered treatment (Rosenbaum, 1981). Pregnant women remained in treatment until delivery, but they often dropped out once they were sure about the baby's health (Anglin and Hser, 1990).

Treatment programs had been designed for male heroin addicts, and at least initially, women who used crack or cocaine joined therapy groups dominated by male drug users. Women found it difficult to discuss sensitive topics like sexual abuse in groups dominated by men. The treatment programs focused on the individual addict and did not typically take into account drug use by partners or other family members. Because women tended to be involved in relationships with drug users, their success in treatment depended on whether they could get help for their partners as well as themselves. In addition, mothers who abused drugs or alcohol required child care for at least the period of treatment. Some mothers could rely on relatives, but those without family support faced a difficult choice. Residential treatment meant turning children over to foster care.

Even so, clinical experiences with women who had used heroin during pregnancy provided a model of sorts for dealing with crack mothers. Methadone maintenance programs were designed to cope with high relapse rates among male heroin users (Landry, 1995). Daily and measured doses of pure methadone are effective for up to 24 hours, and methadone maintenance permits clients to lead a normal life (Landry, 1995). When treatment specialists encountered women heroin addicts, some of whom were pregnant, the question was whether methadone could be administered to pregnant women—and the consensus was encouraging.

Heroin had negative effects on pregnancy, the newborn, and parenting. Heroin-exposed babies were at risk for premature delivery, abruptio placentae, breech births, and intrauterine growth retardation (Finnegan, 1988). Then, too, the supply was uncertain and adulterated, and when the heroin ran out, abstinence produced withdrawal in the mother and induced distress and withdrawal in the fetus (Finnegan, 1988; Finnegan and Fehr, 1980; Kaltenbach and Finnegan, 1986, 353). Methadone, by contrast, provided the fetus with a continuous supply of a long-acting, unadulterated narcotic without significant impact on the pregnancy (Finnegan, 1988). Its effects on fetal growth and birth weight were slight in comparison with the negative effects of heroin (Finnegan and Fehr, 1980; Kron et al., 1988). Following delivery, methadone babies were given drugs to ease the stress of withdrawal. Methadone had an additional benefit: pregnant women enrolled in methadone programs were more likely to receive prenatal care, which reduced infant mortality (Kaltenbach and Finnegan, 1986; Finnegan, 1982).

The lessons of methadone were not directly applicable to crack mothers, however. While researchers had designed drugs to counteract cocaine, severe side effects limited their use, ruling out a pharmaceutical solution for pregnant women (U.S. General Accounting Office, 1991). Acupuncture was used for relaxation and to help prepare the patient for detoxification (U.S. General Accounting Office,

CHAPTER 4

1991). Normally, however, the cravings and depression associated with cocaine detoxification required medication (Abandinsky, 1997; Witters, Venturellis, and Hanson, 1992, 270–71).

In the first several days of cocaine abstinence, the patient experiences agitation, anorexia, depression, thoughts of suicide, and fatigue that turns into exhaustion. Antidepressants and antipsychotic drugs are used to relieve anxiety and psychosis should symptoms appear. In the middle stages of abstinence, which may take as long as 10 weeks, drug cravings increase to the point of obsession. The patient suffers mood swings, but is able to sleep. Dopamine antagonists like L-dopa are used to reduce the intense craving for cocaine.

Finally, during the last stage, the patient experiences normal pleasures, but still faces mood swings and a wide variety of environmental cues that trigger cocaine cravings. Desipramine is used to relieve depression and craving. Unfortunately, powerful drugs designed to ease anxiety, depression, and drug cravings are contraindicated for pregnancy. In addition, some programs take a strong abstinence approach, denying all drugs throughout the course of treatment. It seems, therefore, that most pregnant patients went through cocaine detoxification "cold turkey," without the benefit of stress-relieving drugs.

Other lessons learned from methadone maintenance were more helpful. Before the 1960s, success in drug treatment meant lifelong abstinence. A single lapse in judgment in this all-or-nothing approach to treatment turned success into failure. Methadone maintenance, however, recognized that recovery was a complex process in which relapse played a part (Landry, 1995; U.S. General Accounting Office, 1991). In the methadone model, success means stabilizing the life of recovering drug users by reducing drug use and criminal activity; improving physical health, mental health, and social functioning; and maximizing the benefits of holding a job. Simply reducing the likelihood of using drugs again counts as success, as does the client's preparedness for the possibility of relapse (National Institutes of Health, 1993).

Meeting the practical goals of treatment necessitates a broad range of services (U.S. Department of Health and Human Services, 1992).

122

Patients are tested for illicit drug use, receive job and educational counseling, and are encouraged to recognize and get help for psychological problems (Landry, 1995). Talking therapies, designed to increase the patient's insight into the causes of his or her drug use, are expensive and their track records uncertain. Publicly financed treatment programs are, therefore, more likely to use behavioral techniques, based on the assumption that better relationships and sharper problem-solving skills promote success in treatment.

In behavioral contracting, the client agrees to certain consequences of success or failure in meeting program goals. Should the patient pass a drug test, he or she gets additional privileges. Should a patient fail, the consequences, agreed to beforehand, might include having the spouse begin divorce proceedings. Aftercare is important, too. The client learns stress management and relapse prevention and is encouraged to join a support group—for example, one of the 12-step programs that provides social support for a drug-free lifestyle (National Institutes of Health, 1993).

The Center for Substance Abuse Treatment, charged with designing effective treatments, recommended dealing with "a woman's substance abuse in the context of her health and her relationship with her children and other family members, the community, and society" (1994, 67). For pregnant women, services included prenatal and postpartum care, AIDS testing and counseling, and psychological counseling on issues that may underlie drug abuse—family dynamics; violence, including incest or rape; interpersonal relationships; sexuality; and grief related to the loss of children, family, or partners (Center for Substance Abuse Treatment, 1993; U.S. General Accounting Office, 1991). The goal of self-sufficiency emphasized education and job training. Clients received health education with an emphasis on preventing sexually transmitted diseases and protecting the health and safety of children. Clients were provided with transportation to outside referrals, including health care.

The Center for Substance Abuse Treatment recommended that programs serving pregnant women provide long-term care, for from 6 to 18 months (Center for Substance Abuse Treatment, 1994). While residential treatment was designed for such extended care, Medicaid, Medicare, and most private health insurance companies limited treatment to just 28 days. From residential treatment, a client could go to outpatient services, remaining for anywhere from a month to a year. Intensive outpatient programs required the client to participate in counseling and other services 8 to 10 hours per week. Less intensive programs required once- or twice-weekly visits. Either way, the client participated in group or individual therapy and continued to receive employment counseling. Clients were referred to other agencies for physical or mental health problems and for social services, including housing, AFDC, and public assistance. Outpatient services worked to integrate the client into a 12-step program.

Effective treatment was the goal, but despite federal and state commitments, little was known about what worked. Research on treatment provided some insights (Landry, 1995): The better a women is able to fulfill her parenting responsibilities by providing food, health care insurance, housing, and transportation, the easier it is to enter and remain in treatment. The number and quality of a woman's interpersonal relationships appear to be a factor in treatment outcomes. The most effective programs use case managers to set goals and monitor clients' progress toward them. Adequate funding and ongoing program evaluation make for effective programs. Relapse prevention and follow-up care are especially important. In addition, researchers found, short-term intensive programs are effective when combined with outpatient continuing care and follow-up services, although the minimum effective stay is three months (Landry, 1995). The length of time spent in treatment programs may not by itself be related to successful outcomes (Landry, 1995). Longer periods of intense psychosocial treatment may be effective for clients with significant mental disorders or with heavy involvement in criminal activity.

From a clinical perspective, pregnant substance abusers presented a number of challenges (U.S. Department of Health and Human Services, 1992). The women had parenting responsibilities, but even if a program were to address reproductive and parental issues, the women were typically not married or employed, and many had troubled relationships with family. And even if their involvement with cocaine or crack had been brief, relapse was easily triggered by depression, problems with sex, family pressures, or the environment of drug-using neighborhoods (U.S. General Accounting Office, 1991).

In addition, low-income inner-city communities offered few legitimate employment opportunities. Instead, crack and cocaine remained a feature of street life, a complex nexus for social activity, the backbone of the informal economy, and the source of any number of illicit jobs. In the end, the prospects for crack or cocaine users were far less optimistic than what news accounts of treatment presented. Successful treatment is quite a bit less certain than implied by the networks' optimistic coverage of Sisters, an outreach program in Nashville, or by their coverage of the Christian Community Youth Against Drugs Foundation in New Orleans (NBC, 1992, December 29 and 30; ABC, 1993, June 10). But these segments were effective in conveying the impression that maternal drug use had been institutionalized in programs like these throughout the country.

Media accounts that conveyed a sense of solution were as distorted, one-sided, and simplistic as the accounts that conveyed panic. By providing motive and a narrative that allowed for recovery, selected news segments idealized crack mothers as candidates for recovery. They were made to appear more sympathetic—less like the renegade mothers who had fueled the panic, and more like their white middle-class cocaine-using counterparts. With a few of the trappings of middle-class recovery, crack mothers began to fit more easily into the picture of drug treatment.

Through all this, the networks stressed the addictiveness of crack—it still had the power to enslave its users. What made the difference, however, was an upbeat reaction by the networks to effective outreach and residential treatment programs. These appeared to work, but the networks remained silent on the possibilities of relapse. As the news industry moved on to new and different stories, the problem persisted despite resources shaken loose by the panic. It was left to professionals and researchers to complain (McNeece, 1997). Despite a significant investment in treatment, the women's circumstances remained unchanged, most patients were treated on an outpatient basis instead of in residential facilities, and more states in 1994 than in 1985 reported having unmet treatment needs (Butynski et al., 1991).

CHAPTER 5

Children, Welfare, and Education

The images we were presented in the late 1980s and early 1990s of crack babies changed, for reasons having more to do with institutional reactions than with the children themselves. In chapter 1 we looked at some of the shifts in news images of cocaine-exposed babies. While the cocaine babies shown belonging to white middle-class women appeared to be normal, commentators expressed concern that they might have future learning difficulties. After crack surpassed cocaine in the media's estimation as the most dangerous drug in the world, crack babies belonging to poor women of color appeared on the nightly news as severely impaired. The images offered of crack babies, as chapter 2 showed, exaggerated the problem, reflecting the perceived urgency of the war on drugs, the increasing scientific interest in cocaine-related impairments, and the growing alarm that treating such infants would prove extremely expensive. It would take $500 million annually to provide hospital care for cocaine-exposed newborns (Phibbs, Bateman, and Schwartz, 1991).

Another kind of image played on themes of abandonment or abuse and neglect. What might be called the "child welfare" portrait focused on abused drug-exposed babies and boarder babies left by their mothers in the hospital. As the problem broadened to include older children whose parents and guardians used drugs and alcohol, the number of children at risk for abuse mounted. The news shifted its emphasis from suffering newborns to children left without food, clothing, or care while their mothers smoked crack. Social workers were characterized as frontline soldiers in the war on drugs, and to save the babies and children, they were forced to make the difficult decisions to take custody of the children (ABC, 1992, May 20).

Finally, news segments focused on the much broader problem of children in state care, including the children of homeless, the long-term unemployed, and those with drug and alcohol problems (CBS, 1991, June 24). The crack babies, as we will see in this chapter, thus disappeared—in popular perception and in reality—into a large and increasing population of at-risk children who fell under the jurisdiction of child welfare services.

Then, too, after years of covering crack babies, the networks began to question earlier stereotypes. In a segment on children entering school with learning disabilities, an ABC anchor noted that perhaps there was no such group as "crack babies," since pregnant women, like most people, tended to use a wide variety of licit and illicit drugs that affect pregnancy and compromise the well-being of newborns (1991, July 24). The tremulous and premature babies shown on television news as crack babies might, in retrospect, be simply drug babies.

Second, most drug-exposed babies, according to this report, were not black, as stereotypes would have it. Rather, most of the learning-disabled children shown attending special education programs were white. The singular focus on crack, which seems to have been the drug of preference among black women, produced an image of irresponsible black mothers and damaged black babies. But by expanding the problem to include other drugs, including alcohol, prescription drugs, and marijuana, all of which were used at higher rates by white women, it was correct to say that most drug babies were white.

Third, most crack babies, stated the ABC anchor, were not monsters. Rather, prenatal drug exposure produced a continuum of outcomes, ranging from severely damaged babies to apparently perfectly healthy ones. Most, the anchor noted, fell within the normal range of development, although many would have learning disabilities and require special education services. What had been viewed as the "crack baby population" was swallowed up in the increasing numbers of learning-disabled children who entered public schools in the early 1990s. The cost to public schools was high—$10 thousand more per special education student.

Warnings that "the crack kids are coming" meant that states would be required to do more with less. Meeting the needs of drug-exposed infants and more at-risk children necessitated additional resources, but finding a continuing stream of federal dollars to pay for such services was problematic. The Reagan and Bush administrations had reduced the number of families on AFDC and, as argued in chapter 4, placed more women at risk for homelessness, drugs, and drug-impaired pregnancies. Child welfare services—an essential but flawed part of the safety net—were also targeted for federal cuts. The status of special education as a civil rights entitlement ensured its survival, but it was chronically underfunded. In other words, for drug-exposed babies, the safety net was going to be stitched together—or not—by hard-pressed state bureaucracies.

Child Abuse and Child Welfare Services

When crack babies hit the child welfare system, the system itself was in crisis (U.S. Department of Health and Human Services, 1992). The roots of trouble included Reagan's budget cuts, but they went deeper, reflecting basic differences over the mission of child welfare services. Generally speaking, child welfare services investigate reports of child abuse and neglect, provide support for families at risk of child abuse or neglect, deliver services to abused children and their families, place children in foster care and manage the cases, and process adoptions (Kamerman and Kahn, 1976; Holder et al., 1981; "The Enemy Within," 1990).

For years, professionals in the field have been divided over the desirability of keeping families together. Advocates of substitute care, the technical phrase for foster care, argued the key to resolving the backlog in foster placements was to streamline adoption procedures. In practical terms, child welfare services had already become investigative agencies that removed at-risk children from the custody of abusive or negligent parents (Kamerman and Kahn, 1989; Kamerman, 1990). Removal kept children out of harm's way, but an increasing reliance on foster care was becoming cause for concern (Kamerman, 1990; Downs, Costin, and McFadden, 1996).

If children were to be either adopted or reunited with their families, these events occurred within the first year or so in foster care; if neither occurred then, children tended to remain in foster care until they reached the age of 18 (Burt and Pittman, 1985). Unstable living arrangements, the absence of a caring adult, elevated rates of delinquency, and drug use were among the disadvantages of long-term placement in foster care (Burt and Pittman, 1985). Advocates for substitute care, therefore, urged Congress to attack the backlog by making it easier for families to adopt (Besharov, 1989).

Family preservation advocates, on the other hand, believed that the biological family, not foster care, provided the best long-term hope for safeguarding children (Berry, 1994). Using abuse and neglect statutes, social workers investigated complaints and served as case managers for the sundry services required to preserve the family and thereby to protect the child. In this investigate-and-preserve model of child welfare, the expense of services was justified on the theory that stable living arrangements and caring adults would reduce problems related to foster care. The problem with preservation, however, was this: the remedial effects of social services were often temporary (Berry, 1994). As problems reappeared within the family, the child was again placed at risk, and intervention was required. Overcoming the open-ended nature of preservation efforts raised difficult questions about the expense of support services in an era favoring more cost-efficiency and less government involvement.

Differences in the mission of child welfare services—foster care versus family preservation—were reflected in the zigzagging history of federal policy (Burt and Pittman, 1985; Dorne, 1997). The original federal legislation distinguished between direct payments to children without parental support and welfare services to children at risk for abuse or neglect. Direct payments and services were both authorized by Congress in 1935 as part of the Social Security Act; but legislation

on direct payment tended to strengthen foster care, while laws affecting welfare services tended to support family preservation.

In the 1960s, Congress extended direct payments—Aid to Families with Dependent Children—to children in foster care, added
emergency payments for families in crisis, and authorized Medicaid
coverage for children in foster care. Unfortunately, those reforms
helped create the backlog of children languishing in foster care. Children in foster care received AFDC payments and Medicaid, but adoptive parents had no such aid—unless they were poor enough to qualify
on their own. Thus, foster parents were reluctant to adopt. In the
1970s, Congress capped spending for family preservation services, but
AFDC payments for children in foster care remained an open-ended
entitlement, shaping child welfare services' response to the emerging problem of child abuse (Kamerman and Kahn, 1989; Kamerman, 1990).

The Child Abuse Prevention and Treatment Act in 1978 gave the
upper hand to advocates of foster care, turning welfare services into investigative agencies that removed children from abusive homes (Kamerman and Kahn, 1989). The act provided federal grants to the states,
but to be eligible, states were required to create an extensive child
abuse reporting system: to guarantee legal immunity to people who
reported child abuse, to pass mandatory reporting laws for designated
professionals, including physicians, and to develop programs that distributed information on child abuse.

The states rapidly complied, enacting mandatory reporting laws
and thus widening the net of social control in this area. Medical
personnel, mental health professionals, social workers, teachers and
school officials, day care and child care workers, and law enforcement
personnel were required to report child abuse. Administrative links between child welfare services and the agencies likely to report abuse,
such as schools, hospitals, or day care, reinforced the reporting system.

For over 20 years the number of reported cases of child abuse rose
annually, driven up by an improved reporting system and increased
sensitivity to the behavior in question. For over 20 years caseworkers
referred cases to foster care because federal grants, though not large,

were fully funded (Kamerman and Kahn, 1989). The work of monitoring these placements required child welfare agencies to hire more staff, while other child welfare services were cut (Hagdorn, 1995). By the end of the 1970s, three-quarters of the child welfare monies were spent on foster care (Burt and Pittman, 1985).

To return to the original Social Security Act of 1935, it was also in that piece of legislation that Congress authorized child welfare services, providing federal grants to states to develop services for vulnerable children regardless of income (Burt and Pittman, 1985; Dorne, 1997). In the 1960s, Congress legislated federal-state cost-sharing to develop social service programs, including child welfare services, a policy responsible for the surge in federal expenditures in services in the 1960s.

In 1972, Congress took steps to limit social spending, capping social service expenditures at $2.5 billion. Congress also took steps to create alternatives to foster care. It increased federal funds available to the states but required that the funds be used for family preservation services. Lacking strong sanctions, the states used the new federal funds to support foster care; but in 1975, Congress provided grants specifically for developing family preservation services. The 1972 cap on social service spending limited the impact of these grants, but the 1975 legislation permitted greater flexibility for the states to create alternatives to foster care (Burt and Pittman, 1985).

The Adoption Assistance and Child Welfare Act of 1980 made family preservation and permanency the goals of child welfare services. The act contained the first financial incentives for states to develop alternatives to foster care (Berry, 1994; Burt and Pittman, 1985). Chief among the alternatives was adoption, for which Congress created an open-ended entitlement. The act authorized the use of federal funds to reimburse the states for monies used to support foster child adoption. The act continued payments to adoptees—to AFDC children with "special needs"—and it extended Medicaid coverage to children regardless of the adoptive family's income level.

For the first time Congress placed a conditional ceiling on foster care payments and allowed the states to use unspent portions of foster care funds on prevention and family preservation. Notably, the 1980 act disallowed the use of child welfare service funds for foster care, thus reversing a long-term trend. To receive funds under the Adoption Assistance and Child Welfare Act, states had to make reasonable efforts to preserve the family, and, when family preservation failed, to find adoptive parents (Berry, 1994; Burt and Pittman, 1985).

This meant that child welfare had to come up with a plan and services that could be expected to produce permanent and safe living situations for each child. If, for example, an agency temporarily removed a child from the custody of abusive or negligent parents, then to receive federal reimbursement for the placement or services, the agency had to fashion a creditable plan for the eventual return of that child to the family. Permanency planning emphasized counseling and parent training to stabilize families, family reunification services, as well as pre- and postplacement services.

Reagan's cutbacks, under the rubric of "the New Federalism," frustrated efforts to implement family preservation (Caputo, 1994; Kimmich, 1985; Burt and Pittman, 1985). Although opponents of the cutbacks argued that local control would produce inconsistent standards of child welfare services, Republican complaints about bureaucratic inflexibility, inefficiency, and corruption had helped carry Reagan into office (Burt and Pittman, 1985). Once there, President Reagan and Congress set about reducing the federal commitment to child welfare services (Burt and Pittman, 1985; Kimmich, 1985). Reagan was partially successful in cutting back on block grants, but in 1984 Congress compensated the states for the previous year's losses. In other areas, Reagan funded family preservation services, but he delayed enacting guidelines under which the states could qualify for federal funds.

The impact of the federal cutbacks was variable. States depended more on foster care (Berry, 1994). As federal and state or local dollars disappeared, city agencies shifted remaining resources away from foster care and into child welfare services—protection requests, referrals, investigations, and services (Burt and Pittman, 1985). The reduction in foster care payments was attributed to caseworkers' preference for family preservation; but staff cutbacks, leading to decisions to leave all but the most endangered children in the home, may also have accounted for reductions (Burt and Pittman, 1985).

Heroic efforts to keep children out of foster care, however, failed to offset the effects of staff shortages and net reductions in funding. Cities and states could not do more with less; something had to change. While hardly meaning to stigmatize the children, child protective leaders played a role in fanning the moral panic, seeing in the plight of crack babies the basis for a campaign to rebuild the social safety net—to increase, if not restore, the federal government's portion of funding for state and local child protective services.

The Child Welfare League of America (CWLA) linked child abuse to crack in its 1989 symposium held in conjunction with its annual conference (1990). Of the 900,000 confirmed child abuse cases that year, the majority were attributed by the CWLA to drug- or alcohol-impaired parents, and crack was singled out as a leading cause of the child abuse crisis (1990). Drug-exposed babies and boarder babies added 100,000 more abuse cases each year: abandonment and violence made these extremely complex cases (Office of the Inspector General, 1990a, 1990b).

In its 1989 survey of relevant programs, the Office of the Inspector General found examples of existing services—community projects like Maternity Outreach Mobile in Washington, D.C., designed to lower infant mortality—but these were not expected to meet the increasing demand (1990b, 1990c). The networks gave a full airing to the child abuse crisis, conveying a sense of urgency by portraying the desperate plight of children.

A CBS report featured the Children of the Light Mission in Philadelphia, which ran a 24-hour emergency placement service to save the children "others treated like trash" (1990, June 13). One child featured, Belinda, was a nine year old who had cared for her six siblings. They had been saved from crack-abusing parents, but she and her siblings had been separated. She was in a temporary group home awaiting placement in foster care that the city could ill afford. More placements were needed, but Philadelphia, like other cities, could not pay for them. The CBS segment criticized Reagan's cutbacks, noting that the federal government had capped or underfunded child protective services. According to the CBS correspondent, when the segment was aired, the federal government was $500 million behind in reimbursing states for foster care (1990, June 13).

Child welfare workers were dramatically affected by child abuse cases involving crack (CWLA, 1992; Office of the Inspector General, 1990c). David Liederman, spokesperson for the Child Welfare League of America, said in an ABC news segment that social workers who dealt with children in drug-abusing families had become the "front line in the war on drugs" (1992, May 20). They saved abused and neglected children, pulling some out of filthy, cold apartments, and despaired over the deaths of children they could not save. Some social workers took early retirement, leaving the job to less experienced caseworkers (Feig, 1990).

This and lack of caseworker training were cause for concern among child welfare leaders (Feig, 1990; CWLA, 1992). Under the Adoption Assistance and Child Welfare Act of 1980, caseworkers were required to make "reasonable efforts" to preserve the family or to find other permanent placements for children removed from the home. Making "reasonable efforts" was increasingly perplexing (Berry, 1994). Caseworkers, untrained in addiction, were called on to make complex judgments about parents' drug use and the risk of child abuse or neglect (CWLA, 1990). At what point did drug abuse jeopardize the child's safety?

Any assessment would have to include the nature of the drug, the pattern of drug use, the presence of other problems made worse by drug use, the adults' commitment to parenting, the support of family or other community members, and the availability of appropriate services. Caseworkers were ill equipped to make such assessments; and when they did, without anywhere to refer drug-impaired parents, they were in no position to make efforts to preserve the family. Instead, they seem to have set up an informal triage system, placing only the worst cases in foster care and leaving the rest to the questionable protection of hard-pressed preservation services.

Finally, the ravages of crack led more and more observers to question the wisdom of family preservation (Feig, 1990; CWLA, 1992; Kilborn, 1997). The risks to health and welfare were too serious to permit young children, especially crack-exposed infants, to remain in the home (CWLA, 1990). And it cost more to maintain fragile children in dangerous homes than in out-of-home placements (Kilborn, 1997; CWLA, 1990; but see, Berry, 1994). Foster care, on the other hand, was unsatisfactory. The large caseloads and the inability of caseworkers to provide effective supervision made foster care a poor choice, especially for prenatally exposed infants (Feig, 1990). Even for older children, foster care was not a good option, because as the numbers of foster care children increased, the number of families willing to adopt dwindled (Feig, 1990).

Families preferred healthy children, and handicapped or drug-exposed children were difficult to place. Families balked, thinking twice about the meager subsidies (AFDC, Medicaid) in relation to real medical costs associated with adopting a drug-exposed, or "handicapped," child ("The Enemy Within," 1990; Office of the Inspector General, 1990a). The outcome was inevitable: younger and younger children were shifted from one poorly supervised foster home to another, for longer and longer periods of time (Feig, 1990).

Most child welfare professionals acknowledged that crack created the situations that required the child's removal from the home (CWLA, 1990; Office of the Inspector General, 1990a). Orphanages, a proposal put forward by drug czar William Bennett, were rejected out of hand by policy makers. Laura Feig from the U.S. Department of Health and Human Services put the problem this way: "Current child welfare laws were written under the assumption that virtually all families were redeemable. Many experts dealing with crack-addicted parents, however, are now wondering if that assumption is valid. The current population of cocaine-exposed children and crack families did not exist in 1980 when the foster care system was last revised, and it may be that the system does not suit the needs of this new generation of children" (1990, 19).

Strong advocates of adoption like Douglas Besharov of the American Enterprise Institute argued for the rapid removal of drug-exposed infants from parental custody and for expedited adoption procedures (1989). Such proposals appealed to the law enforcement community, and Bennett took a forceful position favoring revised laws to encourage adoption. The Child Welfare League of America took the narrower view that when parents cannot be found and the court declares the child abandoned, child welfare services should move quickly to terminate parental rights and place the child in kinship care or bypass foster care and put the child up for adoption (CWLA, 1992). But for other babies, CWLA stuck with the language of the Adoption Assistance and Child Welfare Act of 1980: reasonable efforts had to be made to preserve or, depending on circumstances, to reunite the family.

But in *Maternal Drug Abuse and Drug-Exposed Children: Understanding the Problem*, the U.S. Department of Health and Human Services included the following as a principle for developing child welfare initiatives: "When children must be separated from their families, tentativeness cannot be permitted to prolong placement in foster care. When it is not feasible for children to be reunited with their own families, early steps must be taken toward termination of parental rights and adoption" (1992, 50).

All three of the major networks, CBS, ABC, and NBC, followed the child abuse crisis, weighing the alternatives without obviously favoring family preservation on the one hand or adoption on the other. In a segment on kin care, CBS reported on a San Francisco group that gave support to grandmothers who had been pressed into caring for the babies of their crack-addicted adult daughters (1989, June 20). While such arrangements kept families together, caregivers like Precious Moore, a 67 year old who looked after four grandchildren, found it hard to make do on fixed incomes and limited energy.

Orphanages—or their modern equivalent, group homes—promised solutions, or so suggested a CBS segment on boarder babies (1989, December 4). Casey at four months had been placed in foster care because his crack-addicted mother could not care for him. What lay ahead was suggested by Janet, an eight year old who had already been in eight different placements. Group homes offered stability. In

Los Angeles, the Children's Institute International provided care for almost 50 babies and toddlers with primary caregivers. But group homes had their critics, including Rhoda Veney of the Washington, D.C., Family and Child Services, who said they simply warehoused kids. She argued that the foster care system, despite its defects, provided the special care cocaine babies seemed to need.

In another segment, CBS showed the benefits of family preservation (1989, December 11). The case of Janice, a white woman whose children had been removed from her custody by the state of California, illustrated the effects of homelessness, crack, and AIDS on the lives of children. As wards of the state, her children were among the half million children in foster care, juvenile detention, or mental health facilities. But under a family preservation program, she was enrolled in drug treatment and had in-home services, and her children had been returned to her.

Adoption, the last alternative, was explored by both CBS and NBC. White foster parents had been barred from adopting minority crack babies, even though as a result most of the children were placed in foster care (NBC, 1989, November 18; NBC, 1992, December 16). A CBS segment followed a couple as they sought, but ultimately declined to adopt, a cocaine-exposed infant, after they had the baby tested for drugs (1989, December 13). And ABC presented the difficulties faced by a family who had taken in a crack baby: respiratory disease, cerebral palsy, vision and digestive problems, and delays in speech and motor development made the baby a handful (1990, March 7).

Although crack babies had practically disappeared from public consciousness by 1994, the abuse and foster care problems festered, prompting Congress to ease restrictions on interracial adoptions and to provide a $5,000 tax credit for each foster child adopted by families with incomes below $115,000 (Cong. Rec., 1997, April 30). Acting on a bipartisan basis, Congress quickly passed the Adoption and Safe Family Act of 1997 to speed the adoption process for foster children and protect vulnerable children from being returned to unsafe homes, an outcome many attributed to the shortsightedness of family preservation policies (Knutson, 1997, November 19; Cong. Rec., 1997,

April 30; Cong. Rec. 1997, November 8). It was not that the family preservation policies had been wrong; rather, they had left caseworkers in doubt as to what constituted "reasonable efforts," unduly prolonging a child's stay in foster care and increasing the number of children maintained at state and federal expense.

To make drug-exposed children more attractive to potential adoptive parents, the Adoption and Safe Family Act added more subsidies to the package (AFDC, Medicaid, and tax credits) already provided by Congress. The federal law required states to calculate the average number of children actually adopted. For every foster care adoption over this base figure, the federal government paid the states $4,000. For every hard-to-place adoption, the federal government paid the states $6,000. To prevent the states from using these additional funds for foster care, the Adoption and Safe Family Act required states to document the steps they had taken in moving children out of foster care.

The U.S. General Accounting Office estimated that 100,000 crack- or cocaine-exposed babies were referred to child welfare services in 1989, but it commissioned no further surveys (1990). The expectation seems to have been that the number of drug-exposed babies would increase, adding to the child abuse crisis. This much is clear: the number of children in foster care continued to rise in the 1990s. It is too soon to tell, however, how the states fared in finding adoptive homes for foster children. Some states have complied with at least one surprising result. In 1997, a gay couple in the state of New Jersey won the joint right to adopt a foster child. The gay couple qualified as adoptive parents, but only for the narrow purpose of adopting a child in state custody (Gold, 1997).

From Congenital Defects to Developmental Delay

As the war against crack mothers wound down, old stereotypes began to be questioned. In a segment on the sudden increase in public school children diagnosed as learning disabled, ABC set about dispelling myths about crack babies. The term, ABC said, was a misnomer, since most of these infants had been exposed to a variety of drugs in the womb (1991, July 24). In this, ABC acknowledged what medical researchers had already conceded, namely, that the problem was not crack but polydrug use and unhealthy lifestyles. Contrary to another myth, the ABC segment continued, not all drug-exposed children were severely impaired—they experienced problems ranging from serious to nonexistent, with most falling somewhere in between.

Filmed in classroom settings, the largest group—those who fell in between—had learning disabilities and behavioral problems that could be managed within the classroom. In a Seattle elementary school, a seven-year-old boy explained that prenatal exposure to cocaine had made him hyperactive, although the ABC correspondent noted also that the boy had to struggle to learn, to focus his attention, and to control his emotions. He had difficulty reading, and he may have suffered brain damage in the womb (1991, July 24).

The ABC segment helped humanize crack children, but in shifting focus from physical defects to neurobehavioral problems, the segment illustrated educators' confusion about the children. Educators had absorbed the results of clinical studies showing that cocaine-exposed infants were slow to develop language, showed lack of affect and ability for representational play, and were hyperactive or labile (Hicks and Wilson, 1993; Walker, 1993). But educators like Barbara Hicks and Gregory Wilson were also familiar with developmental studies showing that the babies' performance on a variety of tests fell within the normal ranges (1993). These findings were cause for optimism: early intervention and special education might accommodate the needs of the children.

Teachers, however, reported that the children were easily overstimulated and frustrated, withdrew from stressful situations, behaved impulsively, and demonstrated language difficulties (Hicks and Wilson, 1993; Walker, 1993). Like everyone else, educators were perplexed (Cole, 1993). The war on drugs, the search for adverse effects, and the crusade against crack mothers had convinced them that most learning problems were caused by crack. Clinical studies linking cocaine with neurobehavioral deficits in infants and toddlers were widely disseminated, but, as is suggested in chapter 2, the studies were too poorly designed to reliably support conclusions. Subsequent research remained equivocal. Barry Lester and Edward Tronick, for example, in introducing a collection of articles they edited, noted the studies raised many questions but produced few, if any, answers (1994; see also Lester, LaGasse, and Brunner, 1997).

Research reported in the popular press suggested that poverty was to blame for observed learning problems. One study showed that drug-exposed children, while falling below average on IQ tests, performed as well as a control group drawn from the same inner-city population (FitzGerald, 1997). ABC developed a similar point (1992, July 2). Cocaine-exposed babies had performed within the normal range in research conducted by Dr. Claire Coles of Emory University. It was not the drug but rather the mother's lifestyle that made the difference. Mothers who had healthy lifestyles, Coles said, gave birth to healthy babies. Women who used alcohol or drugs, smoked cigarettes, and had no prenatal care risked delivering unhealthy babies.

Crack was singled out as a cause because it was in the public eye, but in reality it was impossible to isolate one factor amid an array of contributing conditions. The tendency to blame learning disabilities on crack/cocaine was, despite research to the contrary, well entrenched, reinforced by the highly publicized studies that reported a host of learning disabilities for cocaine- or drug-exposed infants.

Research from UCLA's Department of Pediatrics was so widely disseminated that its characterization of drug-exposed toddlers and two year olds formed part of the knowledge base for educators (Howard et al., 1989; Beckwith et al., 1994). Dr. Judy Howard, a leader of the UCLA team, had worked with the children of heavy drug users. She found drug-exposed toddlers to be at the low end of the developmental scale, but still within an average range of intelligence. The toddlers had problems, but their difficulties were subtle. In free, unstructured play situations, drug-exposed children were less likely than the control children to combine toys, fantasy, and exploration in pretend games. Instead, they tended to pick up and put down the toys without developing consistent themes in their play.

Because representational play and language acquisition are related, deficits in the area of imaginative play, experts worried, could have implications for the ability to learn. While drug-exposed children did not have less secure attachments than control groups, the comings and goings of caregivers did not elicit strong emotions, like pleasure, anger, or distress. Their neutral responses were difficult to interpret. Did they express avoidance or ambivalence? Because the quality of the relationship between teacher and student may determine learning, neutral responses could have longer-term implications.

Dr. Howard added to the portrait of crack children in testimony given before the Senate Committee on the Judiciary in 1991 ("Cocaine Kindergartners," 1992). The children were awkward. Their language skills were slow to develop, and they had what is called sporadic mastery of tasks—what they learned one day, they forgot the next. The children were emotionally labile, shifting suddenly from pleasure to tears. They seemed passive at times; but without apparent reason, drug-exposed children could become aggressive or impulsive. Teachers would have their hands full when these children arrived at the schoolhouse door.

One of the best-known pilot programs, located in Los Angeles, was designed by Carol Cole and Vicki Ferrara to find ways to overcome factors that made learning difficult for drug-exposed children (Cole et al., 1989; Videro, 1989; "L.A. Program," 1989). Beginning in 1987, the Los Angeles School District offered separate preschool classes for drug-exposed children, but its enrollments were restricted to a small number. The children were young, between the ages of three and five.

Because drug-exposed children were subject to overstimulation, Cole and Ferrara suggested that programs should provide a stable environment and a predictable set of daily routines. A program would also have to be flexible enough to encourage self-directed exploration, because drug-exposed children were reluctant to engage in such behavior. Additionally, Cole and Ferrara found that the children had difficulty in making the transition from one activity to another—from coloring, for example, to group play. They recommended preparing the children for a new activity by allowing extra time for them to anticipate and then adjust to the new activity. Cole and Ferrara recommended that teachers allow more time for the children to form attachments to them. And other things helped: a stable group of classroom teachers and aides as well as a low ratio of teachers to students. And finally, Cole and Ferrara recommended that teachers support and interact with the children's parents, bringing them into the educational project (Videro, 1989; "L.A. Program," 1989).

Another well-known pilot program, at Salvin Special Education School in Los Angeles, incorporated much of what had been learned about drug-exposed children and education (Howard et al., 1989; Videro, 1989; "L.A. Program," 1989). At this school, 24 toddlers who had been followed since birth received a developmentally appropriate, intensive education. But success came at a remarkably high price. The cost of schooling a child at Salvin was $18,000 a year. Other programs in other locations cost considerably less—in every case, though, the cost of preparing a drug-exposed toddler for kindergarten was more than twice what it was for a normal child.

But the cost of programs like this also had to be measured by the extras. Dr. Howard and her team gave educators pause when they reported what it actually took to involve parents or caregivers in the educational project (1989). First of all, substance-abusing parents were difficult to track down. They moved frequently, missed appointments, and dropped out of sight when they were actively using drugs. Many lacked telephones. They distrusted authority, which meant representatives of education, medicine, and especially the law. Friends and family helped in keeping authorities, including teachers, at bay.

Heavy drug users lived in dangerous circumstances, a fact that imperiled the children who lived with them and the people who wanted to initiate or maintain contact. In addition, the children faced other threats, including violent, drug-ridden neighborhoods and abuse or neglect at the hands of drug-using caregivers. Outsiders had to be strongly motivated in their task. Apparently for Howard's team the first goal was to keep the children safe by keeping them visible in the community. And teachers and social workers, in addition to providing transportation, often had to awaken drug-using parents, getting adults as well as the children ready, to keep up a regular routine of clinic appointments.

Little is known about the attitudes of public school teachers toward crack children. According to Debra Harley's study, teachers tended to believe that they could pick out the crack children in their classes (1992). Crack children, they thought, were more disruptive than children who had been exposed to other substances, although no research supported this idea (Harley, 1992). Unfortunately, such labels have the power to become self-fulfilling prophecies: the child becomes the infamous "crack kid," as the expectations of teachers, caseworkers, and others decline. Others, however, worried about the consequences of not identifying the children as drug-exposed ("The Enemy Within," 1990). In dangerous environments, overlooked children may be at greater risk for injury, abuse, and neglect. But because their problems may be subtle, such children would not necessarily appear in need of protective attention or remedial services.

California's plan for incorporating drug-exposed children into special education was based on clinical research and pilot programs (Poulsen, 1992). It recognized that drug-exposed children presented a range of potential abilities. There were the extreme cases—children with serious disabilities like mental retardation, seizure disorders, and cerebral palsy. Highly visible, but few in number, these children would be identified in time for early intervention and require special education services throughout their schooling years. In contrast, there were marginal cases—children born to women who had stopped using drugs (although in some cases not) once they realized they were pregnant. Contrary to stereotypes, many children born to women who continued to use drugs during pregnancy showed no signs of drug exposure. Unless these children had other difficulties, they would not normally require special education services.

And in between the extreme and marginal cases were drug-exposed children at risk for educational failure. These children had normal cognitive abilities, but a range of immaturities (learning, behavioral, and neurobehavioral) would make it difficult for them to achieve school success or develop appropriately (Poulsen, 1992). Their learning problems were subtle. Disorganized children reacted to many situations with aggressive, destructive behavior; other, overly compliant children failed to react to caregivers—they may have been clinically depressed.

These disabilities would be difficult to identify.[1] Since educators did not know which students had been prenatally exposed to drugs, they were urged to develop more refined assessment tools to identify the subtle deficiencies that might indicate drug-exposed children and to evaluate their capacity to function in groups or amid distractions and stresses. Without more sensitive tools, the children would not receive services, or would receive them too late to be helpful. So preschool programs would be needed, but still, extra support—a structured, predictable environment, a consistent set of supportive adults, and a curriculum that stressed learning through experience— would be needed to ensure their success.

Recognition that educating young people could not be accomplished without engaging the family in the process led federal and state levels of government to encourage educators to build bridges between schools and their students' families. Implementing the principle meant finding someone to train outreach workers, to develop contact with parents, and to maintain relationships with caregivers, some of whom may have been struggling with addiction and relapse. It also meant finding someone to train the parents to support and follow through on the educational plan devised for their child.

Interviews, home visits, and participation events were among the ways school districts were to make contact, and the school had responsibility for providing transportation and child care if low-income parents were to be engaged. In working with children who lived in multiproblem families, schools were pressed to coordinate an array of systems, including criminal justice, drug and alcohol treatment, child protective services, and education. The California plan would have required case managers to monitor a child in special education, child protective services, and mental health centers. Leadership in creating coordinating bodies would have fallen to the school district, adding yet another set of responsibilities to a long list of mandatory duties.

The California plan and others like it added up to significant new investments in special education. The high price tag attached to educating drug-exposed children, from $10,000 to $18,000 per child, placed their fate in the much larger arena of federal support for special education.

Learning-Disabled Children and Special Education

Senator Joseph Biden held hearings in 1991 on cocaine-exposed children and public education ("Cocaine Kindergartners," 1992). These hearings were not the first on maternal drug use or on cocaine-exposed babies, but they were the first to address what policy makers and educators had dreaded: the entrance of the first cohort of crack-exposed, developmentally delayed kindergartners into an underfunded, overburdened public school system. Crack children—indeed, all drug-exposed children with discernible disabilities—were eligible for a variety of services falling under the general heading of special education.

Special education had emerged as a focus of federal action in the 1970s, when Congress enacted the Education for All Handicapped Children Act of 1975, establishing for the first time the right of children with disabilities to a "free, appropriate public education." Before this, youths and children with disabilities had been excluded from public schools or received minimal education. The 1975 law, the forerunner of the current system of special education, barred discrimination and required school districts to assess disabled students, develop individualized education programs, involve their parents in the process of designing educational programs, and place the children in the "least restrictive setting." In 1986, Congress passed the Education of the Handicapped Act Amendments; and in 1990, it passed IDEA, or the Individuals with Disabilities Education Act. Both acts mandated services for infants and toddlers with special needs and their families.

Congress amended the Individuals with Disabilities Education Act (IDEA) in 1991 to provide more services for children from birth to age three.

Programs to prepare the very young for later educational opportunities seem to have been designed with crack babies in mind. And as recently as 1994, testimony during hearings sponsored by the House Committee on Education and Labor suggested that these children were still a concern. Speaking about the failings of IDEA in 1994, Dorothy A. Wendel, vice president of Self-Initiated Living Options, pointed out that

> we as a society must realize that not only are the number of disabled children increasing but they are not those typically envisioned when the IDEA was enacted. Today's children are the victims of low birth weight, inadequate prenatal care and drug addicted parents. As a result, they may not appear to have traditional symptoms associated with disability. Instead they have slight neurological disorders which because of improved neonatal care do not necessarily result in losses of mobility or lack of coordination. These children, instead, experience learning difficulties caused by shorter attention spans, hyperactivity, or poor visual motor integration skills, rather than walking, talking, hearing or seeing. ("Reauthorization of Disability-Related Programs," 1994)

Perceptions that drug-exposed babies had swollen the ranks of the disabled, however, missed an important point. Crack babies, once a highly visible category of youngster, were lost in a much broader pool of handicapped children.

Still, this meant a broader constituency for the programs that served them. Because disabilities cut across all social categories, any threat to limit services under IDEA or related federal legislation tended to mobilize middle-class parents whose children benefited from special education. In the 1990s the total number of people designated as having some sort of disability increased from 4.8 million to 5.4 million.

These and earlier increases were attributed to the extension of benefits to children from birth to the age of majority and to children with a wider array of disabilities.

IDEA applies to three types of disability: severe emotional disturbances, specific learning disabilities, and health impairments. "Health impairments" serves as a catch-all category, but the increase in the number of disabled children receiving benefits was also due to provisions found in Section 504 of the Education Rehabilitation Act. This act concerns vocational education, and it extended benefits to people whose disabilities significantly limit one or more major life activities. Efforts by some parents and educators to include "soft" disabilities— for example, attention deficit disorder and hyperactivity—under the "health impairment" category of IDEA and "the major life activity" provision contributed to the growing number of children eligible for special education services.

An impressive array of organizations opposed the inclusion of attention deficit disorder (ADD) and other "soft" disabilities under IDEA and Section 504 of the Education Rehabilitation Act. ADD, elusive and difficult to diagnose, was not well recognized in medical circles. As a result, the risk of mislabeling a child was quite high. ADD, it was feared, could become a catch-all category, used by overextended teachers to banish disruptive children from the classroom. Moreover, leading organizations, including the National Association of Directors of Special Education and others, expressed concerns about the costs of establishing eligibility for thousands and thousands of children with soft disorders. Thus, the addition of soft disabilities came up against increasingly tight funding limits.

Federal funding has never been sufficient to support special education programs mandated by Congress (Smith et al., 1995). The U.S. Department of Education, citing available figures from the 1980s, acknowledged this. The federal government contributed only 8 percent and local sources provided another 36 percent, but the main responsibility for special education fell to the states. About half (56 percent) of the dollars for special education had come from state governments in 1988, according to a Department of Education report (1995). As the costs of special education increased, state budgets remained relatively flat. Not only was an array of agencies and departments competing for static state revenues, but general and special education competed for the same funding.

According to a 1996 report, the portion of school budgets that went to special education increased from 17.8 percent in 1991 to 19 percent in 1996 (Love, 1997). States used general education dollars to fund special education. Fearing a backlash by parents with children in general education, leaders in special education sought ways to control special education costs (Schnaiberg, 1996).

Crack kids required expensive services, driving up the cost of special education and adding to the drain on general education. The resulting increases led policy makers and educators to place a ceiling on expenditures in special education (U.S. Department of Education, 1995). Typically, states reimbursed local school districts for special education on a per-student basis. The more disabled students a district claimed, the more money it received from the state, especially since the rate of reimbursement for disabled students was twice that for regular students.

The rush to do away with this method of payment assumed that increases in the number of students with learning disabilities were spurious—that districts manipulated enrollments to their financial benefit. But such criticisms overlooked obvious explanations: the number of learning-disabled youngsters may actually have increased, or better-informed parents may have been able to negotiate services, including eligibility standards within the special education system. Nonetheless, a new funding formula backed by the federal government, the states, educational administrators, and special education organizations established a ceiling. The states would reimburse local school districts based on their percentage of disabled students.

Learning-disabled students typically accounted for 9 to 11 percent of total enrollments; districts with a much higher proportion of disabled students would be appropriately reimbursed. So in effect, local districts would receive fixed grants with which to implement mandated educational services. They could stretch reimbursements to fund currently enrolled and new special education students, cut the number of students by reclassifying some as less disabled, or make up the losses through administrative efficiencies or local funding sources. Cost cutting had its rewards: unspent portions of the special education allocation could under IDEA be used to fund general education projects, a provision that reversed the flow of money from general to special education.

Crack kids—or teachers' fears about them—played a more direct role in revising disciplinary procedures affecting disabled students. To understand the significance of classroom discipline, one must first recognize that according to the Education for All Handicapped Children Act, a "free, appropriate public education" in the "least restrictive setting" meant that special education students had the right to be placed in general classrooms in public schools. Since the 1980s, the inclusion movement had aimed to eliminate wherever possible special education classrooms and pull-out sessions, or sessions that require students to leave regular classrooms for special instruction ("Inclusion," n.d.). The inclusion movement also foresaw multiple teachers in a single classroom, roving aides, and a much greater reliance on technology.

Inclusion, however, had its critics. The American Federation of Teachers, the main union for public school teachers, was strongly opposed to inclusion ("Inclusion," n.d.). According to the AFT, the normal duties of a classroom teacher were already excessive, and without additional resources that were unlikely to materialize, teachers could not be expected to take on the added and complex responsibilities for teaching the disabled. Crack children needed help in forming relationships, in maintaining self-control, and in concentrating. Second, the AFT was aware of parents' concerns about the dilution of education standards in classes where teachers had to address the needs of general and special education students alike. Most teachers were wary of teaching to the lowest common denominator. Third, disabled students often posed disciplinary problems. The AFT took the position that federal disability law tied teachers' hands when it came to dealing with the disruptive conduct of disabled students ("Disability and Discipline," 1997; "Special Treatment," 1995).

Most school districts had stories about disabled students and violence. The level of violence reported by different school districts ranged from hitting or shoving to serious assault and even murder. In St. Louis, a 15-year-old high school student died after being beaten in a high school rest room. The student accused in the attack had a disability and a record of disciplinary problems of which school administrators were unaware (Greene, 1997).

While the lesser forms of violence were more frequent, teachers who worked with the severely disabled feared that frustration or anger might trigger outbursts on a larger scale—hurting others and destroying property. One six-year-old disabled youngster who entered kindergarten in Huntington Beach, California, hit and bit his teacher, threw chairs, attacked classmates, and kicked staff members ("Special Treatment," 1995). The school suspended the child. On his return, his behavior worsened, but school officials were barred by federal law from removing him from the classroom for more than 10 days.

Such stories fanned educators' fears that the crack babies of the 1980s would become the disruptive students of the 1990s. So did television news stories. In a segment on schools, CBS followed an eight-year-old boy whose mother had used crack during pregnancy (1990, April 5). He was violent: his teacher complained that he hit classmates, destroyed property, and struck a teacher. He suffered mood swings, could not concentrate, and showed increasingly unpredictable behavior. If the child was unmanageable at the age of 8, what would he be like at 15? And what could a teacher be expected to do?

The Individuals with Disabilities Education Act had made it extremely difficult for educators to discipline students with disabilities. Disabled students cannot be punished for behavior that by definition they cannot control. The in-school committees that made these classifications tended to relate disruptive behavior to the disability. But even if the committees ruled otherwise, the child-guidance team, consisting of educators and parents, would still have to agree about discipline. Parents have authority to veto suspension, forcing school districts into court, and the courts generally support the rights of the disabled to remain in the general classroom.

Congress was more inclined to listen to teacher grievances. In the 1992 reauthorization bill for IDEA, disciplinary procedures were amended to allow for suspensions of up to 45 days when disabled students brought firearms to school. These and the 1997 provisions hardly applied to crack children who were still in elementary school, but they may have calmed teachers' worries about managing them in the future. The 1997 reauthorization bill allowed long-term suspensions when disabled students were involved with serious incidents—drugs or weapons (Meckler, 1997; Sanchez, 1997; see also Sacks, 1997).

Reforms gave teachers and school districts greater flexibility in managing disciplinary problems, but critics maintained the amendments simply acknowledged long-standing practices. Districts have not hesitated to place disabled students in separate public schools or, where warranted, in state or private facilities. Thus, the inclusion movement may keep disabled students in the general classroom, but depending on the problems created for the teacher and other students, district officials can suspend them and place them in separate public institutions or a variety of private facilities at public expense.

• • •

It would be incorrect to suggest that crack children by their very existence were responsible for the school districts' seeking greater control over the management of disruptive disabled students. But the addition of their ranks to an increasing number of learning-disabled students, combined with the practice of mainstreaming, brought the rights of general students in conflict with the rights of the disabled. For drug-exposed children, federal revisions in disciplinary procedures actually reduced access to general education. And because separate special education programs have a poor record in linking students with postsecondary employment, reduced access to general education means reduced access to job opportunities. So even if crack children did not initiate reforms, they along with other disabled students face a similar future of limited opportunities.

Cocaine-exposed children vanished from public view before they realized public fears about future criminality. As victims of neglect or abuse, crack children disappeared, along with increasing numbers of other children, into a system of foster care troubled by disputes within child protective services over whether to preserve families or remove children, and over the value of temporary and permanent placements. The direction of federal policy, including a new funding priority for permanent placements, was not set until 1997—too late to help most crack children.

To the extent that the learning difficulties experienced by crack children could be identified, the youngsters were absorbed by special education, blending with the increasing numbers of learning-disabled children who had entered public school in the early 1990s. Once absorbed, their disability status linked crack children to powerful allies—middle-class parents whose learning-disabled children received federal educational benefits. But even middle-class parents were no match for cost cutters: the rising costs of special education prompted state and federal efforts to cap expenditures. The inclusion movement that brought severely disabled students into general classrooms raised serious questions about discipline, and the teachers' union finally prodded Congress to give local districts more flexibility in removing disruptive students from the classroom.

Conclusion

The crack mother episode illustrates the broader pattern of moral panic taking place in the United States in the late 1980s and early 1990s. In the period leading up to the drug scare, news coverage revealed the convergence of images—urban chaos, uncontrolled addiction, and dangerous mothering—that seemed to justify perceptions that crack mothers had broken the law. Perceptions such as these displaced reality, as prosecutors reacted disproportionately to women who had used cocaine during pregnancy. Because the crusade against crack mothers failed to institutionalize maternal drug use in criminal justice, other institutions responded. In the receding phase of the drug scare, news coverage reflected this new reality, revealing a new convergence of images—humanized mothers and real, salvageable children—that seemed to justify the impression that drug treatment, child protective services, and special education adequately addressed the problem. Again, perception displaced reality; the media's "solutions" were at best naively optimistic and at worst patently false.

Chapter 1 reviewed the media portrayal of crack mothers, showing three different images of maternal drug use that could be found in network news coverage from 1983 to 1994. In the 1983–85 period, the stories involved white middle-class women, recreational cocaine use, and psychological addiction. Women started using cocaine believing it to be safe. Once addicted, however, they found pregnancy was not enough to break the drug's hold. Filmed in the home or in treatment facilities, cocaine mothers were shown tending healthy babies, expressing remorse for having put their infants through withdrawal. Experts were concerned about developmental problems that might appear as the children grew up, although no official actions were taken. In the period from 1985–87, news segments about prenatal exposure to cocaine showed underweight, premature babies who suffered withdrawal. Prenatal cocaine exposure was said to have more serious consequences: strokes, heart attacks, cerebral palsy, and mental retardation. However, middle-class women who gave birth to these babies were not subject to punishment.

The second image of maternal drug use, which emerged from 1988 to 1990, incorporated perceived class and race shifts associated with both cocaine and crack use. That image focused on poor women of color, cities, and physical addiction. To the women who smoked it, crack became more important than their pregnancies or their newborns. Filmed in the active stage of addiction, these women who used crack during pregnancy defied expectations about mothers, resisted treatment, or failed to help themselves. Their babies had all the defects associated with cocaine babies, plus a syndrome of neurobehavioral effects—hyperactivity, poor concentration, and impulsive or aggressive behavior. And poor women of color who were blamed for harming their babies were subject to punishment. County prosecutors launched their crusade against crack mothers.

The third image, emerging in the period from 1991 to 1994, stressed crack mothers as survivors. Filmed in recovery, as the beneficiaries of services or wards of the criminal justice system, these newly humanized crack mothers explained their addictions, expressed remorse for having lost their children, and saw treatment as their hope for the future. Their children were less affected by prenatal exposure to crack than had been feared, but they nonetheless presented serious challenges to the public school system, as did drug-using parents whose abandoned, abused, or neglected children required state intervention.

Chapter 2 compared perceptions and realities, showing that the networks misrepresented maternal drug use in the period leading up to and including the prosecutorial campaigns against crack mothers. They neglected to consider the general decline in cocaine use that occurred in the 1980s and 1990s. They misrepresented a short-term, equivocal increase in weekly crack use as the crack "epidemic" of 1988 and 1989. They gave more validity to the estimates of maternal cocaine and crack use than was deserved. And they typically overstated the consequences of prenatal cocaine exposure, omitting altogether coverage of the scientific controversy surrounding these effects.

In the earlier coverage of spreading cocaine use, white middle-class women who used the drug were presented as promiscuous—at some point the compulsion forced many of them to exchange sex for cocaine—and as questionable mothers. Their cocaine use, according to news reports, increased the risk of miscarriage, premature delivery, and infant withdrawal. Still, given these symptoms (infant withdrawal would soon be linked in reports to permanent brain damage), the networks showed a remarkable degree of tolerance toward the mothers. Their status as recovering addicts whose television interviews might discourage recreational cocaine use appeared more important than their failings as mothers.

After the discovery of crack, the networks demonized the new drug and connected it to the inner city, the poor, and minorities. Poor women of color in the active stage of addiction emerged as the dominant image, most ominously as crack mothers. They put the drug before their children and duties of motherhood, with devastating results. Prenatal crack exposure was said to increase infant mortality, cause birth defects, and produce developmental problems. Given the controversy over the research on prenatal crack or cocaine exposure, the networks showed a remarkable degree of intolerance toward these women. By presenting renegade mothers as heedless addicts, the media in general provided county prosecutors with the scapegoats they seemed to require.

The county prosecutors described in chapter 3 essentially invented crimes to punish crack mothers. In the process, they attempted, but ultimately failed, to institutionalize the problem within the criminal justice system. Prosecutors complained about there being too many crack babies, although not all their communities had excessive numbers, and even then, not all the babies suffered irreparable harm. The prosecutors said that to ignore the babies' plight would border on barbarism, and that timely prosecution would discourage drug use among women and save the babies. William O'Malley in Massachusetts, for instance, said accountability worked in relation to how high the penalties were set: If set high enough, people—including pregnant women—would take some responsibility for their drug use. To let crack mothers escape criminal penalties (for example, by letting social services take care of the problem) was seen as condoning drug use.

Because the war on drugs was being lost, some prosecutors looked for easier victories—deterrent prosecutions against crack mothers, a category of people already vilified by the media. Tony Tague took frustration one step further, piggybacking on earlier prosecutions, his cases adding to his reputation as a no-nonsense, high-profile prosecutor. The prosecutions also reflected the widening divide between the inner cities and the rest of America. Paul Logli's crusade aimed to keep big-city problems, like poverty, crime, and drugs, out of Rockford, Illinois. That the label "crack mother" automatically conjured up images of urban chaos made it easy for county prosecutors to mobilize public opinion to punish the mothers.

Finally, it was difficult to disentangle these prosecutions from the advocacy of the pro-life movement. O'Malley and Charles Condon of South Carolina were both explicit about the right of the fetus to be born free of defects. Legal scholars who argued that the state ought to recognize fetal rights applauded the prosecutions, although leaders of the pro-life movement were not so sure, since, according to the public health argument, the threat of prosecution drove women to abortion clinics.

Chapters 4 and 5 concentrated on the institutionalization of solutions to the problems experienced by the mothers and their children. In the end phase of the crusade against crack mothers, network coverage dwindled, but it continued to misrepresent the problem. Networks ignored the downward trend in cocaine use. They continued to refer to the crack "epidemic" and to report questionable estimates of maternal drug use as authoritative. Nevertheless, they altered images of crack mothers and cocaine babies. As the story line took many different directions, the networks covered with unbridled optimism an increasing range of social service solutions.

Women, addiction, and treatment were addressed in chapter 4. Women who used crack had been so marginalized over the course of their lives that by the late 1980s many relied entirely on the informal economy, getting by on prostitution, shoplifting, and small-time drug dealing. In these circumstances, some mothers sent their children to relatives, and others tried to manage, compartmentalizing drug use and protecting their children from its effects. Because pregnancy remained a sign of life, women also found themselves managing pregnancy and drug use, although at delivery most of their babies tested positive for drugs. But even though there was no reason to think circumstances of crack mothers had changed, the networks eventually transformed them from demonized women to recovering addicts. In this new status they looked forward to regaining custody of their children, and their standing as functional mothers was seen as more important than their addiction or the likelihood of relapse.

Addiction is difficult to define, but the chronic abuse of crack—that is, the tendency to sacrifice everything in a compulsive effort to find and use the drug—makes crack especially destructive. Norms that idealize the "high" and settings that easily accommodate binge behavior reinforce chronic abuse. The networks acknowledged this in maintaining their position on the dangers of addiction. But they softened the characterization in the context of treatment. Programs that ministered to addicts' spiritual and physical needs or that broke down the isolation of addicted women were portrayed as effective. In reality, expanding the drug treatment network to approximate demand was a difficult task; ironically, the crusade against crack mothers helped free federal monies to accomplish the expansion. Even though federal funding helped double the capacity of the treatment network, adding special programs for women, the unmet need for treatment was greater in 1994 than it was in 1985.

Children were the focus of chapter 5. Drug-exposed children hit a child welfare system already in crisis. The television networks followed this crisis, their coverage featuring caseworkers demoralized by what drug-impaired parents did to their children, the need for more federal resources to cope with child abuse, and the alternatives available— adoption, group homes, family preservation, and foster care. But spotlighting alternatives underplayed the impact that drug-exposed children had on child welfare services.

Differences in the understanding of these services' basic missions and a zigzag history of federal policy contributed to the crisis. The added burden of drug-exposed babies led policy makers to question the effectiveness of both foster care and of attempts at family preservation. Infants and children could not be left with drug-impaired caregivers, experts agreed, but the other choices were limited: kin care, group homes, or adoption. The federal government removed the ban on interracial adoptions in 1994, but even though adoption was the preferred solution, federal incentives to speed the adoption of children in foster care were not enacted until 1997.

Some educators, drawing on clinical studies that defined drug-exposed children as learning disabled, tailored programs to the children's needs. Statewide plans that recommended these programs classified the subtle problems experienced by drug-exposed children as learning disabilities under federal law and assigned significant new duties to district administrators and classroom teachers. As a group, these children brought with them increasing costs and classroom discipline problems. In the face of increases, Congress capped costs and provided teachers with greater flexibility in dealing with discipline problems.

An Unenviable Target

This book began with a question: Under what circumstances and with what consequence did a group of powerless women become the unenviable target in the war on drugs, the symbol for everything that was wrong in America? Obviously, the circumstances concern the war on drugs, but they also concern perceptions of crack as an underclass drug, distributed and consumed in increasingly chaotic and dangerous cities. The alleged divide between drug-free, middle-class suburbs and drug-infested, inner-city cores both threatened and insulated white America, providing the necessary rationales for police to unleash a strategy of unrelenting (but ineffective) suppression on poor neighborhoods. Perceived by some as an assault on the poor, the war on drugs did not initially differentiate between men and women. But soon attention turned to the crusade against women who used drugs during pregnancy.

As it unfolded, the crusade against crack mothers revealed troubling choices about the poor and the nation's collective responsibility for poverty. True, the families crack mothers came from were among those that AFDC, food stamps, and Head Start were originally designed to protect. Yet critics saw in the "war on poverty," launched in the 1960s, the reinforcement of older prejudices—notably the belief that the longer the poor endured poverty, the more entrenched the cycle became (Katz, 1989). Those who lingered, or, worse, connived to stay, became in popular consciousness welfare families, teenage mothers, and welfare queens. Stereotypes like these raised all the wrong questions. Just as the myth of welfare queens provided an easier explanation than impersonal economic forces, the stereotype of crack mothers diverted attention from the poverty that was at the root of their problems.

Drug scares are not about drugs; rather, drug scares are about lower-class drug use. The perception that crack was more or less controlled by an underclass and confined to inner cities made all the difference. A spokesperson from the Drug Enforcement Administration said in 1989 that he thought crack had leveled off in the suburbs but not in the inner cities. While drug use by the affluent was tolerated, among lower classes it signaled the breakdown of order: rising crime rates, drive-by shootings, drug gangs, and street battles over turf.

Contagion was a factor in the menace, as well. Drug supermarkets threatened to spill over into middle-class enclaves. Images of degraded addicts and filthy crack houses contributed to the sense of menace. Politically astute prosecutors understood that an anti-drug campaign sent middle-class voters a message they wanted to hear: their elected officials would protect them from big-city problems—poverty, crime, violence, and drugs. Moreover, the war on drugs encouraged officials to scapegoat the poor, blaming crack dealers and crack mothers for an array of endemic problems. It was easier and far less costly, for example, to blame high infant mortality rates in Washington, D.C., on women who used crack during pregnancy than to guarantee health care for all the district's poor residents.

The image of crack mothers also activated racial fears. According to prevailing wisdom, crack mothers were black. Television news reporters interviewed inner-city black and Hispanic crack users in an effort to find out about the mysterious new drug. Pregnant and black, Tracy Watson smoked crack on national television; an addicted Stephanie abandoned her newborn at the hospital. At the height of the drug panic and after, the main story line was crack mothers and their children. Most of the women shown were black, and, judging from the large number of babies, most were mothers. So many of the defendants in the criminal cases were black that a South Carolina defense attorney complained of racism. "Of all the women I've represented," said Rauch Wise, "only two have been white. The vast majority of them are black. And all of them are poor" (CBS, 1994, March 10). Imprisoned crack mothers interviewed for television news were invariably black. Film footage showing the inside of drug treatment facilities also connected black women and crack: waiting rooms, group therapy sessions, recreational activities were dominated by black women (Humphries, 1998).

The networks constructed maternal drug use in racial terms without ever addressing questions about discrimination. News reports were true to documentary sources—black as opposed to white or Hispanic females were more likely to have ever used crack—but never acknowledged differences in interpreting such findings. Were those statistics accurate or were they biased?

The National Institute on Drug Abuse's *National Pregnancy and Health Survey*, for instance, showed that pregnant black women used crack and cocaine at significantly higher rates than white or Hispanic women.

But although a Florida study found that black women were more likely to use cocaine, it also found that black women were significantly more likely than whites to be tested for drugs at the time of delivery. Race and class biases in the procedures for identifying maternal drug use made experienced researchers wary. So even though ethnographic studies suggested that black women were overrepresented among women who exchanged sex for crack, researchers also noted that middle-class drug users have the resources to avoid detection and arrest, and thus not show up in statistics.

Drug scares have historically played on racial fears. Southern fears of black rebellion precipitated an anti-cocaine crusade at the beginning of this century (Grinspoon and Bakalar, 1976). At the end of the nineteenth century, the crusade against opium targeted Chinese immigrants (Morgan, 1978; Musto, 1987). And in the crack mother episode, again policy makers played on racial fears. The national leadership had demonstrated hostility toward minorities in its efforts to turn back affirmative action. It is easy to see that labels like "crack mother" eased lawmakers' consciences, enabling liberals and conservatives alike to reduce spending for social programs seen as supporting marginalized groups.

Crack mothers raised long-standing concerns among lawmakers about the social costs of maintaining dysfunctional black families. The Moynihan Report had made black matriarchs principal characters in debates about the culture of poverty and welfare dependency. Poverty and Republican cutbacks took their toll on black families. And despite everything that is known about racism, economic marginalization, the vulnerabilities of female-headed households, and the burdens black families shoulder to support kin and near kin, a stereotype like "crack mother" still activated racist fears. To many legal scholars who wrote about the criminal cases, crack prosecutors were racists. Socially isolated and blinded by misconceptions about black women and stereotypes about crack mothers, these prosecutors filed cases that appealed to the prejudices of white audiences.

Finally, in targeting women the crusade animated fears about traditional family values. Whether they used manslaughter, abuse or neglect, or drug-trafficking statutes, prosecutors aimed to "leverage" women into treatment; but in the process, their actions—had they not been stopped—would have imposed new legal duties on mothers. Encouraged in the 1980s by the anti-abortion planks in the Republican Party's election platforms, pro-life advocates saw in the prosecutions a potential new front in the abortion-related conflict between fetal and maternal rights. The New Right had long perceived feminism—with its emphasis on reproductive rights—as an organized attack on male prerogatives, a conscious attempt to downgrade the traditional authority of the male in the family. Right-wing evangelicals cited biblical sources to the effect that the husband is head of the family as Christ was head of the church; they also blamed feminists for the decline of the family. If women have careers, then their children and families will suffer. If welfare permits poor women to set up independent households, then they too contribute to the decline of the traditional family (Faludi, 1991).

The new conservatives and the religious right sought to reverse the gains of women. They called for a ban on abortion, censorship of birth control information until after marriage, a chastity bill, revocation of the Equal Pay Act, and defeat of the Equal Rights Amendment. Their agenda, according to Susan Faludi (1991), reflects the aspirations of downwardly mobile white males, the spiritual values of television evangelists, and the analyses of intellectuals housed in conservative think tanks. It appealed to white males who felt passed over, whose declining economic prospects and family roles contrasted sharply with the perceived progress of women in professional circles and in the making of family decisions (Faludi, 1991). This is the group from which the anti-abortion movement arose, demanding among other restrictions the father's right to veto his partner's decision to terminate a pregnancy.

The answer to the second part of the question—with what consequence were crack mothers targeted?—concerns the institutionalization of maternal drug use within social service bureaucracies. In most states, crack mothers and their drug-exposed babies were referred to social services for investigation, to family preservation services, or, where warranted, to family court. Within social services, issues of custody for drug-exposed children, boarder babies, and children whose parents abused drugs also required attention. So did drug treatment for the mothers and special education for children with learning disabilities.

The influence that the crack mothers crisis had on updating and expanding services was examined at the federal level, where officials, operating under the New Federalism, made decisions that affected what funds states would have. Efficiencies in federal, state, and local government were, according to the New Federalism, expected to pay off in reduced costs without sacrificing services. The grand design of the New Federalism was found in the Budget Reconciliation Act of 1981, which authorized spending cutbacks that reduced the number of people receiving benefits under the Social Security Act and ancillary legislation. Whatever impact the crack mother episode had on drug treatment, child protective services, or special education would have to be negotiated by the states in this new funding environment.

John Hagdorn, who had participated in efforts to reform child welfare in Milwaukee County, concluded that state bureaucracies place control over their funding environments ahead of meeting demands for services (1995). Advocacy groups in child welfare and special education secured a continuing flow of federal dollars by supporting budgetary restrictions and caps on services. The addition of crack children to the already increasing numbers of students with learning disabilities produced spending limits supported by leaders in special education. The 1997 reauthorization bill for IDEA capped federal reimbursements at a percentage of disabled students. As younger and younger children entered foster care for longer periods of time, the federal government provided incentives for adoptions. The 1997 Adoption and Safe Family Act provided the necessary incentives, but sponsors also hoped to effect savings by the shift taking place away from discredited family preservation services.

Federal funding for drug treatment seems to have been the exception to the New Federalism. Pressure had built during the 1988 presidential campaign to enact the Anti-Drug Abuse Act of that year.

Although President George Bush did not increase the amount of funds available, which still represented only 30 percent of the budget for his war on drugs, the 1988 law allowed federal dollars to finance state treatment projects directly. Under this legislation, the U.S. Department of Health and Human Services earmarked funds to develop treatment programs for pregnant women and their families. Increased federal expenditures helped double the nation's treatment capacity. And while expansion has to be counted as one of the significant consequences of the crack mother episode, capacity still fell short of demand.

Panics, Policy, and Polemics

Moral panics will not disappear, and for this reason I hope to have encouraged a healthy skepticism toward the kind of exaggerated claims made during the crusade against crack mothers. For me the most difficult claims to challenge were the ones based on medical research. Not only were they published in prestigious medical journals, meaning that a panel of experts had reviewed and recommended them for publication, but their premise—prenatal exposure to cocaine resulted in significant damage to the fetus and newborn—seemed irrefutable. As it turned out, however, basic insights—sample size, comparison groups, the inability to rule out alternative explanations—put the research in perspective.

Science is built on the reliability and validity of research findings. Few, if any, scientists generalize beyond the limits of their studies. The news media, on the other hand, evaluate scientific findings for their news value. The more shocking the effects, the higher the news value. The limits of the study hardly qualify as news. In moving from science to advocacy, limits and qualifications disappear entirely, leaving questionable assertions as guides for actions.

But to get to the heart of the matter—whether it be in drug scares or other panics—there is no substitute for evaluating the studies and drawing independent conclusions. Doing this, I sometimes felt like a detective on the trail of cocaine's elusive teratogenic effect. Was cocaine a teratogenic drug or not? Hundreds of articles said that cocaine produced grave congenital defects. Was sheer volume replication enough to establish the defects as fact? Or was I going to be swayed by the two or three articles that raised questions about the research cited? In a test to see where medical consensus lay, I turned to a dozen or so medical reviews and found that consensus had shifted from a broad acceptance of many defects to a qualified support for a very few. In the end, the answer to the question about teratogenesis depended on the point of the inquiry. Even small risks play a role in the clinical management of high-risk obstetrical patients. But weak evidence cannot show that cocaine ingested by the mother actually causes the injury suffered by the fetus or newborn.

For most of this century, medicine and criminal justice have fought over the problem of drug use. After *Robinson v. California* (1962), addiction was legally defined as a disease, subject to medical treatment, but the possession and distribution of controlled substances remained in the jurisdiction of law enforcement. The medical model for approaching the problem of drug abuse had come under increasing attack in the 1970s because the results of therapeutic interventions were difficult to assess. Some treatments—including methadone—appeared to work, but not for all patients. Programs had high dropout and relapse rates.

The war on drugs, which according to one account grew out of treatment's failures, took the law enforcement model to new levels of suppression (Inciardi, 1986). It sought to cut off the supply of drugs, obviating the need for treatment. But the war on drugs not only failed to cut the supply lines, it pushed illicit drug use further underground, driving women away from hospitals that might have helped, and trampled on civil liberties, outraging women, public health officials, and doctors alike.

Public health offers a third approach. The goal in public health is to promote healthy conduct or, where unhealthy conduct cannot be changed, to reduce the harm associated with it. One such step, for example, is the establishment of needle exchanges, which provide clean needles to heroin addicts to reduce the risk of AIDS (Reinarman and Levine, 1997b). The first principle of harm reduction is that drug user not outlaws. No judgments are made about drug use. The second principle of harm reduction is that outreach workers approach addicts with goods and services that they value, such as sterile needles and referrals to treatment, health facilities, or housing. A third principle, which can only operate if addicts' basic needs are met, is to enlist them in taking responsibility for their drug use and its consequences.

One of the objections to harm reduction is that it appears to condone drug use. But opposing harm reduction on this basis is like opposing seat belts because they condone reckless driving. No one ever suggested that seat belts would discourage the police from enforcing the traffic laws. Seat belts help people survive the accidents the police are unable to prevent. Similarly, needle exchanges, condoms, information about safe sex, and prenatal care for pregnant addicts all help drug users survive dangers that law enforcement cannot prevent. Making drug rehabilitation and prenatal care attractive to pregnant addicts does not mean that the police would halt reasonable efforts to suppress drug trafficking. But the emphasis has to be on "reasonable."

If harm reduction is to work, the law—in its moral authority—has to be uniformly and consistently applied. The anti-drug laws have, unfortunately, never been enforced uniformly. People from all walks of life use drugs; yet only the poor and marginalized feel the full force of law enforcement. Any reasonable enforcement effort would attempt to bridge the divide between suburb and inner city, recognizing that the middle class is implicated in the distribution and consumption of illicit drugs, too. In addition, the anti-drug laws have never been applied consistently. Drugs have been used in the United States since its inception; yet, periodically, drug scares have targeted a single drug and its users for high-intensity suppression. Again, any reasonable enforcement effort would attempt to convey a constant level of disapproval, not a variable one.

Those who have enforced the anti-drug laws have promised what cannot be delivered—namely, that with the elimination of drugs, problems of poverty, crime, and idleness will also disappear. The inability to realize such goals, however, is not a matter of will or leadership; it is, instead, a matter of social structure. Drugs do not create

167

poverty; rather, poverty, as we have seen in this book, provides a fertile environment for drugs. The illegal economy, in fact, fills the void created by the disappearance of jobs, the concentration of poverty, the cutbacks in social services. And in the long run, until the economy produces jobs with wages high enough to sustain individuals, families, and communities, harm-reduction programs, along with fair, consistent, and practical enforcement, are the best we can do to protect the people most affected by illicit drugs.

Notes

1. Celebrities whose cocaine use became news included Roxanne and Peter Pulitzer, Mercury Morris, Richard Dreyfuss, Jodi Foster, Stacy Keach, John Belushi, former representative John Burton, and Washington, D.C., mayor Marion Barry.

2. The terms *psychological addiction* and *physical addiction*—used in a later news segment—confuse two concepts: addiction and dependence. "Physical dependence," which implies tolerance and withdrawal, comes closest to the original meaning of addiction. Tolerance occurs when increased doses of a drug like heroin are required to achieve the original euphoric effects. Withdrawal occurs when drug use is stopped abruptly. Withdrawal from alcohol is life-threatening, but heroin withdrawal, although dramatic, is not. "Psychological dependence" on a drug instills a feeling of satisfaction and psychic drive that requires periodic or continuous administration of the drug to produce a desired effect or to avoid psychological discomfort.

3. The hotline was a standard feature in CBS reports on facilities designed to address the cocaine problem. Such reports supplied information on who used cocaine, on the prevalence of cocaine use among women, and on the extent of addiction (1984, May 30 and 31; 1984, November 28).

4. In primary dependence, a user repeatedly administers the drug to achieve the high. In secondary dependence, the user repeatedly administers the drug to avoid the effects of withdrawal. In the case of heroin, for instance, users are initially motivated by the euphoria until tolerance builds up and withdrawal symptoms set in. Once symptoms appear, drug users administer the drug to forestall withdrawal.

5. Even so, white mothers were represented (ABC, 1989, February 28; ABC,

1989, July 12). One white woman featured, Ginger, had used crack during her pregnancy, and after completing a drug treatment program she enrolled in another program aimed at keeping families together. Back at home, she nonetheless worried about her ability to remain drug free (CBS, 1990, December 17). Another white woman who used cocaine during pregnancy, Tina, said that every time she thought about the baby she got high so she would not have to deal with it (CBS, 1990, June 13).

6. See note 2.

7. ABC's report linked cocaine use to premature birth and miscarriage, continuing a pattern established in earlier accounts of drug-exposed babies (1988, October 13). NBC's report on crack mothers Tracy, Erocelia, and Stephanie departed from earlier accounts of middle-class women who used cocaine during pregnancy (1988, October 24). For this reason, NBC's report is treated as the breaking story.

CHAPTER 2

1. The National Household Survey neglects to include college students living in dormitories, the homeless, and transient populations. College students are included in the National High School Senior Survey, but the omission of the homeless and transients leaves out people who are believed to use drugs frequently. The National High School Senior Survey overlooks dropouts, another group thought to use drugs frequently. One might think that reports from Drug Use Forecasting, compiled by the National Institute of Justice, would shed some light on the prevalence of drug use in groups not included in the NIDA surveys. The jailhouse samples, however, are assembled on a voluntary basis, meaning that results cannot be generalized to the larger population of inmates, nor can they be used to balance out samples for the National Household Survey (National Institute of Justice, 1990, 1995).

2. A less reliable source noted a similar increase over the same period. According to the Drug Use Forecasting reports, cocaine use among jail inmates peaked between 1988 and 1991 and then declined (National Institute of Justice, 1990, 1995). Prevalence rates vary widely from city to city, however (see Golub and Johnson, 1997).

3. Normally, the total sample or a sizeable portion of it—for example, lifetime cocaine use—is used to compute prevalence rates in the National Household Survey. Weekly or daily prevalence rates are rarely published because sample sizes are too small. The U.S. General Accounting Office report calculated weekly and daily prevalence rates and used as the total past-month cocaine use, thus decreasing the stability of its findings (1991).

4. Crack use moved from large metropolitan areas to smaller ones, from the Northeast and the West to all regions of the country, from those with less than a high school education to those with some college (NIDA, 1990; SAMHSA, 1995b).

5. The Drug Awareness Warning Network (DAWN), sponsored by the National Institute of Justice, reports the number of deaths and emergency-room episodes that mention drugs, licit or illicit, as a factor. DAWN reports provide an indication of the consequences of drug use—deaths or medical problems related to drug use—but the measure is flawed. Changes in procedures for collecting and processing drug-related information raise questions about trends based on the data set. Breaks in the collection of information, in addition, make the series noncontinuous. The measure is reactive: whether emergency-room personnel suspect and report drug use will depend on institutional policy, the degree of attention focused on a drug, and the drug's reputation. It is a better indicator of the medical system's response to drugs than a measure of drug prevalence.

6. For example, reports told of a middle-class man leaving a child in his parked car as he went to buy crack from a street dealer (NBC, 1986, May 23) and of out-of-state buyers driving to Washington Heights to get crack (NBC, 1986, August 4).

7. Generally speaking, assertions that drug use had increased in cities are based on the *Drug Use Forecast* surveys, compiled by the National Institute of Justice. *Drug Use Forecast* surveys report the number of arrestees in the criminal justice system who test positive for drugs. Anonymous urine specimens are voluntarily collected from arrestees at central booking facilities in large urban areas. The data series is continuous. The program began in New York City in 1984, expanded to include 20 cities in 1988, and in 1994 it included 23 cities. Estimates, reported for each of the cities, are relatively independent of shifts in criminal justice resources, but they are not based on representative or probability samples and cannot be generalized.

8. Hispanic crack users interviewed on the street talked about the intensely vivid high (NBC, 1986, May 23). Addicts said they felt powerless to resist drug cravings (ABC, 1989, February 28). One addict explained the violence of crack users (ABC, 1986, July 28), while Senator Alfonse D'Amato said he considered the drug epidemic more dangerous to the U.S. than terrorism (ABC, 1986, July 15). In New York City in 1986, 50 percent of the emergency room admissions were reportedly for crack (but see my discussion in note 5 on the limitations of the Drug Awareness Warning Network). And Arnold Washton, drug-treatment expert, described crack users as violent and as suffering from paranoia and severe depression (ABC, 1986, May 27).

9. In 1989, hospitals in eight cities had reported 8,974 crack/cocaine baby cases to the child welfare system (Office of the Inspector General, 1990). But interviews with welfare administrators, caseworkers, and others suggested that this number underestimated the actual number of crack/cocaine-exposed babies by half. As a result, the Inspector General's Office increased the national projection to 100,000 (1990)—a figure that matched the one reported in President Bush's National Drug Control Strategy document.

10. For CBS coverage see the following dates: 1989, January 9; 1990, April 5; 1990, June 13; 1990, December 17; 1991, March 12; 1991, June 24.

11. That 11 percent of the women could not be identified racially raises some questions about this finding. However, if one assumes that 11 percent of the women who could not be identified racially were white, the data would still show a pattern of racial disparity (Humphries, 1998).

12. Some reviewers accepted cardiac, cranial, and intestinal defects (Singer, Garber, and Kliegman, 1991; Kain, Kain, and Scarpelli, 1992; Holtzman and Nigel, 1994); another found support for several minor or one major abnormality (Slutsker, 1992).

13. Social scientists have also questioned the validity of early medical studies. See, for example, Reinarman and Levine (1989), and more recently, Inciardi (1997a).

14. Given the icon status of withdrawal, it is surprising that the networks ignored a key medical finding. The single most consistently reported result for cocaine use by pregnant women was that their infants were underweight, falling into the category of low-birth-weight babies, in other words weighing less than 2,500 grams. In reviewing 24 studies on birth weight Holtzman and Nigel concluded: "The causal argument for the existence of cocaine-induced impaired fetal growth is strengthened by replication of the association in different populations, by the use of different study designs, some of which used universal screening, by controls for important confounding variables in several studies, and by the development of animal models" (Holtzman and Nigel, 1994, 329). Yet no news correspondent explicitly reported that cocaine babies were small or underweight, though film footage consistently showed tiny, premature infants, usually in incubators.

CHAPTER 3

1. Laura Gomez's book *Misconceiving Mothers* focuses on the legislature and the judiciary, arguing that key actors in these institutions rejected pleas to criminalize pregnancy (1997). On this point: the county prosecutors profiled in this chapter practiced in states with lower-level judges sympathetic to their

arguments. Appellate judges overturned lower-court decisions, however. Gomez goes on to suggest that the strength of social services in relation to the courts played a role in California's reliance on treatment rather than on prosecution. And on this point: South Carolina had probably the least developed social service delivery system, which may help explain that state's continued reliance on prosecution.

2. Maschke argues that, pressed by the war on drugs and the desire to stop child abuse, prosecutors had in fact invented new crimes, and she takes the opportunity to review the crack mothers cases as collective instances of this phenomenon (1995).

3. Frequently included in discussions of cocaine mothers is Brenda Vaughan, who was ordered to jail to protect her unborn fetus. Because the judge, not the prosecutor, acted, I have omitted the Vaughan case in this chapter but include a brief summary here. Brenda Vaughan was charged with wrongfully cashing over $700 in checks from the employment agency where she worked. She plead guilty in a Washington, D.C., superior court to second-degree theft. Before being sentenced Vaughan spent 30 days in jail, and she complained of weight loss, which combined with her pregnancy led to her release. She had, however, missed drug checks; when she appeared, she tested positive for cocaine. At the sentencing hearing, superior court associate judge Peter Wolf singled Vaughan out: "You've got a cocaine problem, and I'm not going to have this baby born addicted" (Moss, 1988). He continued, "I'm going to keep her locked up until the baby is born because she's tested positive for cocaine when she came before" (Moss, 1988). Judge Wolf sentenced Vaughan to 180 days in jail, although by the time she was released in September 1988, just before the baby was due, she had already received two sentence reductions.

4. California Penal Code reads in part, "If a parent of a minor child willfully omits, without lawful excuse, to furnish necessary clothing, shelter or medical attendance, or other remedial care for his or her child, he or she is guilty of a misdemeanor" (Cal. Penal Code P 270). The statute was designed for use against fathers who refused to support the women they had impregnated. The statute was amended in 1974 to apply to women, establishing that women as well as men are financially responsible for their children.

5. In an article "Reining in Runaway Prosecutors," B. D. Colen praised the grand jurors for their compassion and common sense in protecting Green's rights, and criticized the prosecutor for showing no compassion and little sense (1989).

6. In addition to the ACLU, the American Medical Association, American Public Health Association, American Society of Law and Medicine, and National

Association for Perinatal Addiction Research and Education opposed the prosecutions as antithetical to sound public health policy.

7. Jackson pleaded guilty in superior court in January 1990 and began serving his two-year sentence for assault and battery (Guerreo, 1990).

8. The text describes the MUSC program based on an evaluation that appeared in the *Journal of the South Carolina Medical Association* (Horger, Brown, and Condon, 1990). As an evaluation purporting to show the efficacy of arresting women who used drugs during pregnancy, it justified the program. As a piece of research, however, it was to come back and haunt Attorney General Charles Condon. The team of Horger, Brown, and Condon had not gotten the consent of their subjects, an oversight that enabled the Center for Reproductive Law and Policy to petition the National Institutes of Health to shut the program down.

9. The judiciary played an instrumental role in halting the panic by rulings against the questionable legal strategies prosecutors employed. South Carolina is an exception. In *Whittner v. South Carolina* (1996), the Supreme Court of South Carolina reversed a lower court's decision to grant postconviction relief to the defendant. The defendant pled guilty to criminal child neglect after her baby tested positive for cocaine. The circuit court judge sentenced her to eight years in prison. The defendant petitioned for postconviction relief, arguing that the circuit court lacked subject-matter jurisdiction to accept her plea of ineffective counsel. Her attorney had not informed her that the child-neglect statute used to convict her may not apply to a cocaine-exposed baby. The appellate court granted her relief on both grounds, and the state appealed. In reversing the postconviction relief, the supreme court ruled that the word *child* in the child-neglect statute included fetuses.

10. The American Prosecutors Research Institute supported a traditional criminal justice approach. Under existing laws, hundreds of thousands of drug users pass through the criminal justice system every year—a fact that makes the criminal justice system a better point of intervention than hospitals if the aim is to identify and provide treatment for as many drug-using parents (men and women) as possible. Inevitably, pregnant women pass through the criminal justice system, brought in under a variety of charges. And while pregnancy is neither an element of any crime nor a defense to criminal charges, it can be a factor in assessing penalties. For lesser offenses and first-time offenders, noted Dinsmore, diversion may be appropriate for pregnant women or new mothers, especially since successful completion of treatment and prenatal care result in the dismissal of charges. For more serious offenses, making treatment and prenatal care conditions of probation or sending the mother to treatment in place of jail may be required. Long-term treatment in jail or prison would be used only as a last resort ("Pregnant Addicts," 1990).

CHAPTER 4

1. Chapter 5 shows the sense of closure also involved a new approach to drug-exposed children and institutionalization of their problems in child protective services and special education.

2. In this and the following paragraph, statements about cocaine and crack use are for the most part restricted to young adults (18–25) and apply to past-month crack use, which remained even lower, at 0.2 percent of the sample (see figure 2.2). The figures for crack use among black and white women are for females of all ages.

3. Still, more white than black women reported past-year crack use in 1991 and 1993. In 1991, 131,000 white and 106,000 black women reported past-year crack use; in 1993, 105,000 white women and 84,000 black women reported past-year crack use (NIDA, 1992; SAMHSA, 1994).

4. An exceptional ABC segment challenged stereotypes that all crack babies were black, stating that most of the babies were white (1991, July 24). The ABC broadcast had no impact on perceptions of crack mothers as black or as heavily involved in illicit drug use, since the other networks continued to develop the story along racially specific and drug-specific lines. The ABC broadcast did, however, have an impact on moderating claims about the harmfulness of prenatal exposure to crack or cocaine. See chapter 5.

5. More than anything else the civil rights movement and the urban riots of the 1960s shattered portrayals of the urban poor as helpless or passive. Black Americans mobilized against desegregation at lunch counters, in schools, and in housing. They registered voters and faced down white racism in the South. Black Americans succeeded in getting the federal government to pass the Civil Rights Act of 1964 and the Voting Rights Act of 1965. Elsewhere, the urban riots, beginning in Watts in 1965, revealed the depths of rage provoked by an accumulating and persistent pattern of injustices. Militant young blacks rejected the civil rights goal of integration and embraced an internationalist perspective that linked the oppression of black Americans to national liberation struggles in Africa and Asia. Just as Europeans had colonized Africa and Asia, setting up local elites to manage the exploitation of the colony, American policy makers used compliant black elites to manage the ghetto as colony, argued militant black organizations.

6. In other words she missed the association of female relatives that Ladner found so important in imparting resourcefulness to overcome obstacles (1971).

7. The generational effects of alcohol and drug use are a matter of concern for Bourgois and Dunlap, who link maternal heroin use in the mother's generation

with crack use in the daughter's: "Trauma often starts in the womb. Several of the prostitutes were born addicted to heroin. The future promises an even larger cohort of survivors of neonatal substance abuse" (1993, 111). This precedes a discussion of pregnancy, prostitution, and crack, although the biological determinism suggested by this passage is neither explained nor justified.

8. The service-sector jobs proved a temporary way station. Most of the 35 women who participated as respondents in Inciardi's ethnography had previously worked in the service sector, e.g., as fast-food cashiers, but only one held a legal job at the time of the interview (1993, 48).

9. Sudarkasa argues that the increase in female-headed households resulted from welfare policies that exclude men from the household unit (1997). Others relate the increase to demographic trends. "The combined impact of greater marital delay, more nonmarriage, a very high divorce rate, and a continuing high rate of births out of wedlock (all interrelated phenomena) is observed most acutely through the living arrangements of children and the burden of responsibilities borne by women" (Tucker and Mitchell-Kernan, 1995).

10. Litt and McNeil (1994, 105) interpreted this passage differently. They were alarmed that Bourgois and Dunlap had linked emancipation with maternal irresponsibility and neglect. If street culture was dominated by crack, then that was the context in which women expressed their newfound freedoms, said Litt and McNeil. That freedom found expression in addiction is a measure of the oppressiveness of racism, sexism, and poverty.

11. Bourgois and Dunlap reported contrary findings: "Some of these expecting women were able to capitalize on their pregnant status to increase their consumption of crack. Standing on the corner in midwinter, Lorie, one of the respondents, was opening her coat to display her distended belly as a sexual enticement to potential customers. When we interviewed her, she explained that she was eight months pregnant and that she received benefits from people on the street for being pregnant: food, protection, free hits of crack" (1993, 111).

12. Law enforcement defined addiction as a crime, but the U.S. Supreme Court recognized it as a "disease"—hence not subject to prosecution in *Robinson v. California* (1962). Regarding the disease model of addiction, disputes had arisen about the relative importance of physical, psychological, and sociological processes. For a discussion of differences between physiologists and sociologists, see A. R. Lindesmith (1938).

13. In 1993, of the 18 million people who had tried marijuana in the previous year, 44.6 percent had used the drug in the past month.

Chapter 5

1. Pilot programs had tracked drug-exposed infants from birth. Indeed, Dr. Howard's description of the difficulties in maintaining contact with the drug-using parents of the infants was as much about managing a longitudinal study as it was about educating the children (1989). The public school system, however, was not in a position to know the drug status of the children entering kindergarten. Nor was it especially interested. Its job was to ascertain the capacity of children to learn and to provide services for those who had trouble. Thus, in encouraging educators to identify assessment tools, the California plan stressed learning deficits over drug status, explaining why the drug children disappeared into the public school system.

Works Cited

Abandinsky, H. (1997). *Drug abuse: An introduction*. Chicago: Nelson-Hall Publishers.

ABC evening news. (1985, July 16). Cocaine hearings. On *Media services videotape, 1983–1994* (Compilation tape). Nashville, Tenn.: Vanderbilt University. (1994).

———. (1986, May 27). Drugs/"crack." On *Media services videotape, 1983–1994* (Compilation tape). Nashville, Tenn.: Vanderbilt University. (1994).

———. (1986, July 11). Cocaine babies. On *Media services videotape, 1983–1994* (Compilation tape). Nashville, Tenn.: Vanderbilt University. (1994).

———. (1986, July 15). Cocaine. On *Media services videotape, 1983–1994* (Compilation tape). Nashville, Tenn.: Vanderbilt University. (1994).

———. (1986, July 28). Special assignment (crack). On *Media services videotape, 1983–1994* (Compilation tape). Nashville, Tenn.: Vanderbilt University. (1994).

———. (1986, August 5). Special assignment (crack). On *Media services videotape, 1983–1994* (Compilation tape). Nashville, Tenn.: Vanderbilt University. (1994).

———. (1986, September 17). Special assignment (crack). On *Media services videotape, 1983–1994* (Compilation tape). Nashville, Tenn.: Vanderbilt University. (1994).

———. (1988, July 13). Sanford, Florida/cocaine mother trial. On *Media services videotape, 1983–1994* (Compilation tape). Nashville, Tenn.: Vanderbilt University. (1994).

———. (1988, October 13). Medicine: Cocaine and pregnancy/Florida "cocaine babies." On *Media services videotape, 1983–1994* (Compilation tape). Nashville, Tenn.: Vanderbilt University. (1994).

———. (1989, February 28). American agenda (Drugs: Crack addiction). On

Media services videotape, 1983–1994 (Compilation tape). Nashville, Tenn.: Vanderbilt University. (1994).

———. (1989, March 21). American agenda (Drugs: "Crack" in rural America). On *Media services videotape,* 1983–1994 (Compilation tape). Nashville, Tenn.: Vanderbilt University. (1994).

———. (1989, July 12). American agenda (Medicine/Crime: Pregnant women and drugs). On *Media services videotape,* 1983–1994 (Compilation tape). Nashville, Tenn.: Vanderbilt University. (1994).

———. (1989, July 13). Sanford, Florida/Cocaine mother trial. On *Media services videotape,* 1983–1994 (Compilation tape). Nashville, Tenn.: Vanderbilt University. (1994).

———. (1989, November 14). Medicine: Cocaine babies. On *Media services videotape* 1983–1994 (Compilation tape). Nashville, Tenn.: Vanderbilt University. (1994).

———. (1990, January 13). Medicine: Infant mortality/Washington, D.C. On *Media services videotape* 1983–1994 (Compilation tape). Nashville, Tenn.: Vanderbilt University. (1994).

———. (1990, March 7). American agenda (Drugs: Crack babies). On *Media services videotape,* 1983–1994 (Compilation tape). Nashville, Tenn.: Vanderbilt University. (1994).

———. (1991, July 24). American agenda (Education: Crack and learning disabilities). On *Media services videotape,* 1983–1994 (Compilation tape). Nashville, Tenn.: Vanderbilt University. (1994).

———. (1991, September 17). Medicine: Crack babies. On *Media services videotape,* 1983–1994 (Compilation tape). Nashville, Tenn.: Vanderbilt University. (1994).

———. (1992, May 20). American agenda (Family: Social workers). On *Media services videotape,* 1983–1994 (Compilation tape). Nashville, Tenn.: Vanderbilt University. (1994).

———. (1992, July 2). Medicine: Crack babies. On *Media services videotape,* 1983–1994 (Compilation tape). Nashville, Tenn.: Vanderbilt University. (1994).

———. (1992, September 10). War on drugs/Crack mother case. On *Media services videotape,* 1983–1994 (Compilation tape). Nashville, Tenn.: Vanderbilt University. (1994).

———. (1993, June 10). American agenda (Drugs: Sisters program). On *Media services videotape,* 1983–1994 (Compilation tape). Nashville, Tenn.: Vanderbilt University. (1994).

Adoption and Safe Family Act of 1997, Pub. L. No. 105-89.

Adoption Assistance and Child Welfare Act of 1980, Pub. L. No. 96-272, 94 Stat. 500, Title 42, Sec. 670 *et seq.* (1980).

Anglin, M. D., and Hser, Y. I. (1990). Treatment of drug abuse. In M. Tonry and

J. Q. Wilson (Eds.), *Drugs and crime* (pp. 393–460). Chicago: University of Chicago Press.

Associated Press. (1994, September 8). Hospital gives up notifying the police of cocaine abusers. *New York Times*, p. 18A.

Baxley, C. (1997, January 9). Cocaine policy upheld. *Post and Courier* (Charleston, S.C.), p. A1.

Beachum, S. (1989, November 11). Abuse charge unfair, says "crack mom." *Muskegon Chronicle and Sunday Chronicle*, pp. 1A, 3A.

Beckwith, L., Rodning, C., Norris, D., Phillipsen, L., Khandabi, P., and Howard, J. (1994). Spontaneous play in two-year-olds born to substance-abusing mothers. In G. H. Smith, C. D. Coles, M. K. Poulsen, and C. K. Cole (Eds.), *Children, families, and substance abuse: Challenges for changing educational and social outcomes* (pp. 198–201). Baltimore, Md.: Paul H. Brooks Publishing.

Berry, M. (1994). *Keeping families together.* New York: Garland Press.

Besharov, D. J. (1989). The children of crack: Will we protect them? *Public Welfare*, (Fall), 6–11.

Bourgois, P., and Dunlap, E. (1993). Exorcising sex-for-crack: An ethnographic perspective from Harlem. In M. S. Ratner (Ed.), *Crack pipe as pimp: An ethnographic investigation of sex-for-crack exchanges* (pp. 97–132). New York: Lexington Books.

Boyle, K., and Anglin, M. D. (1993). "To the curb": Sex bartering and drug use among homeless crack users in Los Angeles. In M. S. Ratner (Ed.), *Crack pipe as pimp: An ethnographic investigation of sex-for-crack exchanges* (pp. 159–85). New York: Lexington Books.

Burns, R. (1990, June 2). Appeals court agrees to hear coke mom case. *Muskegon Chronicle and Sunday Chronicle*, p. 1A.

Burt, M. R., and Pittman, K. J. (1985). *Testing the social safety net: The impact of changes in support programs during the Reagan administration.* Washington, D.C.: Urban Institute Press.

Butynski, W., Record, N., Yates, J. L., and National Association of State Alcohol and Drug Abuse Directors. (1991). *State resources and services for alcohol and drug abuse problems, FY 1985: A report for the National Institute on Alcohol Abuse and Alcoholism and the National Institutes of Health.* Rockville, Md.: U.S. Department of Health and Human Services, Public Health Service.

Cahill, J., and Scaglione, D. (1989, August 22). A cocaine pregnancy? Police charge woman in unprecedented case. *Enterprise* (Brockton, Mass.), pp. 1, 4.

California Penal Code P 270 (West 1970 and Supp. 1988).

Caputo, R. K. (1994). *Welfare and freedom American style II: The role of the federal government, 1941–1980.* Lanham, Md.: University Press of America.

CBS evening news. (1983, February 7). Cocaine. On *Media services videotape, 1983–1994* (Compilation tape). Nashville, Tenn.: Vanderbilt University. (1994).

———. (1984, May 30). Cocaine part 1. On *Media services videotape, 1983–1994* (Compilation tape). Nashville, Tenn.: Vanderbilt University. (1994).

———. (1984, May 31). Cocaine part 2. On *Media services videotape, 1983–1994* (Compilation tape). Nashville, Tenn.: Vanderbilt University. (1994).

———. (1984, November 27). Cocaine part 1. On *Media services videotape, 1983–1994* (Compilation tape). Nashville, Tenn.: Vanderbilt University. (1994).

———. (1984, November 28). Cocaine part 2. On *Media services videotape, 1983–1994* (Compilation tape). Nashville, Tenn.: Vanderbilt University. (1994).

———. (1985, September 11). Cocaine and pregnant mothers. On *Media services videotape, 1983–1994* (Compilation tape). Nashville, Tenn.: Vanderbilt University. (1994).

———. (1985, December 4). Cocaine/Crack. On *Media services videotape, 1983–1994* (Compilation tape). Nashville, Tenn.: Vanderbilt University. (1994).

———. (1985, December 30). Cocaine use. On *Media services videotape, 1983–1994* (Compilation tape). Nashville, Tenn.: Vanderbilt University. (1994).

———. (1986, August 29). Cocaine babies/Florida custody fight. On *Media services videotape, 1983–1994* (Compilation tape). Nashville, Tenn.: Vanderbilt University. (1994).

———. (1989, January 9). Medicine: Florida/Cocaine babies. On *Media services videotape 1983–1994* (Compilation tape). Nashville, Tenn.: Vanderbilt University. (1994).

———. (1989, May 10). Norfolk, Virginia/Child abuse case/Cocaine babies. On *Media services videotape 1983–1994* (Compilation tape). Nashville, Tenn.: Vanderbilt University. (1994).

———. (1989, May 26). Illinois/Greene cocaine case. On *Media services videotape 1983–1994* (Compilation tape). Nashville, Tenn.: Vanderbilt University. (1994).

———. (1989, June 20). An American crisis: Cocaine's victims. On *Media services videotape, 1983–1994* (Compilation tape). Nashville, Tenn.: Vanderbilt University. (1994).

———. (1989, August 25). Drug abuse/Heroin-crack cocaine combination. On *Media services videotape, 1983–1994* (Compilation tape). Nashville, Tenn.: Vanderbilt University. (1994).

———. (1989, December 4). Children/Orphanages. On *Media services videotape 1983–1994* (Compilation tape). Nashville, Tenn.: Vanderbilt University. (1994).

———.(1989, December 11). Government report/Children. On *Media services videotape 1983–1994* (Compilation tape). Nashville, Tenn.: Vanderbilt University. (1994).

———. (1989, December 13). Adoption/Cocaine babies. On *Media services video-*

tape 1983–1994 (Compilation tape). Nashville, Tenn.: Vanderbilt University. (1994).

―――. (1990, April 5). War on drugs: Crack cocaine. On *Media services video-tape 1983–1994* (Compilation tape). Nashville, Tenn.: Vanderbilt University. (1994).

―――. (1990, June 13). Drugs/Child welfare/Philadelphia, Pa. On *Media services videotape, 1983–1994* (Compilation tape). Nashville, Tenn.: Vanderbilt University. (1994).

―――. (1990, December 17). Medicine: Pregnancy and cocaine. On *Media services videotape 1983–1994* (Compilation tape). Nashville, Tenn.: Vanderbilt University. (1994).

―――. (1991, March 12). Medicine: Georgia/Cocaine babies. On *Media services videotape 1983–1994* (Compilation tape). Nashville, Tenn.: Vanderbilt University. (1994).

―――. (1991, June 24). Children in America/The pressure. On *Media services videotape 1983–1994* (Compilation tape). Nashville, Tenn.: Vanderbilt University. (1994).

―――. (1994, March 10). Eye on America (Medicine: Crack babies). On *Media services videotape 1983–1994* (Compilation tape). Nashville, Tenn.: Vanderbilt University. (1994).

Center for Reproductive Law and Policy. (n.d.). *Punishing women for their behavior during pregnancy: A public health disaster* (Mimeograph). Available: Center for Reproductive Law and Policy, New York, N.Y.

Center for Substance Abuse Treatment. (1993). *CSAT comprehensive treatment model for alcohol and other drug abusing women and children.* Rockville, Md.: U.S. Department of Health and Human Services, Public Health Service.

―――. (1994). *Practical approaches to the treatment of women who abuse alcohol and other drugs.* Rockville, Md.: U.S. Department of Health and Human Services, Public Health Service.

Chasnoff, I. J. (1989). Drug use and women: Establishing a standard of care. *Annals of the New York Academy of Science, 562,* 208–10.

―――. (1991). Cocaine and pregnancy: Clinical and methodological issues. *Clinics in Perinatology, 18,* 113–23.

―――. (1992). Cocaine, pregnancy, and the growing child. *Current Problems in Pediatrics, 22,* 302–21.

Chasnoff, I. J., Landress, H. J., and Barrett, M. E. (1990). The prevalence of illicit drug or alcohol use during pregnancy and discrepancies in mandatory reporting in Pinellas County, Florida. *New England Journal of Medicine, 322,* (April 26), 1202–6.

Chavkin, W. (1989). Testimony before the House Select Committee on Children, Youth, and Families. U.S. House of Representatives, April 27.

Child *Abuse Prevention and Treatment Act* of 1978, Pub. L. No. 95-266. 92 Stat. 205, Title 42, Sec. 1501 et seq. (1980).

Child Welfare League of America (CWLA). (1990). Crack and other addictions: Old realities and new challenges for child welfare. In *Proceedings of a symposium and policy recommendations: March 12-13, 1990*. Washington, D.C.: Child Welfare League of America.

———. (1992). *Children at the front: A different view of the war on alcohol and drugs.* Washington, D.C.: Child Welfare League of America.

Coakley, T. (1990, October 17). Judge rejects charge that woman gave drug to her unborn child. *Boston Globe*, (Metro section) p. 1.

Coakley, T., and Richard, R. (1989, August 22). Mother charged with exposing fetus to cocaine. *Boston Globe*, (Metro section) p.1.

Cocaine babies on the rise in Florida. (1989, July 13). UPI, regional news, Florida. Available: Lexis-Nexis/News/US.

Cocaine kindergartners: Preparing for the first wave, 102 Cong., 1st Sess. 1 (1992).

Cocaine mother gets 15 years probation. (1989, August 26). *Los Angeles Times,* (Home Edition) p. 2.

Cohen, S. (1972). *Folk devils and moral panics: The creation of the mods and the rockers.* London: McGibbon and Kee.

Cole, C. K. (1993). Classroom interventions for young children at risk. In G. H. Smith, C. D. Coles, M. K. Poulsen, and C. K. Cole (Eds.), *Children, families, and substance abuse: Challenges for changing educational and social outcomes* (pp. 121–53). Baltimore, Md.: Paul H. Brooks Publishing.

Cole, C. K., Ferrara, V., Johnson, D., Jones, M., Poulsen, M. K., Schoenbaum, M., Tyler, R., and Wallace, V. (1989). Today's challenge: Teaching strategies for working with young children prenatally exposed to drugs/alcohol. Los Angeles: University School District, Division of Special Education.

Colen, B. D. (1989, June 6). Reining in runaway prosecutors. *Newsday,* (Nassau and Suffolk Edition) p. 13.

Coles, C., Platzman, K. A., Smith, I., James, M. E., and Falek, A. (1992). Effects of cocaine and alcohol use in pregnancy on neonatal growth and neurobehavioral status. *Neurotoxicology and Teratology,* 14, 23–22.

Collins, P. H. (1990). *Black feminist thought.* Boston: Unwin Hyman.

Commonwealth v. Pelligrini, 414 Mass. 402; 608 N.E.2d 717 (Mass. 1993).

Condon, C. M. (1995). Clinton's cocaine babies: Why won't the administration let us save our children? *Policy Review,* 72 (Spring), 12–15.

Cong. Rec. 105th Cong. H. R., 1st. Sess. pp. 2012–15 (April 30, 1997).

———. 105th Cong. Senate, 1st Sess. pp. 12210–13. (November 8, 1997).

Curriden, M. (1990). Holding mom accountable, *ABA Journal,* 76, 50–53.

Davidson, J. (1989, July 13). Newborn drug exposure conviction a "drastic" first. *Los Angeles Times,* (Home Edition) p. 1.

Doering, P. L., Davidson, C. L., LaFauce, L., and Williams, C. A. (1989). Effects of cocaine on the human fetus. *DICP, The Annals of Pharmacotherapy*, 23, 639–45.

Disability and discipline. (1997, May 19). *Times-Picayune* (New Orleans, La.), p. B4.

Dorne, C. K. (1997). *Child maltreatment: A primer in history, public policy, and research*. Guilderland, N.Y.: Harrow and Heston Publishers.

Downs, S. W., Costin, L. B., and McFadden, E. J. (1996). *Child welfare and family services: Policies and practice*. White Plains, N.Y.: Longman Publishers.

Eddy, N. B., Halback, H., Isbell, H., and Seevers, M. H. (1965). Drug dependence: Its significance and characteristics. *Bulletin of the World Health Organization*, 32, 721–33.

Education for All Handicapped Children Act, Pub. L. No. 94-142, 89 Stat. 77, Title 20, Sec. 1400 *et seq.* (1975).

Education of the Handicapped Act Amendments, Pub. L. No. 99-457, 100 Stat. 1145 (1986).

Eisen, L., Field, T., Bandstra, E., et al. (1991). Perinatal cocaine effects on neonatal stress behaviors and performance on the Brazelton scale. *Pediatrics*, 13, 229–33.

The enemy within: Crack-cocaine and America's families, 101st Cong., 2d Sess. 1 (1990).

Fagan, J., and Chin, K. (1991). Social process of initiation into crack. *Journal of Drug Issues*, 21, 313–43.

Faludi, S. (1991). *Backlash: The undeclared war against American women*. New York: Crown Publishers.

Feig, L. (1990). Drug-exposed infants and children: Service needs and policy questions. Mimeograph: U.S. Department of Health and Human Services, Office of the Assistant Secretary for Planning and Evaluation. (January 1990, updated August 1990).

Finnegan, L. (1982). Outcomes of children born to women dependent upon narcotics. In B. Stimmel (Ed.), *Advances in alcohol and substance abuse: The effects of maternal alcohol and drug abuse on the new born* (pp. 55–102). Boston: Haworth Press.

————. (1988). Influence of maternal drug dependence on the newborn. In S. Kacew and S. Lock (Eds.), *Toxicologic and Pharmacologic Principles in Pediatrics* (pp. 183–98). New York: Hemisphere Publishing.

Finnegan, L., and Fehr, K. O. (1980). The effects of opiates, sedative-hypnotics, amphetamines, cannabis, and other psychoactive drugs on the fetus and newborn. In O. Kalant (Ed.), *Alcohol and drug problems in women: Research advances in alcohol and drug problems* (pp. 653–723). New York: Plenum Publishing.

Fishman, M. (1978). Crime waves as ideology. *Social Problems*, 25, 531–43.

FitzGerald, S. (1997, June 15). Coming up with the wrong answers. *Inquirer Magazine: The Philadelphia Inquirer*, pp. 12, 14, 26, 31.

Frank, D., Zuckerman, B. S., Amaro, H., et al. (1988). Cocaine use during pregnancy: Prevalence and correlates. *Pediatrics*, 82 (December), 888–94.

Goetz, E., Fox, H., and Bates, S. (1990). Poor and pregnant: Don't go to South

Carolina (Memoranda February 1). Available: American Civil Liberties Union, New York, N.Y.

Gold, J. (1997, December 18). N.J. gays win right to adopt. *AP Wire*, U.S. news. Available: http://wire.ap.org.

Golub, A. L., and Johnson, B. D. (1997). Crack's decline: Some surprises across U.S. cities. *NIJ Research Brief* (July). Washington, D.C.: National Institute of Justice, U.S. Department of Justice. Available: http://www.ncjrs.org/txtfiles/165707.txt.

Goode, E. (1989). *Drugs in American society.* New York: McGraw-Hill.

Gomez, L. E. (1997). *Misconceiving mothers: Legislators, prosecutors, and the politics of prenatal drug exposure.* Philadelphia: Temple University Press.

Gramlich, E., Laren, D., and Sealand, N. (1992). Mobility into and out of poor urban neighborhoods. In A. V. Harrell and G. E. Peterson (Eds.), *Drugs, crime, and social isolation: Barriers to urban opportunity* (pp. 241–55). Washington, D.C.: Urban Institute Press.

Greene, D. (1991). Abusive prosecutors: Gender, race, and class discretion and the prosecution of drug-addicted mothers. *Buffalo Law Review, 39,* 737–802.

Greene, D. L. (1997, June 5). New law tracking disciplinary records of disabled students. *St. Louis Post-Dispatch,* p. A8.

Grinspoon, L., and Bakalar, J. B. (1976). *Cocaine: A drug and its social evolution.* New York: Basic Books.

Guerreo, A. B. (1990, October 17). Fetus-cocaine ruling greeted by jubilation. *Enterprise* (Brockton, Mass.), pp. 1, 4.

Hagdorn, J. M. (1995). *Forsaking our children: Bureaucracy and reform in the child welfare system.* Chicago: Lake View Press.

Hall, S., Critcher, C., Jefferson, T., Clarke, J., and Roberts, J. (1978). *Policing the crisis: Mugging, the state, and law.* London: MacMillan.

Hancock, M., and Thompson, N. (1995, April 3). Plymouth County DA O'Malley dies. *Enterprise* (Brockton, Mass.), pp. 1, 4.

Harley, D. A. (1992). *Early childhood educators' beliefs and knowledge about the effects of prenatal exposure to alcohol, crack, cocaine, and a combination of substances on infants and young children.* Unpublished doctoral dissertation, Southern Illinois University, Carbondale.

Harrell, A. V., and Peterson, G. E. (Eds.). (1992). *Drugs, crime, and social isolation: Barriers to urban opportunity.* Washington, D.C.: Urban Institute Press.

Hatchett, S. J., Cochran, D. L., and Jackson, J. S. (1991). Family life. In J. S. Jackson (Ed.), *Life in black America* (pp. 46–83). Newbury Park, Calif.: Sage Publications.

Hicks, B. B., and Wilson, G. A. (1993). *Kids, crack, and the community: Reclaiming drug-exposed infants and children.* Bloomington, Ind.: National Education Service.

Hill, R. B. (1997). Social welfare policies and African American families. In H. P.

McAdoo (Ed.), *Black families* (pp. 349–63). Thousand Oaks, Calif.: Sage Publications.

Hoey, J. T. (1993, August 11). O'Malley weighs in on crime: Clinton plan bears stamp of local DA. *Enterprise* (Brockton, Mass.), pp. 1, 4.

Hoffman, J. (1990, August 19). Pregnant, addicted, and guilty? *New York Times,* p. 34.

Hogan, J. (1991, January 17). Judge questions "coke mom" charges. *Muskegon Chronicle and Sunday Chronicle,* p. 1B.

Holder, W. M., Mouzakitis, C., Romera, M., Sahd, D., and Salisbury, O. (1981). *Helping in child protective services.* Englewood, Colo.: American Humane Association.

Holtzman, C., and Nigel, P. (1994). Maternal cocaine use during pregnancy and perinatal outcomes. *Epidemiologic Reviews,* 16, 315–34.

Horger, E. O., Brown, S. B., and Condon, C. M. (1990). Cocaine in pregnancy: Confronting the problem. *Journal of the South Carolina Medical Association,* 86, 527–31.

Howard, J., Beckwith, L., Rodning, C., and Kropenska, V. (1989). The development of young children of substance-abusing parents: Insights from seven years of intervention and research. *Zero to Three,* 9, 8–16.

Humphries, D. (1993). Crack mothers, drug wars, and the politics of resentment. In K. D. Tunnel (Ed.), *Political crime in contemporary America: A critical approach* (pp. 31–48). New York: Garland Press.

———. (1998). Crack mothers at 6. *Violence against Women,* 4, 45–61.

Humphries, D., Polak, H., Behrens, K., Weiner, J., and Schulter, V. (1992). Drug use and pregnancy: Issues in evaluation and treatment. Paper presented at the Eastern Sociological Meetings, Baltimore, Md.

Hutchings, D. E. (1993). The puzzle of cocaine's effects following maternal use during pregnancy: Are there reconcilable differences? *Neurotoxicology and Teratology,* 15, 281–86.

Inciardi, J. A. (1986). *The war on drugs: Heroin, cocaine, and public policy.* Mountain View, Calif.: Mayfield.

———. (1993). Kingrats, chicken heads, slow necks, freaks, and blood suckers: A glimpse at the Miami sex-for-crack market. In M. S. Ratner (Ed.), *Crack pipe as pimp: An ethnographic investigation of sex-for-crack exchanges* (pp. 37–67). New York: Lexington Books.

———. (1997a). *Cocaine-exposed infants: Social, legal, and public health issues.* Thousand Oaks, Calif.: Sage Publishing.

———. (1997b). *The war on drugs II: The continuing epic of heroin, cocaine, crack, crime, AIDS, and public policy.* Mountain View, Calif.: Mayfield.

Inclusion. (n.d.). *Education Week on the Web* (On-line). Available: http://www.edweek.org/context/issues/inclusion.

Individuals with Disabilities Education Act of 1990, Pub. L. No. 101–476, 104 Stat. 1142 (Title IX, Sec. 901 (a) (22)) (1990).

Individuals with Disabilities Education Act of 1991, Pub. L. No. 102–119, 105 Stat. 607 (Title IX, Sec. 25 (b)) (1991).

Jacoby, J. E. (1979). *The American prosecutor: A search for identity.* Lexington, Mass.: Lexington Books.

Johnson v. State, 602 So.2d, 1290–91 (Fla. Supreme Ct. 1992).

Kain, Z. N., Kain, T. S., and Scarpelli, E. M. (1992). Cocaine exposure in utero: Perinatal development and neonatal manifestations—review. *Clinical Toxicology, 30,* 607–36.

Kaltenbach, K., and Finnegan, L. (1986). Neonatal abstinence syndrome: Pharmacotherapy and developmental outcomes. *Neurobehavioral Toxicology and Teratology, 8,* 353–55.

Kamerman, S. B. (1990). If CPS is driving child welfare—where do we go from here? *Public Welfare,* 48 (Winter), 9–13.

Kamerman, S. B., and Kahn, A. J. (1976). *Social services in the United States: Policies and programs.* Philadelphia: Temple University Press.

———. (1989). *Social services for children, youth, and families in the United States.* New York: Columbia University Press (Annie E. Casey Foundation).

Kandall, S. R. (1996). *Substance and shadow: Women and addiction in the United States.* Cambridge, Mass.: Harvard University Press.

Kasinsky, R. G. (1994). Child neglect and "unfit" mothers: Child savers in the progressive era and today. *Women and Criminal Justice, 6,* 97–129.

Katz, M. (1989). *The undeserving poor: From the war on poverty to the war on welfare.* New York: Pantheon Books.

Kennedy, J. H. (1989, August 23). Cloudy future after infant-cocaine case: DA rejects vision of legal morass, *Boston Globe,* (Metro section) p. 1.

Kilborn, P. T. (1997). Priority on safety is keeping more children in foster care. Cong. Rec. 105th Cong. H. R., 1st Sess. pp. 2019+ (April 30, 1997).

Kimmich, M. H. (1985). *American's children—who cares? Growing demands and declining assistance in the Reagan era.* Washington, D.C.: Urban Institute Press.

Knutson, L. L. (1997, November 19). Clinton signs adoption law. *AP Wire,* U.S. news (On-line). Available: http://wire.ap.org.

Koren, G., Gladstone, D., Robeson, C., and Robieux, I. (1992). The perception of teratogenic risk of cocaine. *Teratology,* 46, 567–71.

Koren, G., Shear, H., Graham, K., and Einarson, T. (1989). Bias against the null hypothesis: The reproductive hazards of cocaine. *Lancet,* (December 16), 1440–42.

Kreiter, M. S. (1989, May 10). ACLU offers to represent Rockford mother. *UPI,* regional news, Illinois, Chicago. Available: Lexis-Nexis/News/US.

———. (1989, May 27). Cocaine mothers and cocaine babies: Whose rights prevail? UPI, domestic news, Illinois, Chicago. Available: Lexis-Nexis/News/US.

Kron, R. W., Litt, M., Phoenix, M. D., and Finnegan, L. (1988). Neonatal narcotic abstinence: Effects of pharmacotherapeutic agents and maternal drug usage on nutritive sucking behavior. *Journal of Pediatrics*, 4 (Part 1), 637–41.

L. A. program stresses nurturance, understanding. Archives. (1989). *Education Week on the Web.* Available: http://www.edweek.org.

Ladner, J. A. (1971). *Tomorrow's tomorrow: The black woman.* Garden City, N.Y.: Doubleday and Co.

Lamb, J. (1989, May 27). Melanie Green, focus of national attention. . . . *Gannet News Service.* Illinois, Rockford. Available: Lexis-Nexis/News/US.

Landry, M. J. (1995). *Overview of addiction treatment effectiveness.* (DHHS Publication No. (SMA) 96-3081.) Rockville, Md.: Substance Abuse and Mental Health Services Administration.

Lane, R. (1992). Black Philadelphia then and now: The "underclass" of the late twentieth century compared with poorer African-Americans of the late nineteenth century. In A. V. Harrell and G. E. Peterson (Eds.), *Drugs, crime, and social isolation: Barriers to urban opportunity* (pp. 45–98). Washington, D.C.: Urban Institute Press.

Lester, B. M., LaGasse, L., and Brunner, S. (1997). Data base of studies on prenatal cocaine exposure and child outcome. *Journal of Drug Issues*, 27, 487–99.

Lester, B. M., and Tronick, E. Z. (Eds.). (1994). Prenatal Drug Exposure and Child Outcome (Special Issue). *Infant Mental Health Journal*, 15(2).

Levine, H. G. (1978). The discovery of addiction: Changing conceptions of habitual drunkenness in America. *Journal of Studies on Alcohol*, 39, 143–74.

Lewin, T. (1990, February 5). Drug use in pregnancy: New issue for the courts *New York Times*, p. 14A.

Lindesmith, A. R. (1938). A sociological theory of addiction. *American Journal of Sociology*, 43, 593–613.

Lissauer, T., Ghaus, K., and Rivers, R. (1994). Maternal drug abuse—effects on the child. *Current Pediatrics*, 4, 235–39.

Litt, J., and McNeil, M. (1994). "Crack babies" and the politics of reproduction and nurturance. In J. Best (Ed.), *Troubling children: Studies of children and social problems* (pp. 93–113). New York: Walter de Gruyter.

Little, B. B., Snell, L. M., Palmores, M., and Gilstrap, L. C., III. (1988). Cocaine use in pregnant women in a large public hospital. *American Journal of Perinatology*, 5 (July), 206–7.

Logli, P. (1990). Drugs in the womb: The newest battlefield in the war on drugs. *Criminal Justice Ethics*, (Winter/Spring), 23–29.

———. (1992). The prosecutor's role in solving the problems of prenatal drug use and substance abused children. *Hastings Law Journal*, 43, 559–67.

Love, A. A. (1997, December 11). Study: Special education budget rising. *AP Wire*, U.S. news. Available: http://wire.ap.org.

Lutiger, B., Graham, K., and Einarson, T. R. (1991). Relationship between gestational cocaine use and pregnancy outcome: A meta-analysis. *Teratology*, 44, 405–14.

MacDougall, D. W. (1991, July 31). Charles Condon: Ninth circuit solicitor's motto is "do the right thing." *News and Courier/Evening Post*, p. 1E.

MacNeil/Lehrer newshour. (1990, June 28). Pregnant addicts. (Transcript 3804). New York and Washington, D.C.: Educational Broadcasting and GWETA.

Mahan, S. (1996). *Crack cocaine, crime, and women*. Thousand Oaks, Calif.: Sage Publications.

Maher, L. (n.d.). Cocaine mothers: (Re)constructing the crack mom. Unpublished manuscript.

———. (1995). *Dope girls: Gender, race, and class in the drug economy*. Unpublished doctoral dissertation, Rutgers University, Newark, N.J.

———. (1997). *Sexed work: Gender, race, and resistance in a Brooklyn drug market*. Oxford and New York: Clarendon Press.

Maher, L., and Curtis, R. (1992). Women on the edge of crime: Crack cocaine and the changing contexts of street-level sex work in New York City. *Crime, Law, and Social Change*, 18, 221–58.

Maschke, K. J. (1995). Prosecutors as crime creators: The case of prenatal drug use. *Criminal Justice Review*, 20, 21–33.

Mayes, L. C., Granger, R. H., Bornstein, M. H., and Zuckerman, B. (1992). The problem of perinatal cocaine exposure: A rush to judgment. *Journal of the American Medical Association*, 267, 406–8.

McGuire, K., and Pastore, A. L. (Eds.). (1995). *Sourcebook of criminal justice statistics, 1994*. U.S. Department of Justice, Bureau of Justice Statistics, Washington, D.C.: U.S. Government Printing Office.

McNeese, C. A. (Guest Ed.). (1997). Pregnancy and substance abuse (Special Issue). *Journal of Drug Issues*, 21(3).

McNulty, M. (1988). Pregnancy police: The health policy and legal implications of punishing pregnant women for harm to their fetuses. *New York University Review of Law and Social Change*, 16, 277–319.

Meckler, L. (1997, December 17). Disability kids get second chance. *AP Wire*, U.S. news. Available: http://wire.ap.org.

Medendorp, L., and Walsh, M. G. (1989, October 19). "Crack baby" mom sought. *Muskegon Chronicle and Sunday Chronicle*, pp. 1A, 2A.

Michigan v. Hardy, 188 Mich. App. 305; 469 N.W.2d 50 (Mich. App. 1991).

Minkler, M., and Roe, K. M. (1993). *Grandmothers as caregivers: Raising children of the crack cocaine epidemic*. Newbury Park, Calif.: Sage Publications.

Morales, E. (1989). *Cocaine: White gold dust in Peru.* Tucson: University of Arizona Press.

Morgan, P. (1978). The legislation of drug laws: Economic crisis and social control. *Journal of Drug Issues, 8,* 53–62.

Moss, D.C. (1988, November 1, November 29). Pregnant? Go directly to jail: Suits hit prenatal care for women inmates. *American Bar Association Journal, 74,* 20.

Moss, K., and Crockett, J. (1990). Testimony on children of substance abusers before U.S. Senate subcommittee on children, family, drugs, and alcoholism. (February 22).

Mother's cocaine conviction overturned. (1992, July 24). Houston Chronicle, p. 7.

Moynihan, D. P. (1965). The Negro family: The case for national action. Washington, D.C.: U.S. Government Printing Office. Department of Labor, Office of Policy Planning and Research.

Murphy, S. (1992). It takes your womanhood: Depersonalization, resistance and the persistence of self. Unpublished doctoral dissertation, University of California, San Francisco.

Murphy, S., and Rosenbaum, M. (1997). Two women who used cocaine too much: Class, race, gender, crack, and coke. In C. Reinarman and H. Levine (Eds.), *Crack in context: Demon drugs and social justice* (pp. 98–112). Berkeley: University of California Press.

———. (1999). *Pregnant women on drugs: Combatting stereotypes and stigma.* New Brunswick, N.J.: Rutgers University Press.

Murray, C. (1984). *Losing ground.* New York: Basic Books.

Musto, D. F. (1987). *The American disease: Origins of narcotic control.* New Haven, Conn.: Yale University Press.

National Center for Health Statistics. (1994). *Vital statistics of the United States, 1990, vol. 2, morality, part A.* Washington, D.C.: Public Health Service.

———. (1996). *Vital statistics of the United States, 1992, vol. 2, mortality, part A.* Washington, D.C.: Public Health Service.

National Institute of Justice (NIJ). (1990). *DUF: 1988 drug use forecasting report.* Washington, D.C.: Office of Justice Programs, U.S. Department of Justice.

———. (1995). *Drug use forecasting: 1994 annual report on adult and juvenile arrestees.* Washington, D.C.: Office of Justice Programs, U.S. Department of Justice.

National Institute on Drug Abuse (NIDA). (1988). *National household survey on drug abuse: Main findings 1985.* (DHHS Publication No. (ADM) 88-1586). Rockville, Md.: Public Health Service, U.S. Department of Health and Human Services.

———. (1989). *National household survey on drug abuse: Population estimates 1988.* (DHHS Publication No. (ADM) 89-1636). Rockville, Md.: Public Health Service, U.S. Department of Health and Human Services.

———. (1990). *National household survey on drug abuse: Main findings 1988.* (DHHS

Publication No. (ADM) 90-1682). Rockville, Md.: Public Health Service, U.S. Department of Health and Human Services.

———. (1991). *National household survey on drug abuse: Population estimates 1990.* (DHHS Publication No. (ADM) 91-1732). Rockville, Md.: Public Health Service, U.S. Department of Health and Human Services.

———. (1992). *National household survey on drug abuse: Population estimates 1991 (Revised).* (DHHS Publication No. (ADM) 92-1887). Rockville, Md.: Public Health Service, U.S. Department of Health and Human Services.

———. (1996). *The national pregnancy and health survey: Drug use among women delivering livebirths: 1992.* (NIH Publication No. (ADM) 96-3819). Rockville, Md.: National Institutes of Health, U.S. Department of Health and Human Services.

National Institutes of Health (NIH). (1993). *Recovery training and self-help: Relapse prevention and aftercare for drug addicts.* (NIH Publication No. 93-3521). Rockville, Md.: National Institute on Drug Abuse.

NBC nightly news. (1984, August 9). Special segment (The cocaine epidemic, part 1). On *Media services videotape, 1983–1994* (Compilation tape). Nashville, Tenn.: Vanderbilt University. (1994).

———. (1984, August 10). Special segment (The cocaine epidemic, part 2). On *Media services videotape, 1983–1994* (Compilation tape). Nashville, Tenn.: Vanderbilt University. (1994).

———. (1985, December 1). Crack/Cocaine. On *Media services videotape, 1983–1994* (Compilation tape). Nashville, Tenn.: Vanderbilt University. (1994).

———. (1986, May 23). Crack/"Cocaine." On *Media services videotape, 1983–1994* (Compilation tape). Nashville, Tenn.: Vanderbilt University. (1994).

———. (1986, August 4). Cocaine/Crack. On *Media services videotape, 1983–1994* (Compilation tape). Nashville, Tenn.: Vanderbilt University. (1994).

———. (1987, February 27). Drugs/Crack. On *Media services videotape, 1983–1994* (Compilation tape). Nashville, Tenn.: Vanderbilt University. (1994).

———. (1988, January 13). Cocaine/High school use. On *Media services videotape, 1983–1994* (Compilation tape). Nashville, Tenn.: Vanderbilt University. (1994).

———. (1988, May 16). War on drugs (Deadly demand, part 1). On *Media services videotape, 1983–1994* (Compilation tape). Nashville, Tenn.: Vanderbilt University. (1994).

———. (1988, May 17). War on drugs (Deadly demand, part 2). On *Media services videotape, 1983–1994* (Compilation tape). Nashville, Tenn.: Vanderbilt University. (1994).

———. (1988, October 24). Cocaine kids (Part 1). On *Media services videotape 1983–1994* (Compilation tape). Nashville, Tenn.: Vanderbilt University. (1994).

———. (1988, October 25). Cocaine kids (Part 2). On *Media services video-*

tape, 1983–1994 (Compilation tape). Nashville, Tenn.: Vanderbilt University. (1994).

———. (1989, July 7). Drugs/Cocaine mothers. On *Media services videotape* 1983–1994 (Compilation tape). Nashville, Tenn.: Vanderbilt University. (1994).

———. (1989, August 10). Medicine: Cocaine mothers. On *Media services videotape* 1983–1994 (Compilation tape). Nashville, Tenn.: Vanderbilt University. (1994).

———. (1989, August 16). Drugs/Chasing the dragon (Crack cocaine and heroin). On *Media services videotape*, 1983–1994 (Compilation tape). Nashville, Tenn.: Vanderbilt University. (1994).

———. (1989, September 12). War on Drugs? Miami, Florida. On *Media services videotape*, 1983–1994 (Compilation tape). Nashville, Tenn.: Vanderbilt University. (1994).

———. (1989, September 30). Medicine: D.C. infant mortality rate. On *Media services videotape* 1983–1994 (Compilation tape). Nashville, Tenn.: Vanderbilt University. (1994).

———. (1989, November 7). '89 elections/Drug issues. On *Media services videotape*, 1983–1994 (Compilation tape). Nashville, Tenn.: Vanderbilt University. (1994).

———. (1989, November 18). Weekend journal (Interracial adoptions). On *Media services videotape*, 1983–1994 (Compilation tape). Nashville, Tenn.: Vanderbilt University. (1994).

———. (1990, January 3). War on drugs/Commuters. On *Media services videotape*, 1983–1994 (Compilation tape). Nashville, Tenn.: Vanderbilt University. (1994).

———. (1990, October 4). Guns and drugs (Crack generation). On *Media services videotape*, 1983–1994 (Compilation tape). Nashville, Tenn.: Vanderbilt University. (1994).

———. (1991, June 24). American children/Commission report/Funding. On *Media services videotape*, 1983–1994 (Compilation tape). Nashville, Tenn.: Vanderbilt University. (1994).

———. (1991, September 17). Drugs: Crack cocaine. On *Media services videotape*, 1983–1994 (Compilation tape). Nashville, Tenn.: Vanderbilt University. (1994).

———. (1992, December 16). Texas/Racial adoption case. On *Media services videotape*, 1983–1994 (Compilation tape). Nashville, Tenn.: Vanderbilt University. (1994).

———. (1992, December 29). American close-up (Crack cocaine) (Part 1). On *Media services videotape*, 1983–1994 (Compilation tape). Nashville, Tenn.: Vanderbilt University. (1994).

————. (1992, December 30). American close-up (Crack cocaine) (Part 2). On *Media services videotape*, 1983–1994 (Compilation tape). Nashville, Tenn.: Vanderbilt University. (1994).

Nelkin, D. (1987). *Selling science: How the press covers science and technology*. New York: W. H. Freeman.

Neuspiel, D., Hamel, S., Hochberg, E., Greene, J., and Campbell, D. (1991). Maternal cocaine use and infant behavior. *Neurotoxicology and Teratology*, 13, 229–33.

Nightline. (1990, June 19). Jailing pregnant users: Does it help or hurt? (Transcript). ABC News. New York: American Broadcasting Company. Available: Lexis-Nexis/News/Script.

Norton-Hawk, M. A. (1997). Frequency of prenatal drug abuse: Assessment, obstacles, and policy implications. *Journal of Policy Issues*, 2, 447–62.

Office of the Inspector General (OIG). (1990a). *Crack babies*. (OEI-03-89-01540). Washington, D.C.: Office of Evaluations and Inspections, U.S. Department of Health and Human Services.

————. (1990b). *Crack babies: Selected models of practice* (OEI-03-89-01542). Washington, D.C.: Office of Evaluations and Inspections, U.S. Department of Health and Human Services.

————. (1990c). OIG management advisory report: "Boarder babies" (Memorandum) (OEI-03-89-01541). Washington, D.C.: Office of Evaluations and Inspections, U.S. Department of Health and Human Services.

O'Neal, D. (1992, March 7). Court hears coke-babies case; Lawyer: Mom who used drugs was illegally prosecuted. *Orlando Sentinel Tribune*, p. A1.

Parson, C. W. (1993, January 24). When drug-addicted babies, die, is it murder? *Chicago Tribune*, p. 1C.

Peterson, G. E., and Harrell, A. V. (1992). Introduction: Inner-city isolation and opportunity. In A. V. Harrell and G. E. Peterson (Eds.), *Drugs, crime, and social isolation: Barriers to urban opportunity* (pp. 1–26). Washington, D.C.: Urban Institute Press.

Phibbs, C. S., Bateman, D. A., and Schwartz, R. M. (1991). The neonatal costs of maternal cocaine use. *Journal of the American Medical Association*, 226, 1521–26.

Pitts, K. S., and Weinstein, L. (1990). Cocaine and pregnancy: A lethal combination. *Journal of Perinatology*, 10, 180–82.

Pluta, R. (1991, April 2). Charges against a woman whose cocaine use led to the birth of an infant affected by the drug were thrown out Tuesday by the Michigan Court of Appeals. UPI, regional news, Michigan. Available: Lexis-Nexis/News/US.

Poulsen, M. K. (1992). *Schools meet the challenge: Educational needs of children at risk due to prenatal substance exposure*. Sacramento, Calif.: Resources in Special Education.

Pregnant addicts: The debate over prosecution. (1990). *Update: National Center for Prosecution of Child Abuse*, 3 (August), p. 1.

Primetime live. (1989, September 7). The most innocent. (Transcript). Available: Lexis-Nexis/News/US.

Ratner, M. S. (1993a). *Crack pipe as pimp: An ethnographic investigation of sex-for-crack exchanges*. New York: Lexington Books.

———. (1993b). Sex, drugs, and public policy: Studying and understanding the sex-for-crack phenomenon. In M. S. Ratner (Ed.), *Crack pipe as pimp: An ethnographic investigation of sex-for-crack exchanges* (pp. 1–35). New York: Lexington Books.

Reardon, P. (1989, May 11). "I loved her," mother says "shocked" over arrest in baby's drug death. *Chicago Tribune*, p. 1.

———. (1989, May 14). Baby's cocaine death adds to the debate on protection of the unborn. *Chicago Tribune*, p. 1.

———. (1989, May 28). Drugs and pregnancy debate far from resolved. *Chicago Tribune*, p. 1.

Reauthorization of disability-related legislation. 103rd Cong. 1st Sess. (March 10, 1994).

Reinarman, C., and Levine, H. G. (1989). Crack in context: Politics and media in the making of a drug scare. *Contemporary Drug Problems*, (Winter), 535–77.

———. (1995). The crack attack: America's latest drug scare, 1986–1992. In J. Best (Ed.), *Images of issues* (pp. 147–90). New York: Aldine de Gruyter.

———. (1997a). *Crack in America: Demon drugs and social justice*. Berkeley: University of California Press.

———. (1997b). Real opposition, real alternatives: Reducing the harms of drug use and drug policy. In C. Reinarman and H. G. Levine (Eds.), *Crack in America: Demon drugs and social justice* (pp. 345–66). Berkeley: University of California Press.

Reeves, J. L., and R. Campbell. (1994). *Crack coverage: Television news, the anti-cocaine crusade, and the Reagan legacy*. Durham, N.C.: Duke University Press.

Richardson, G. A., Day, N. L., and McGauhey, P. J. (1993). The impact of prenatal marijuana and cocaine use on the infant and child. *Clinical Obstetrics and Gynecology*, 36, 302–18.

Roberts, D. (1991). Punishing drug addicts who have babies: Women of color, equality, and the right to privacy. *Harvard Law Review*, 104, 1419–81.

Robinson v. California, 370 U.S. 660 (1962).

Roe v. Wade, 410 U.S. 113 (1973).

Roland, E. H., and Volpe, J. J. (1989). Effect of maternal cocaine use on the fetus and newborn: Review of the literature. *Pediatric Neuroscience*, 15, 88–94.

Rosenak, D., Diamant, Y. Z., Yaffe, H., and Hornstein, E. (1990). Cocaine: Maternal use during pregnancy and its effect on the mother, the fetus, and the infant. *Obstetrical and Gynecological Survey*, 45, 348–59.

Rosenbaum, M. (1981). *Women on heroin*. New Brunswick, N.J.: Rutgers University Press.

Sacks, J. L. (1997, October 29). Proposed IDEA rules: Target testing, accountability. *Education Week on the Web* (On-line). Available: http://www.edweek.org/context/tpics/include.html.

Sanchez, R. (1997, May 15). Bill to revamp public education of disabled passes Senate, goes to President. *Washington Post*, p. A7.

Sataline, S. (1991, October 10). State grapples with issue of child abuse before birth. *Hartford Courant*, p. A1.

Scaglione, D. (1989, November 4). O'Malley defends prosecution of women to protect the unborn. *Enterprise* (Brockton, Mass.), pp. 1, 8.

Scaglione, D., and Cahill, J. (1989, August 21). Mother faces drug charge in abuse case. *Enterprise* (Brockton, Mass.), pp. 1, 6.

———. (1989, September 28). Pelligrini indicted in drug case. *Enterprise* (Brockton, Mass.), pp. 1, 8.

Schnaiberg, L. (1996, November 27). States rethink how to pay for special education. *Education Week on the Web* (On-line). Available: http://www.edweek.org.

Schools for disabled children (Editorial). (1996, July 10). *Washington Post*, p. A16.

Sharp, D. (1989, August 25). Drug-baby case sentence today: Ex-addict mother is first convicted. *USA Today*, p. 3A

Shillington, P. (1991, April 20). Mom's conviction upheld in cocaine-to-infant case. *Miami Herald*, (Section 2) p. 5.

Siegel, B. (1994, August 7). In the name of the children get treatment or go to jail, one South Carolina hospital tells drug-abusing pregnant women. Now it faces a civil-rights investigation. *Los Angeles Times Magazine*, p. 14.

Singer, L. T., Garber, R., and Kliegman, R. (1991). Neurobehavioral sequelae of fetal cocaine exposure. *Journal of Pediatrics*, 119, 667–72.

Slutsker, L. (1992). Risks associated with cocaine use during pregnancy. *Obstetrics and Gynecology*, 79, 778–89.

Smith, G. H., Coles, C. D., Poulsen, M. K., and Cole, C. K. (1995). *Children, families, and substance abuse*. Baltimore, Md.: Paul H. Brooks Publishing.

Sobell, M. B., and Sobell, L. C. (1978). *Behavioral treatment of alcohol problems: Individualized treatment and controlled drinking*. New York: Plenum Press.

Social Security Act of 1935, 42 U.S.C. 301 *et seq*.

Special treatment. (1995, February). Teacher Magazine. *Education Week on the Web* (On-line). Available: http://www.edweek.org.

Spitzer, B. C. (1987). A response to "cocaine babies" amendment of Florida's child abuse and neglect laws to encompass infants born drug dependent. *Florida State University Law Review*, 15, 865–84.

Stack, C. (1974). *All our kin: Strategies for survival in a black community*. New York: Harper Torchbooks.

State v. Johnson, 578 So.2d 419 (Fla. App. 5th DCA 1991).

Stein, S. (1989, May 21). Prosecuting a drug baby's mom. *Newsday* (Nassau and Suffolk Edition) p. 15.

Stone, A. (1990, February 26). Experts split on prosecution of pregnant drug users. *Gannett News Service.* Available: Lexis-Nexis/News/US.

Substance Abuse and Mental Health Services Administration (SAMHSA). (1993a) *National household survey on drug abuse: Main findings 1991.* (DHHS Publication No. (SMA) 93-1980). Rockville, Md.: Public Health Service, U.S. Department of Health and Human Services.

———. (1993b). *National household survey on drug abuse: Race/ethnicity, socioeconomic status, and drug abuse 1991.* (DHHS Publication No. (SMA) 93-2062). Rockville, Md.: Public Health Service, U.S. Department of Health and Human Services.

———. (1994). *National household survey on drug abuse: Population estimates 1993.* (DHHS Publication No. (SMA) 94-3017). Rockville, Md.: Public Health Service, U.S. Department of Health and Human Services.

———. (1995a). *National household survey on drug abuse: Main findings 1992.* (DHHS Publication No. (SMA) 94-3012). Rockville, Md.: Public Health Service, U.S. Department of Health and Human Services.

———. (1995b). *National household survey on drug abuse: Main findings 1993.* (DHHS Publication No. (SMA) 95-3020). Rockville, Md.: Public Health Service, U.S. Department of Health and Human Services.

———. (1995c). *National household survey on drug abuse: Population estimates 1994.* (DHHS Publication No. (SMA) 94-3063 Rockville, Md.: Public Health Service, U.S. Department of Health and Human Services.

———. (1997). *Treatment episode data set, 1992–1995* (Advance Report No. 12, February). National Administration of Substance Abuse Treatment Services. Available: http://www.samhsa.gov/oas/teds.

Substance abused infants: A prosecutorial dilemma (1990, September/October). *Update: National Center for Prosecution of Child Abuse,* 3, p. 1.

Sudarkasa, N. (1997). African American families and family values. In H. P. McAdoo (Ed.), *Black families* (pp. 9–40). Thousand Oaks, Calif.: Sage Publications.

Thompson, N., and Reardon, M. (1995, April 4). O'Malley suffered heart attack. *Enterprise* (Brockton, Mass.), pp. 1, 6.

Townsend, R. J. (1991, April 23). Last of charges dismissed in mother-child drug case. *Enterprise* (Brockton, Mass.), pp. 1, 6.

Trial to start on case of baby born addicted to drugs. (1990, May 28). UPI, regional news, Michigan. Available: Lexis-Nexis/News/Wire.

Tucker, M. B., and Mitchell-Kernan, C. (1995). Trends in African American family formation: A theoretical and statistical overview. In M. B. Tucker and C. Mitchell-Kernan (Eds.), *The decline in marriage among African Americans: Causes, consequences and public policy* (pp. 3–26). New York: Russell Sage Foundation.

U.S. Department of Education. (1995). Seventh annual report to Congress on the implementation of the Individuals with Disabilities Education Act (On-line). Available: http://www.cd.gov/pubs/OSE95AnlRpt/index.html.

U.S. Department of Health and Human Services. (1992). Maternal drug abuse and drug-exposed children: Understanding the problem (DHHS No. (ADM) 92-1949). Washington, D.C.: U.S. Government Printing Office.

U.S. General Accounting Office (GAO). (1990). Drug-exposed infants: A generation at risk. (GAO/HRD-90-138). Washington, D.C.: Report to the Chairman, Committee on Finance, U.S. Senate.

———. (1991). Drug abuse: The crack cocaine epidemic: Health consequences and treatment. (GAO/HRD-91-155FS). Washington, D.C.: Fact Sheet for the Chairman, Select Committee on Narcotics Abuse and Control, House of Representatives.

Videro, D. (1989, October 25). Drug-exposed children pose special problems. Archives. Education Week on the Web. Available: http://www.edweek.org.

Vielmetti, B. (1990, January 28). Lawyer advocates prosecuting mothers of cocaine babies. St. Petersburg Times (Brandon Times section), p. 5.

Walker, M. B. (1993). Crack affected children: A teacher's guide. Newbury Park, Calif.: Corwin Press.

Walsh, M. G. (1989, November 13). Suspected "crack mom" surrenders to police. Muskegon Chronicle and Sunday Chronicle, p. 1B.

———. (1990, February 2). Mom who used crack charged with abuse. Muskegon Chronicle and Sunday Chronicle, pp. 1A, 2A.

———. (1990, April 16). Newborn removed in cocaine case. Muskegon Chronicle and Sunday Chronicle, pp. 1A, 2A.

———. (1990, April 19). Coke baby's mother may face arrest. Muskegon Chronicle and Sunday Chronicle, p. 1A.

———. (1990, April 20). Coke baby's mom charged. Muskegon Chronicle and Sunday Chronicle, p. 1A.

———. (1990, June 20). Hardy case draws national attention. Muskegon Chronicle and Sunday Chronicle, p. 1B.

———. (1990, June 27). Tague may widen "coke mom" probe. Muskegon Chronicle and Sunday Chronicle, pp. 1A, 2A.

———. (1990, July 19). Mom faces "coke baby" trial. Muskegon Chronicle and Sunday Chronicle, pp. 1A, 2A.

———. (1990, August 10). "Coke baby" will be reunited with mom. Muskegon Chronicle and Sunday Chronicle, p. 1A.

———. (1991, February 4). "Coke baby" charge dumped. Muskegon Chronicle and Sunday Chronicle, pp. 1A, 2A.

———. (1991, April 2). "Coke mom" case dumped. Muskegon Chronicle and Sunday Chronicle, pp. 1A, 2A.

Walsh, M. G., and Medendorp, L. (1989, October 21). Mother of "crack babe" located, arrest is delayed. *Muskegon Chronicle and Sunday Chronicle*, p. 3A.

Warner, J. (1994). In another city, in another time: Rhetoric and the creation of a drug scare in eighteenth-century London. *Contemporary Drug Problems*, 21, 485–511.

Warren, L. (1990, July 18). Judge orders lawyer to stand trial in cocaine-baby case. UPI, regional news, Michigan. Available: Lexis-Nexis/News/US.

Webster v. Reproductive Health Services, 492 U.S. 490 (1989).

Whittner v. South Carolina, S. C. Lexis 120 *2 (1996).

Wilkerson, I. (1991, April 3). Woman cleared after drug use in pregnancy. *New York Times*, p. 15.

Williams, T. (1990). *The cocaine kids*. Reading, Mass.: Addison-Wesley Publishing Co.

Witters, W., Venturellis, P., and Hanson, G. (1992). *Drugs and society*. Boston: Jones and Bartlett Publishers.

Zatz, M. (1987). Chicano youth gangs and crime: The creation of a moral panic. *Contemporary Crisis*, 11, 129–58.

Zimmerman, E. F. (1991). Substance abuse in pregnancy: Teratogenesis. *Pediatric Annals*, 20, 541–44, 546.

Zinberg, N. E. (1984). *Drug, set, and setting: The basis for controlled intoxicant use*. New Haven, Conn.: Yale University Press.

Index

pregnancy, 106; costs of, 101–2, 107;
desirability of, 106, 176 n. 11; difficulty obtaining drugs due to, 107;
obstacles to terminating, 106
pregnant addicts, treatment for, 41
prenatal care, 39–40
prenatal cocaine exposure, 29, 53
pro-life movement, 157. See also *Roe v.
Wade*
promiscuity, to obtain crack, 105
prosecution, 5–7, 34–35, 67–72, 173 n.
6; arguments for, 2–3, 16, 35, 69–71,
73–74, 76, 77, 81, 86, 157; in
Charleston, SC, 87–93; dangers of, 35,
79, 91–92, 94; for delivery of drugs
to a minor, 75–79; for fatal vs. nonfa-
tal injury to fetus, 73; first conviction,
35–36; for involuntary manslaughter,
72–75; of Jennifer Johnson, 75–79; of
Josephine Pelligrini, 79–82, 93; of
Kimberly Hardy, 82–87; of Lynn
Bremer, 82, 85–87; of Melanie Green,
72–75, 93; race and, 71, 94, 161;
sociodemographics and, 67–68, 156,
157. See also imprisonment; MUSC program; punishment
prosecutors, 71, 94, 156–57, 173 n. 2,
173 n. 5
prostitution: to obtain crack, 105, 119;
pregnant, addicted prostitutes, 106,
107
psychological counseling for drug use,
123
public health approach, 166–67
punishment vs. treatment approaches,
36, 40–41, 174 n. 10. See also imprisonment; MUSC program; prosecution;
treatment

racial fears and stereotypes, 97, 128,
161, 162

Rapoport, Alan, 87
Ratner, Mitchell, 98
Reagan, Ronald: budget cutbacks under,
133–34
Reinarman, Craig, 9, 11
reproductive freedom, 7
right to be born without defect, 81
right to privacy, 81
Roberts, Dorothy, 7
Roe, Kathleen, 108
Roe v. Wade, 12, 69, 73
Rosenbaum, Marsha, 97–98

scapegoating. See moral panic(s); war on
drugs
school dropouts, 101–2
Schwacke, David, 91
sexual activity, to obtain crack, 105
Sisters program, 118
social programs, 99, 103. See also *specific
programs*
social services, 164; costs, 34; outreach
programs, 37, 118; overwhelming
need for, 13–14. See also special education; *specific services*
social workers: decision-making authority, 38. See also child welfare workers
special education, 140; learning disabilities and, 146–53
Stack, Carol, 100
Stephanie, 1–2, 52–53
students: disruptive, 150–53; dropouts,
101–2. See also classroom problems
Stutman, Robert, 28, 46, 47
sudden infant death syndrome (SIDS),
23

Tague, Anthony D., 71, 82–87, 157
teratogenesis, 54–55, 64, 165–66
treatment, 29–30, 33, 158; effectiveness, 124; federal funding, 119–20,